CCCC Studies in Writing & Rhetoric

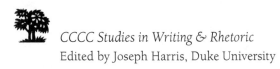

CCCC Studies in Writing & Rhetoric
Edited by Joseph Harris, Duke University

The aim of the CCCC Studies in Writing & Rhetoric (SWR) series is to influence how writing gets taught at the college level. The methods of studies vary from the critical to historical to linguistic to ethnographic, and their authors draw on work in various fields that inform composition—including rhetoric, communication, education, discourse analysis, psychology, cultural studies, and literature. Their focuses are similarly diverse—ranging from individual writers and teachers, to classrooms and communities and curricula, to analyses of the social, political, and material contexts of writing and its teaching. Still, all SWR volumes try in some way to inform the practice of writing students, teachers, or administrators. Their approach is synthetic, their style concise and pointed. Complete manuscripts run from 25,000 to 40,000 words, or about 125–200 pages. Authors should imagine their work in the hands of writing teachers as well as on library shelves.

SWR was one of the first scholarly book series to focus on the teaching of writing. It was established in 1980 by the Conference on College Composition and Communication (CCCC) to promote research in the emerging field of writing studies. Since its inception, the series has been copublished by Southern Illinois University Press. As the field has grown, the research sponsored by SWR has continued to articulate the commitment of CCCC to supporting the work of writing teachers as reflective practitioners and intellectuals. For a list of previous SWR books, see www.ncte.org/books/swr.

We are eager to identify influential work in writing and rhetoric as it emerges. We thus ask authors to send us project proposals that clearly situate their work in the field and show how they aim to redirect our ongoing conversations about writing and its teaching. Proposals should include an overview of the project, a brief annotated table of contents, and a sample chapter. They should not exceed 10,000 words.

To submit a proposal or to contact the series editor, please go to http://uwp.aas.duke.edu/cccc/swr/.

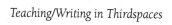

Teaching/Writing in Thirdspaces

Teaching/Writing in Thirdspaces

The Studio Approach

Rhonda C. Grego
and
Nancy S. Thompson

SOUTHERN ILLINOIS UNIVERSITY PRESS

Carbondale

Publication partially funded by a subvention grant from The Conference on College
Composition and Communication of the National Council of Teachers of English.

Library of Congress Cataloging-in-Publication Data
Grego, Rhonda C., 1959–
Teaching/writing in thirdspaces : the studio approach / Rhonda C. Grego and
Nancy S. Thompson.
    p. cm. — (Studies in writing and rhetoric)
Includes bibliographical references and index.
ISBN-13: 978-0-8093-2772-0 (pbk. : alk. paper)
ISBN-10: 0-8093-2772-4 (pbk. : alk. paper)
1. English language—Rhetoric—Study and teaching (Higher)—United States.
2. Report writing—Study and teaching (Higher)—United States. I. Thompson,
Nancy S., 1941–. II. Conference on College Composition and Communication
(U.S.) III. Title.
PE1405.U6G74 2008
808'.0420711—dc22   2007023191

The paper used in this publication meets the minimum requirements of American
National Standard for Information Sciences—Permanence of Paper for Printed Library
Materials, ANSI Z39.48-1992. ∞

To John, Caroline, and Emily—*Rhonda C. Grego*

For my students and colleagues—*Nancy S. Thompson*

Contents

Illustrations

Acknowledgments

First and foremost, our thanks and deep appreciation go out to those students and colleagues with whom we have worked in all three of the Studio programs discussed in this volume. At the original University of South Carolina Writing Studio: graduate student assistant directors Mike Barnes, Chris Fosen, and Mark Sutton; staff/group leaders Mary Alm, Jennie Ariail, Eddy Ball, Mike Barnes, Rhonda Brock-Servais, Terry Carter, Denise Comer, Lee Davinroy, Chris Fosen, Anita Guynn, Hayes Hampton, Christine Helms, Jill Hufnagel, Keaghan Kay, Sonja Launspach, Bill McSweeney, Randy Miller, Clay Motley, Dick Norwood, Daniel Robinson, Randy Smith, Tom Smith, Mark Sutton, Sid Watson, and Dagmar Zuefle; and the 2001 Writing Center–Writing Studio assistant director Mark Sutton and group leaders Brian Cooney, Karen Culver, Joe Goeke, Carl Jenkins, Ladka Khailova, Ronald Miller, Jennifer Reid, Lisa Wills, and Dagmar Zuefle. At the Benedict College first-year composition (FYC) Bridges Writing Program (BWP): Cheryl Jackson, administrative specialist; English lab specialists Anne Imperato Colgate, Doris Greene, Vareva Harris, and Pamela Martin; and FYC English faculty and instructors Ruby Blair, Stephen Criswell, Farrida Cassimjee, Emmie Davis, Max Smith, and Ethel Taylor. At The University of South Carolina Research Communications Studio: codirector Libby Alford; engineering faculty members Roger Dougal, Edward Ernst, Jed Lyons, and Mike Matthews; and staff/group leaders John Brader, Beth Davidson, Lori Donath, Sirena Hargrove-Leak, Nadia Kellam, Rod Leonard, Chris Long, Roxanne Spray, and Eric Vilar.

Other colleagues who were supportive or helped at crucial moments include Ruth Strickland, Opportunity Scholars Program, University of South Carolina; former Benedict College dean and co–principal investigator of the BWP, Christopher Chalokwu; Benedict College administrators Gwenda Greene and Carolyn Drakeford;

University of South Carolina English Department chair Steven Lynn; program coordinator for the Fund for the Improvement of Postsecondary Education (FIPSE), Cassandra Courtney; and National Science Foundation (NSF) program coordinator Sue Kemnitzer. The Bridges Writing Program work was funded by the U.S. Department of Education through FIPSE from 1997 to 2000 (#P116B971289) under the title "The Bridges Writing Program (BWP) at Benedict College: Participatory Inquiry for Student-, Faculty-, and Program-Development" from 1997 to 2000. The Research Communications Studio was funded by the National Science Foundation (NSF EEC 0212244), "Enhanced Learning in Undergraduate Education: A Research Communications Studio Model" from August 2002 to May 2006.

In our professional lives, colleagues have offered much appreciated support and encouragement over several years of our work, often both personally and in print. Our heartfelt thanks go out to Peter Elbow; John Tassoni and Cindy Lewiecki-Wilson; Bruce Horner; Ira Shor; Annie Duménil; and Linda Ferreira-Buckley.

Many thanks for the thoughtful reading given to our manuscript by reviewers Kristie Fleckenstein and Stuart Selber, whose thorough comments challenged us to bring forward our essential ideas more clearly. They engaged in a full dialogue with our manuscript, for which we are most grateful. And finally our immense thanks go out to SWR editor extraordinaire Robert Brooke, someone who saw the value of our ideas and helped us in indispensable ways as we worked over the course of several years to create and shape this book.

Teaching/Writing in Thirdspaces

Prologue: Awakenings and Recollections

Realizing Our Compositional Situation

Despite an understandable disciplinary drive to unify (and uniformly package) composition's work with student writing, compositionists cannot help but be aware of the diversity of our workplaces: size, infrastructure, resources, student bodies, institutional and programmatic histories, and faculty composition are just a few of the many variables that influence the everyday realities of composition's work. When we leave our conferences and return to our institutional homes, we become reimmersed not just in the places of our work but in what feminist cultural geographer Doreen Massey would term the "spaces" constructed by the relationships and interactions therein and by the Foucauldian power relations maintained by the institution in those places/spaces—where *institution* can refer to both the real, particular higher education site and the imagined societal idea(l)s we carry about the "Academy" as an overarching institution (Caputo and Yount). When we look at these flows, forces, and tensions at work in our lives on so many levels within higher education, it becomes clear why we as compositionists may at times feel like just so much flotsam.

Clear, too, is why we move outside our home territory, become a part of national organizations, local community issues, service-learning projects, and online outreach, connecting with and commenting on the life (of writing) outside our everyday institutional existence. But there are times when we are compelled to deal with home matters, to turn the light of our critical faculties on the particular mix of those flows, forces, and tensions within our own compositional places/spaces, when being forced to face our location can help us better see our situation.

One such moment for the two of us was in the early 1990s. In 1990, 1991, and 1992, the South Carolina Commission on Higher Education (CHE) was concerned about duplication of programs across state-run higher-ed institutions in the wake of budget cuts. The South Carolina CHE has for some time attempted to streamline our state's higher education institutions by restructuring the state university and college system. An argument frequently floated has been that given the size of our state, we have too many higher education institutions and cutbacks would allow more efficient use of state tax dollars. Of course arguments for such streamlining often discount the social history of segregation and deep socioeconomic class divisions that have created South Carolina's differing higher education constituencies and historical demands for our state's numerous institutions, including historically black colleges and universities as well as public and private four-year universities, regional campuses, and a burgeoning system of technical and community colleges. Nonetheless, the CHE moved to streamline with its decision in 1990 that all "remedial" courses would be offered for credit at two-year technical and community colleges only. If such courses were to continue at four-year public institutions, students would receive no (not even elective) credit for them.

The University of South Carolina's ambitions in the 1990s to raise standards and thus gain research institution status from the Association of American Universities, along with its English department's history of using the Writing Center and other kindred activities as a financial buffer in recent years of budget crunch, made it clear to us that further departmental funding cuts would soon disproportionately affect composition's work. As compositionists, we knew that basic writing held a key position as ethos-defining work in its connection to a twentieth-century history of access to higher education for successive nontraditional student populations in the United States. But at that time, state, institutional, and departmental forces converged such that we no longer felt a part of our discipline's narrative of progressive social action.

The backgrounds we brought to this convergence in the early 1990s amplified our awareness of the political forces affecting our fate: Nancy is an English educator who grew up in Missouri farm country, attended a one-room schoolhouse where her mother taught, and earned a Ph.D. in English and education under Bob Shafer and Ken Donelson at Arizona State University. She first came to the University of South Carolina in 1971 to work with the Social Problems Research Institute at a time when South Carolina, including the university, was still in the throes of desegregation. Rhonda is a compositionist who attended elementary schools in several states, following a father who left the farm to enlist in the Navy. In the 1970s she attended the historically black middle and high schools in her native Florence, South Carolina; upon completing her doctoral degree in composition and rhetoric at Penn State in the late 1980s, she returned to her home state in 1989 to teach research methods in the University of South Carolina's doctoral program in composition and rhetoric. With both of us being from working-class families, the issues of place and the politics of race, class, and gender embedded in our personal and professional histories brought us together initially in a friendship and then a collaboration based on similar perceptions of the elite university system and literature-focused department in which we had both found ourselves.

Then came the CHE decision to abolish basic writing at four-year state-supported colleges and universities. What could we do? We spent fall 1991 considering the question with a group of graduate teaching assistants and concerned basic writing and first-year-composition (FYC) instructors. Although we knew that some entering students needed extra help adjusting to college and developing their writing, we could not pretend that there was any one answer for work with "basic writing"—or even one institutional definition of that disciplinary designation. Within our own state university system of campuses, there existed different local conditions and outcomes for the placement and teaching of basic writing courses. Many approaches seemed correlated to the relatively higher or lower entrance criteria (SAT scores, high school standing, etc.) and a priori assumptions about attendant student writing abilities, backed by placement tests (enacted in a variety of ways) that served as self-fulfilling prophecies. Under these conditions, we became even more aware that students placed in a writing course that would not count toward the university's required semester credit hours in English (or even as an elective) resented what they saw as a nameless, faceless bureaucratic intervention. We were being pushed from both above and below out of our previously comfortable assumption that an institutional space would continue to be available for students—or that any disciplinary entity known as basic writing necessarily matched the actual circumstances and forces at work in the different campus sites of which we now were more aware. In a sense freed from the constraints of what "should" be, we began focusing on possible alternative approaches and operational structures, figuring out how we might work within the system to help student writers entering the university.

In a specially created research seminar in fall 1991, the two of us, three experienced graduate teaching assistants (Mary Alm, Gloria Underwood, and Miriam Moore), the director of the university's Opportunity Scholars Program, Ruth Strickland, and visiting adjunct Marilyn DeMario (who had recently earned her Ph.D. from the University of Pittsburgh) all taught either English 100 Basic Writing or English 101 Freshman Composition, or both. Mindful of Glynda Hull and Mike Rose's compelling injunction that we rethink remediation, we met each week to compare notes on our classes and students and to review our discipline's relevant literature.

We saw then that increasingly qualitatively focused research on student writers within educational settings—from Janet Emig's early *Composing Processes of Twelfth Graders* (1971) to Elizabeth Chiseri-Strater's *Academic Literacies* (1991) and Linda Miller Cleary's *From the Other Side of the Desk* (1991)—admirably exemplified composition's work, at the end of the twentieth century, to place our view of student writers within the network of relationships and immediate surroundings that contextualize students' development as college writers. But our pedagogies for beginning student writers seemed bound, on the one side, by primarily linguistics-derived terminology for describing writing structures. After intensive work with open-admissions student writers at SUNY, Mina Shaughnessy channeled her greater understanding of the relationships that construct student writing, of "errors and expectations," into a curriculum for teaching students how to manage the different sentence structures available for the better placement or flow of information in their prose. And we were bound on the other side by how the academy prefers to see itself, exemplified in the curriculum of David Bartholomae and Anthony Petrosky, which identifies academic culture with philosophical debate carried out in texts over time. Basing a pedagogical approach on an idealized (and wonderfully democratic) conception of academic culture was also exemplified in the liberatory pedagogy of Ira Shor and composition's Freireans, resting as it does on another preferred view that we academics have of ourselves as public intellectuals—guardians of democracy, defenders of deliberative discourse, the academy being a kind of social critic and safe harbor for those who would become thereby social or community activists, acting in and to change the world outside the academy's higher education institutions.

But none of these approaches seemed to acknowledge the institutional power relations and politics that, we found, dominated our work as compositionists and affected the lives of writing teachers and students. In composition research and accompanying pedagogies, the classroom as institutional space/place was often neutralized, while the rest of the institution's geography seemed typically only a generalized part of the picture provided—if it was attended to at all. But through the situation in which we found ourselves, we better saw how institutional location (both locally and more abstractly in the hierarchy of positions that construct daily life in the academy) influenced our work with student writers on both local and disciplinary fronts. And though we may not have articulated this thought so neatly at the time, we began to suspect that our work with student writing (both products and processes) was influenced by institutional politics, preferences, and power relations at many more levels than currently attended to then in our discipline.

Could there be a systematic approach to helping student writers that would also help us to pursue further this understanding of composition's work? Our initial response to the South Carolina CHE's action was to enact a program that combined (a) our heightened awareness of the institutional power relations that defined not only "basic writing" but also "student writing" and (b) our desire to engage in local action, to explore a very located (in place) and situated (in space) view of student writing. We called that program the "Writing Studio," and it lived from 1992 to 2001 within the first-year writing program at the University of South Carolina. We termed our operational methodology "interactional inquiry," based as it was on our affinity for feminist research methodologies and action inquiry methods in the social sciences. As our work within this original Writing Studio expanded through the Fund for the Improvement of Postsecondary Education–supported Bridges Writing Program (BWP) in Benedict College's first-year composition program and more recently through the University of South Carolina's National Science Foundation (NSF)–funded Research Communications Studio (RCS) in the College of Engineering, which supported the communications development of advanced undergraduates engaged in research experiences (Thompson, Alford, Liao, Johnson, and Matthews), we have developed a sense of the far greater locational and situational complexity—what we call the "compositional situation"—faced by college student writers.

The "rhetorical situation" introduced to students in so many rhetorics of that day called students' and teachers' attention to the exigencies of communication within the scenarios and texts assigned for discussion and writing, but the social and institutional situations in which writing students and teachers were embedded seemed much more complex and contingent on forces well outside our individual powers of control—in fact, they still do. Not only has the postprocess movement in composition since the early 1990s brought issues of race, gender, sexuality, and culture to the attention of our discipline as influences on the social construction of student writing and the teaching of writing, but our own experiences have focused our attention on the institutional construction and influences as well. Our purpose in writing this book is to explore and share what we have learned about this compositional situation in and through our work since 1992 with a variety of Studio programs across institutions and disciplines.

What Is Studio?

But first, some definitions. What exactly are we referring to by "Writing Studio"? In his 1999 dissertation, Bill Macauley examines higher education's use of the studio concept in general; his motivation was to explore an educational environment—the art studio—that he had found conducive to learning himself, both in high school and in college as an undergraduate working-class student. By Macauley's definition, a studio learning environment is one where activities of production are undertaken individually but in a place where others are working and discussing their work simultaneously, where teachers provide, along with other students, guidance, suggestions, input.

When we began our first Writing Studio at the University of South Carolina in the fall of 1992, we had several of these qualities of *studio* in mind. But Macauley's dissertation focuses on the method of studio as a self-contained course, albeit one that can be implemented in many different educational contexts. The major characteristics of a studio in these different contexts are that learners are producing work, of which they take ownership, and that they work both individually and collaboratively in some way. In the version Macauley generates at the end of his dissertation for a four-hour writing course, the writing projects are free-floating assignments created for the course, with a great deal of choice in what students write.

Here, however, the studio concept is differently configured. We have developed "Studio" as a writing program model that provides a highly adaptable approach. It is not limited to a course per se but is a configuration of relationships that can emerge from different contexts. Writing Studio has what might be a fourth credit-hour (or an otherwise-configured small group meeting) attached to an existing course. These Studios can appear anywhere across the curriculum, tied to first-year English, undergraduate research, or any course or academic activity that requires writing or communication assignments. A Studio program organizes small groups of students to meet frequently and regularly (typically once a week) to bring to the table the assignments they are working on for a writing course, another English course, or a disciplinary course or undergraduate research experience that requires communication products (what RCS calls "deliverables"). At these meetings student writers, with the help of a staff group facilitator, focus on the process of production by discussing progress each week, bringing a piece of work or a question about their work to their Studio group, getting feedback from others in the group, and giving helpful feedback to the others. The work of the individual is thus supported and further developed through the interaction of the group.

Our Writing Studio attaches, to an existing course or academic pursuit, a one-hour-per-week workshop, where students bring their work, sometimes to "work on it" but more often to present the work and obtain feedback so they can go away and work on it further. This Studio is a space for reflective communication. Presenting the work for one's own and other group members' reflection allows the writer to use the help of group members to generate ideas and refine not only approaches to content but also processes and attitudes toward the work. Like Macauley's studio approach, though, Writing Studio also focuses on "generative learning": "building understanding through work and experience" and "through your own work" (Macauley 214, 216).

Like the general studios Macauley found in higher education, Writing Studios require a dedicated space conducive to the kind of production and interactions that make it possible to learn "through your own work." Studios seem most productive in a room with at least one table and enough chairs for the size of the group—usually a group leader and three to seven student participants. Students should be in fairly close proximity for group intimacy. The room might have posters or other appropriate or interesting visuals on the wall, especially materials that enhance the work at hand. A white board for sign-in and other writing or visual work is helpful, as is a computer with a large monitor on which students can see one another's writing (that they e-mail or bring on a disk or memory stick) or an Elmo projector to show a piece of writing through the computer monitor or on a screen. Reference tools, such as dictionaries, guides, sample documents, magazines, newspapers, and writing materials, in the environment both visually signal and support the multilayered literacies and interests that Studio students bring. The table, equipment, and resources accommodate the people representing the different abilities, interests, intelligences—and facilitate group work on and awareness of texts and different kinds of communications.

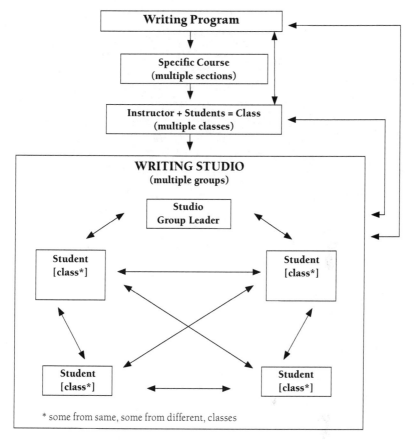

Relationship of Writing Studio to university courses. Studio can be attached to any course or experience in the academy that requires students to produce communications. In the case of the Writing Studio Program for English 101 at the University of South Carolina, the specific courses were part of an overall approach, instructors decided which students needed the supplemental help of a Studio group, and multiple small groups were composed of students from different classes. In the interactional inquiry approach, communications from Studio staff back to instructors inevitably affect teaching and the program approach.

Whereas Macauley's studio instructor is the teacher of the course, the Writing Studio small group leader is an experienced teacher (graduate teaching assistant, faculty member, or learning specialist) who serves as a "facilitating expert" (Macauley 23) for the group meeting, elicits critique and other feedback from the students, keeps the group moving along so everybody gets some attention during the weekly meeting, and otherwise organizes the weekly work and the program. Working outside the course, the facilitator can provide expansive perspectives and can lead other group members to do so. Like the experienced teacher, who is better able to relinquish control of the studio classes that Macauley studied (168–69), the Writing Studio leader is a facilitator of the group process and an experienced educator who can recognize when instruction or an outside resource is needed and can provide it "at the point of need" (Nelson). With an orientation toward responding to what students say, do, and need and not toward dictating a set curriculum to cover content, a Studio group meeting might look chaotic—but giving time to each student's work is the structure that matters most.

What Happens in a Writing Studio Session?

At the first session, after a short introduction or organizing-and-orienting opening by the group leader, the group time is turned over to student interaction, for their introductions to one another and to the work they are going to be bringing to Studio sessions. The students and their work, not any course instructor's plan, provide the "curriculum" of the studio sessions. The sessions will be focused on production of student work and, in tandem, on the processes students engage in to produce that work. Students learn from one another not only about the different versions of first-year composition (or undergraduate research, or history, or biology, etc.) assignments but also about the content of one another's thinking and the different approaches they take to accomplish their work. These views into the work of another for a similar situation—for different types of essays, for research assignments such as writing an abstract for a conference, or for the different versions and interpretations of assignments connected to any other academic situation—help to enlarge students' understanding of the rhetorical and compositional situations they will encounter in academic work.

Often students' assignments are open to interpretation and application to different topics, which helps students take ownership of their academic tasks. The act of bringing that assignment to a Studio session further encourages the student's sense of ownership of it. Though it was assigned by a teacher in another course or academic environment, bringing it to a Studio group is a step removed from the teacher's assignment and thus it becomes more the student's own piece of work to represent as her own to the group. And when different types of writing assignments are reported in a Studio group, students may draw generalizations about what the assignments are leading students to do and think.

Though Studio programs differ according to the programmatic and institutional niches they live within, at this introductory moment we offer the following overview of typical weekly Studio practice within a college writing program:

- The Studio group leader sits at a small conference table, waiting for the students, greeting each as they enter, getting to know each as a person, perhaps commenting on or asking a question about events of the week in the world, on campus, or in the student's class since the group's last meeting.
- Students sign in on the white board or sheet of paper to indicate what they are working on and what they bring to as well as need from the session.
- When everybody has arrived, the leader forms an initial agenda (usually rehearsed orally but sometimes written quickly where all can see) based on what this group needs or "brings to the table" this week.
- Some students' needs can be handled in tandem if they are similar. For example, two student group members working on the generation of ideas for different writing assignments could have the floor together, articulating their initial ideas (or writing blocks) or soliciting suggestions or questions

from the group, with the group leader facilitating reflection on or comparison of different or similar strategies for getting started.

- When a student has a piece of writing in progress, she tells the group what she is working on, presents a hard copy or brings it up on the computer, and asks for particular input. It is important that the student ask for specific feedback and not be allowed to just throw out a piece for whatever others give back. Asking for particular feedback is another way of getting the student to think more deeply about her work. In addition to answering the need articulated by the student writer, group members can provide other suggestions.

- Often students discuss the assignments their teachers have given, rehearsing for other student group members the explanations given by the teacher, perhaps airing questions and misunderstandings or concerns they have about the assignments. Sometimes students discuss their resistance to classes and assignments; the group leader and other students help the student figure out how to deal with this resistance and how to approach the teacher to ask questions to clarify comments, to obtain further explanation, and so forth.

- Though Studio does not grade a piece of writing or a communication, students will bring to the group the teachers' comments and grades on their work, which then are discussed.

- In addition to facilitating student discussion, the group leader listens to what students say about their work, their class, or their assignments and, where appropriate, provides contextualizing information about the genre or the kind of assignment being asked for, based on her knowledge of the way in which the disciplinary affiliation of the student's instructor influences the design of the class and assignments therein or perhaps based on her knowledge of composition's history and goals as a discipline both generally and specifically in her institution's program.

- These kinds of interactions constitute the "interactional inquiry"—the methodology that informs Studio work instead of any set curriculum. Students are encouraged to compare, contrast, define, question, and otherwise collect, as it were, the patterns to be found in the "moments" represented by each student writer at the table and his work that week. Over time, lessons are thus generated about the everyday work of student writing.

- The group leader keeps an eye on the time and decides when to move to another student's work (or another topic that is illustrated in the student group's work that week). If time runs out and a student is missed, the next meeting can begin with that student. The time constraint pushes students to articulate and focus quickly on specific points and needs, though some group members may stay past the allotted time to continue working with each other, enact specific revisions, or get started on drafting, if the Studio space and scheduling allow it.

- At the end of a session, the group leader reminds students to think about what they want or need to bring to the studio group the next week, even perhaps asking each student to make a specific projection. Students may also be asked to write (by hand or electronically) brief meeting reflections for the group file or for other record keeping.

- Studio group leaders keep records of group attendance and, depending on the program, may be asked to provide their own brief narrative of what occurred during the meeting. Notes on areas addressed are also helpful to the group leader as she builds on students' experiences and learning from week to week. Brief narratives or notes are useful for communicating with students' course instructors as needed and in constructing each group leader's own weekly reflections on her overall Studio work (successes, problems, conflicts, recurring issues, observations, questions).

- Studio group leaders meet regularly (once a week or once every two weeks, depending on teaching obligations and loads) to share these reflections and help each other see the larger patterns, possibilities, and needs that arise in the course of Studio work. Thus Studio staff also engage in their own interactional inquiry, looking at issues and patterns across student group meetings held in any given week.

• At the beginning of the next Studio student group session, the group leader may again ask for comments on progress made during the time between Studio meetings, using understandings from previous sessions and staff meetings and other reminders of the territory last traversed.

Studio Repositioning: A Deepening Sense of Space

Embedded in the practicalities of Studio programmatic processes and practice is the defining dilemma that gave rise to Studio work; the same dilemma arose as our fall 1991 research group wrestled with the CHE's abolition of "basic writing," and it continually arises within any Studio work we have since undertaken. At advanced graduate and professoriate levels, composition as a discipline engages in research on writing and, in that location, must depict the object of its research as an open system. At the same time, composition lives at the beginning levels of first-year composition courses largely by depicting its object—writing—as a closed system of known processes and practices that can be encapsulated in handbooks and rhetorics, easily purveyed to those beginning graduate compositionists and noncompositionists alike who act as teaching assistants in large writing programs or to the numerous noncomposition-degree faculty who are charged with teaching college writing courses to undergraduates at so many smaller institutions.

This dilemma, this divorce, this distance between how composition as a discipline sees itself and how it functions in the everyday life of a majority of higher education institutions in the United States was responsible for the South Carolina CHE's ease in affecting basic writing in state institutions—even when the entity "basic writing" existed in such differing states at different institutions. While compositionists may well see basic writing as a space for essential research on the development of student writing, and while composition has historically invested its ethos in socially progressive championing of access for nontraditional students to counter higher education's tendency to use writing as a barrier to such access, the larger higher education institution sees basic writing as a fundamental instructional duty, as territory that is well known and thus easily transportable to institutions with a faculty workforce of whom less is expected (in terms of disciplinary research) and, indeed, of whom less is required in the way of research, since they typically work with students in those well traveled (and, it is assumed, well known) areas of beginning writing.

For those of us who live everyday lives with one foot in both disciplinary research and beginning institutional locations, this disjunction is difficult, to say the least. Why? Because to allow this view of our everyday work is in essence to deny that we have any disciplinary work to do, that we have any place in the kinds of research that define disciplines in higher education. Indeed, this institutional positioning of our discipline is at the heart of the continuing problems and inequities faced by compositionists, graduate teaching assistants, and adjuncts who teach composition, particularly those in more traditional English or literature departments, where literature, linguistics, and even rhetorical studies face much less of this kind of institutional pressure to deny the very institutionally required foundations of their disciplinary status. Writing center, writing-across-the-curriculum, and (though perhaps to a lesser extent) writing-in-the-disciplines programs all suffer in their association with the positioning of composition and the teaching of writing at these beginning levels (writing in the disciplines perhaps less so because it has attempted to define itself as a program of research on writing in the disciplines, as that writing constitutes the knowledge base within those disciplines, a different way of positioning itself within institutional power relations and hierarchies).

It is exactly this positioning that our initial Studio design (and most subsequent manifestations of the program) worked to thwart. In our initial resistance to that which was being forced on us, we worked within the system openings (both conceptual and physical) that were available to us: in the late 1980s and early 1990s we were both graduate faculty at an institution with a doctoral program in comp-rhet, so we first developed the Studio to take advantage of that positioning and our responsibilities to develop the teaching and research abilities of graduate students in the department. In a Writing Studio proposal submitted to our department in spring 1992, we cited (a) a Harvard Assessment report (Light) that argued the value of small-group, collaborative, and cooperative learning opportunities (playing to our institution's "wannabe" impulses and as a nod to the oft-repeated intimation of our disciplinary beginnings with the Harvard Report of 1872); (b) advances in the use of qualitative research methods in composition research to further explore student writing processes in particular; and (c) our responsibilities as a department and graduate program to develop opportunities for graduate student teaching and research. In doing so, we reminded our department of the institutional history of composition and that it is both a discipline and a duty, not just a closed system of repetitive delivery, semester after semester and course after course, but also an open system of ongoing knowledge construction—a (teaching) duty, yes, but also a (research) discipline.

Our use of *positioning* and other spatial terms in the preceding discussion calls on us to revisit—and deepen—terminology we originally used in an early *CCC* article: "repositioning remediation" (Grego and Thompson, "Repositioning Remediation"). Looking back, we can see that because of the fierceness of the debate over the mainstreaming of basic writing in the 1990s, the focus of most of our disciplinary readers was probably on the remediation aspect—particularly since we were playing off Mike Rose's earlier "rethinking remediation" title. But because of the political issues of location and institution narrated above as context for initial Studio work, our own focus was much more on the repositioning. Our discipline was rethinking remediation, but our circumstances forced us away from the term *remediation* altogether, as we were presented with a reality check on our discipline's position within South Carolina's higher education administration and our home institution.

In the years since the early 1990s when we began Studio work, composition as a field has taken its own "spatial" turn, as indicated most recently by the 2006 National Council of Teachers of English collection of articles published in composition's major journals, many by authors who have also recently published book-length works, a collection clearly designed for a graduate-level introduction to the field: *Relations, Locations, Positions: Composition Theory for Writing Teachers*, edited by Peter Vandenberg, Sue Hum, and Jennifer Clary-Lemon. As this collection illustrates, in recent years many compositionists have grown more aware of and articulate about issues of position, location, and space, becoming critical of spatial metaphors and exploring a plethora of theorists who work in fields that combine interests in postmodernism, architecture, education, cultural geography, cultural criticism, feminism, and others.

Compositionists such as Nedra Reynolds are spurred by interest in cultural geography theory and questions about how spatial awareness can become, in essence, part of student writers' critical, analytical tools, much as ethnographic awareness contributed analytical tools and assignments approaches (cultural artifact analyses, for example) to composition's pedagogical repertoire. Reynolds's study in Great Britain and her work with geography students at the University of Leeds are recounted in her book *Geographies of Writing: Inhabiting Places and Encountering Difference*, in which her goals are not just to affect pedagogy, to "teach writing as a set of spatial practices," but also to reimagine composing as "spatial, material, and visual" and to understand "the sociospatial construction of difference" (3). Her work, like that of most compositionists interested in spatial theory and analyses, carries forward a postprocess interest in issues of gender, race, and class. Reynolds aims to imbue composition as a discipline overall with a greater spatial awareness: "Places, whether textual, material, or imaginary, are constructed and reproduced not simply by boundaries but also by practices, structures of feeling, and sedimented features of habitus. Theories of writing, communication, and literacy, this book argues, should reflect this deeper understanding of place" (2). Others, such as Sidney I. Dobrin and Christian R. Weisser, are similarly interested in outlining a new, more spatial paradigm for understanding writing as well. In *Natural Discourse*, these compositionists seek to move from a beginning in "ecocriticism" and writing about nature and the environment to what they term "ecocomposition": reseeing all writing from an ecological perspective and rejuvenating interest in the more broadly defined environments of and in which writing is accomplished.

Morgan Gresham and Kathleen Blake Yancey, as well as Paul Butler, use spatial terminology taken from architecture and postmodernist cultural criticism, respectively, to deepen descriptions of their work and form a new writing and communications program or to rejuvenate an old one. Gresham and Yancey use a spatial view to deepen their description of the evolution of the Communication Studio at Clemson (their use of *studio* based in some small part on our Writing Studio work) as both a physical and virtual site with ties to the institution's past (particularly through the class of 1941 alumni who provided funds) and hopes for the future. Their work is with spatial relationships and the implications for the relations between people who use their studio site to produce actual communications, to do the work that supports the longer-standing and award-winning Communication across the Curriculum initiative at Clemson University. Like Gresham and Yancey, Butler uses spatial concepts of "monument" and "countermonument," adapted from the work of James Young (*The Texture of Memory*), to provide a more analytical description of the shift within Syracuse University's Writing Program itself to a greater emphasis on analytical writing, making use of assignments that borrow from both cultural criticism and critical geography. In Young's analysis, writing programs can, like monuments, through everyday reification of the same event, "kill" that which is thus memorialized, whether it be a moment in time or "a" writing process approach. Thus, writing programs must be like "countermonuments," not afraid to call attention to inadequacies, to invite the opinions and voices of "passersby," to remake themselves, as at Syracuse.

Both Butler's and Gresham and Yancey's works invoke spatial terms to focus on relationships between program participants, as well as between the program and its institutional home base, and thereby raise awareness of the interactions among institutional, disciplinary, and program politics at their higher education sites, four-year state-supported institutions with either supporting graduate programs or alumni.

Johnathan Mauk, however, writing in 2003 from his position at a small community college, makes use of spatial terms and concepts not only to advocate the use of cultural geography within assignments and pedagogy but also to put forth pointed institutional critique. He argues that the first-generation college students of a community college do not or cannot "buy into" the traditional space of academe. Their presence is changing academic space. Mauk says that we need to expand our notions of space to include the spaces in which these new college students live. He sees this situation (*kairos*) as a "placelessness," which "calls for a pedagogy and theoretical lens that accounts for and engages the spatial and material conditions that constitute the everyday lives of students" (370). And he proposes using the concept of thirdspace as "a heuristic for orienting the acts of teaching and learning writing in increasingly spaced-out college environments," beginning "where students are" (370, 373). Mauk cites Nedra Reynolds's idea that "it is time to think smaller and more locally" (Reynolds, "Composition's Imagined Geographies" 30) to support his point that "any exploration of *how* to teach must also be a thorough exploration of *where*—of the geographical complexities that constitute the materiality and the conceptual elements of place" (Mauk 374–75).

We too have found spatial analysis, terms, and concepts helpful. And, as you know from the title of our book, we too tap into the "thirdspace" concept to name the places/spaces in which collide what Edward Soja would term the "real and the perceived/conceived." And, we have used and will use that concept of thirdspace to describe what we believe to be the value of Writing Studio for composition's work in higher education institutions. Our own readings in cultural geography and spatial analysis, coupled with our years in Studio programs with student and staff interactional inquiry groups, enable us at this point to articulate a redefinition of student writing. This redefinition, however, is *not* based on a new theoretical approach to pedagogy that would result in a new reader with additions to composition's repertoire of postprocess assignments fostering greater cultural awareness/criticism of the world at large. This redefinition arises, instead, from Studio's intensive exploration of the impact of composition's institutional and disciplinary locations on student writing, on the teaching and learning of writing within institutions where there is little luxury of pretending we have the ability to control courses or even protect programs.

We agree with both Mauk's and Soliday's ("Class Dismissed") argument that socioeconomic class represents perhaps the great silence in our work and add that it may be so because silence about class is found in (and is even foundational to) our disciplinary failure to interrogate composition's own position in higher education hierarchies, to more fully explore the way in which our positioning affects everyday material and spatial realms of our work with student writers. That silence is actually inhabited space, full of material practice. Compositionists want to escape the old by devising the newest transportable pedagogy, but the institutional systems and what Foucault calls the institution's "surveillant gaze" (Caputo and Yount) remain the same. Studio presents not a new way of representing the world around us for classroom consumption but a different way of "being" with student writers, a way of being that calls attention to the system and its gaze. While Mauk and Reynolds charge either their discipline or the larger academy with the need to include spatial perspectives and analyses, we see Studio itself as a spatialized and spatializing methodology for effecting institutional change: not just preparing student writers for the "real" world outside academe or for what lies beyond the writing classroom but for turning our attention to the more immediate space that lies outside the classroom but within the institution, to promote an analysis and greater awareness of the institutional power relations and influences thereof on student writing and assignments within particular institutional sites and within academe's hierarchy of institutional locations. Between the specific, individual classroom and the largely amorphous concept of a larger society so often invoked by our ideas of the social construction of reality and of knowledge lies a complex institutional life within higher education, one that makes for a wide variety of student and teacher experiences in writing programs. Both we and our student writers need to learn about these complexities and how to address them.

What Lies Ahead

While we were working out these analyses, we saw the death of the original Writing Studio in the University of South Carolina's FYC program, the starvation of the BWP program at Benedict College, and the emergence and evolution of the Studio concept in USC's College of Engineering and Information Technology, through Nancy's work with colleague Libby Alford and the RCS inquiry groups that moved not only outside the homeland of English departments but up the institutional hierarchy of undergraduate education. At the same time that both our Studio programs operating within first-year writing programs died, Studio-adapted programs sprang up in FYC and writing-across-the-curriculum programs at several other higher education institutions, including Miami University–Middletown (Tassoni and Lewiecki-Wilson), University of Wisconsin–Milwaukee, Florida International University, and Stetson College. These developments across so many different institutional, disciplinary, and programmatic places/spaces have made even clearer the need for spatial theory and terms both inside and outside our own discipline for naming and thinking about composition's higher education space/place. We always try to talk about the adaptation of Studio approaches, never wholesale adoption. We believe that Studio is not a pedagogy so much as an institutionally aware methodology, and we hope to avoid Studio becoming just one more means of effecting the oppressive time-space compressions that occur when disciplinary desires to move beyond the classroom into issues and critique of some larger society run roughshod over the complexities of difference and power relations where writing teachers and students daily work and live.

In the chapters that follow, key theorists and terms of spatial analysis are introduced and applied so as to deepen both the general analyses begun here and specific examples of interactions recorded in the course of our Studio work since 1992.

In chapter 1, "Composition's A/Rhetorical Situation," we argue for increased attention to the "institution," specifically those relations of power within colleges and universities that affect composition in general and those programs within which we have initiated Studio-based program designs. To calls for change put forth by scholars such as Nedra Reynolds; Johnathon Mauk; Sidney I. Dobrin and Christian R. Weisser; and James E. Porter, Patricia Sullivan, Stuart Blythe, Jeffrey T. Grabill, and Libby Miles, we add our own analysis of the need for institutional critique that proceeds from the bottom up—to reinstate a more inclusive approach to building educational programs from within institutional settings that should themselves be seen as complex rhetorical contexts. The dilemma academic disciplines face is the need for building rhetorically on local conditions, while academe (the "imagined" academy that informs the general idea of higher education) prefers to reward research and knowledge that is generalizable across wider spaces. Rather than building on the idealizations of institutions and disciplines that seek to generalize arhetorically across places and spaces, no matter what the details actually encountered, we argue that research and teaching, analysis and critique must proceed from a framework that considers the impact of the space/place from which these activities proceed, within which they live. In chapter 1 we also introduce Studio methodology—a variant of the participatory human inquiry approach that we adapted from British social sciences and feminist research methodologies and which we have named "interactional inquiry": Studio staff members (experienced teachers) not only lead their students in regular meetings, interacting and inquiring into the assignments they are working on, but also engage in their own group meetings to discuss effective approaches for their small groups, to take action based on those discussions, and to negotiate and renegotiate the scripts of life in the particular site. The challenge we present in chapter 1 is this: instead of basing composition pedagogies and research on globalized arhetorical maps of student writing that have trickled down, oftentimes from research at the higher levels of other institutions, what if we look at our knowledge as an open system, as an institutionally sited system, acknowledging the rhetorical differences represented by our students, by our teachers and staff, and by everyday realities, in order to illuminate the gaps in our knowledges at both local and global levels?

In chapter 2, "Institutional Critique and Studio as Thirdspace," we introduce concepts and frameworks found in the work of several theorists who have helped us better understand composition's position in the institutional hierarchy of academic life and the ways in which the "thirdspace" nature of Studio works for change within this hierarchy. We begin with Kenneth Burke's pentad and his own language—"scene"—for calling our attention to space/place. Then, Edward Soja's new urban studies show how the previous conception of a traditional city, such as Chicago, planned and built from the center out, gives way to a more decentralized, organic, even "uncontrolled" growth pattern of a city such as Los Angeles. Soja's comparison provides a parallel for a discipline of composition, which has been controlled by English departments but gives way to eruptions in thirdspaces across the institution. For Soja, the "firstspace" of perceived space (everyday reality) collapses into the "secondspace" of conceived space (as theorized in academic disciplines and imagined by society), spawning what we present as the arhetorical foundations of our discipline in generalized curricula that can effect oppressive time-space compressions.

According to Soja, thirdspace is where this collapse of first- and secondspace is realized and where alternatives (that can appear chaotic by previous standards) begin. Research by Kris Gutierrez and colleagues provides a look at thirdspaces arising within the classroom, where openings for rapprochement between teacher scripts and student counterscripts result in a thirdspace in which each lets go of his or her own culture and an unscripted improvisation disrupts conventional classroom power relations. We propose that Studio small groups operating outside but alongside class work provide a supportive space for extending exploration of such "off-script" moments that Gutierrez noted within classroom settings. Homi Bhabha's work furthers the concept: in his analyses the scripts and counterscripts constitute polarities of master narratives that maintain hegemony. To him, thirdspace exists between these polarities, where, for example, as in Studio, teacher scripting and student counterscripting do not quite fit because the usual teacher-student power relationships are disrupted and the nature of discourse therein necessarily shifts. Doreen Massey provides a redefinition of space that focuses on the social relations of power operating in a space/place—still acknowledging sociality and historicality but centering on the momentary social relations operating in a given space/place. Studio provides a space/place where these relations among students and teachers and institutions can be attended to, thus stimulating an external, metarhetorical analysis to illuminate the problems that student writers face and to provide a sense of possibility and potential empowerment.

In chapter 3, "Higher Education's Geographies of Student Writing," and chapter 4, "Studio Staff and Interactional Inquiry," we turn from the more abstract explorations to concrete examples of practice, delving further into Studio interactional inquiry in both student and staff groups. Beginning in chapter 3 with specific examination of the contrasting material conditions and historical contexts at those institutions where the Writing Studio, BWP, and RCS were located, we explore how each site reinforced in different ways the distances placed between student writers and advanced knowledge and knowledge construction at upper levels of the idealized institutional hierarchy outlined in chapter 1. Extending Burke's pentadic analysis, we look at ways in which Studio thirdspaces help us realize and negotiate the intersections of (sometimes collisions between) writing assignments and the institutional contexts for that work. And we use examples of Studio student group sessions (with names changed) to discuss basic Studio practices and to illustrate the different kinds of rhetorical action for change that result from interactional inquiry in our three different institutional sites.

Chapter 4 focuses on staff interactional inquiry, also detailing the contrasting material conditions and historical contexts in which different configurations of staff live at the institutional home of the Writing Studio, BWP, and RCS. Examples illustrate external pentadic factors and their influence on our work as teachers with the internal pentadic scenes of course readings and writing assignments. Studio staff interactional inquiry helps us to formulate our own plans and proposals for local change at each institutional site, working within the history, hierarchy, and spaces particular to each Studio manifestation. As communication is the medium in which interactional inquiry occurs, the communication both with teachers and with other group leaders helps us to resist the isolation from each other effected by higher education institutional structures, with the goal of making institutional critique realistic and reachable through our everyday work with students writers and other teachers of writing.

In our epilogue we turn to the broader implications of Studio work for our discipline. As mentioned earlier, each of the three specific Studio programs examined in chapters 3 and 4 no longer exists or has evolved substantially from its beginnings. The reasons are varied but can be understood in terms of the analyses presented in previous chapters: as rhetorical agents for change, Studio programs take advantage of gaps and fissures in institutional landscapes that inevitably shift and change. Interactional inquiry can be the agency for institutional change across these different landscapes. But just because Studio programs may not live forever does not mean that their benefit to our discipline is fleeting or even that it is too local to be more useful to our discipline as a whole. Instead of producing theory, pedagogy, research, conference papers, and journal articles that tend to assume all readers live at the same kind of institution, we propose that "theorizing the cross-section" across Studio programs can help compositionists generate a body of knowledge about academic writing across the different kinds of higher education institutions.

1 / Composition's A/Rhetorical Situation

Toward Institutional Critique

The ideals of activism that permeate liberatory, postprocess, and service-learning pedagogies and have occupied composition in the past decade seem to be coming home to roost. In "Institutional Critique: A Rhetorical Methodology for Change," James Porter and colleagues Patricia Sullivan, Stuart Blythe, Jeffrey T. Grabill, and Libby Miles cite their frustration with current disciplinary discourse in composition aimed at change, contending that "global critiques exist only in the form of ideal cases or statements, which all too often bracket off discussions of materiality and economic constraints in favor of working out the best case scenario—which, all too often, does not come to pass" (615). They give as an example the Council of Writing Program Administrators' statement on tenure and promotion for administrators, the idealized standards that may not be rhetorically persuasive in specific institutional circumstances. They assert,

> Attacking institutional problems only at a global and disciplinary level doesn't work, because institutions can too easily ignore global arguments for local reasons (such as lack of available faculty). Universities are not likely to be swayed by arguments within particular fields and disciplines. Idealized wish lists are far too easy to dismiss using "budgetary realities" as a rationale. *In short, there exists a gap between global ideals and either local or systemic institutional change.* Somewhere between the macro-level national critiques and the micro-level practices on individual campuses is space for an action plan informed by critique yet responsive to local conditions. (616; emphasis added)

This point—that global critiques leave more local problems and material conditions of work unaddressed—should sound familiar: it has been increasingly made by scholars working in composition and related areas, including several authors whose works appear in the most recent gathering of articles designed to introduce graduate students to composition, the 2006 Vandenberg, Hum, and Clary-Lemon collection *Relations, Locations, Positions* (see Street; Reynolds; Mauk; Mahala and Swilky; and others in that volume). If liberatory and postprocess pedagogies are helping student writers work as informed citizens for change in their communities, to connect the global to their local, then why can't we?

Of course, the move to connect more global theory with local classroom practice to effect change and improvement is one that has defined the field of composition since it became more of an institutionalized discipline in the mid-twentieth century. Rhonda recalls several summer graduate seminars in composition and rhetoric at Penn State University in the 1980s that used Robert Connors, Lisa Ede, and Andrea Lunsford's *Essays on Classical Rhetoric and Modern Discourse*, then the seminal collection for introducing graduate students to the field. Each essay ended with a move to pedagogical implications. In Rhonda's work with Penn State's summer rhetoric conference, there was a recurring need to draw in the teacher audience, to make the papers and presentations seem more relevant for that constituency. Much postprocess work in the 1990s answered this application question with a turn to the social, focusing college student writers' readings and writings on public issues beyond the classroom (*social* and *beyond* being favored, frequently used terms in composition literature of the 1990s and first decade of the twenty-first century) in a disciplinary desire to foster the deliberative rhetoric that many scholars increasingly found and still find lacking in the United States.

Unfortunately, shifting the space for change from the classroom to society (or community) only further avoids analysis of our spatial and material conditions and of the interaction of systems and relationships (past, present, and future) within any given institutional site that affect students and teachers of writing. We give student writers the tools of rhetorical analysis and cultural critique with which to articulate what they see happening in their communities and in our society, and we supply teachers of writing with many ways to understand and parse classroom issues, from syntax to interpersonal relationships to identity formation. But how can we effect needed change in our institutional situations if our disciplinary tools and approaches for analysis do not help us speak in meaningful ways about the effects of the systems and relationships that affect our classrooms and pedagogies? As Porter and colleagues note, composition researchers and pedagogues who focus on the classroom as a site for change do so "without adequately theorizing the institution . . . [thus making] institutions seem monolithic and beyond an individual's power for change" (617).

Composition's Focus on the Classroom

The absence of attention to institutional geographies and material conditions noted recently by scholars in our disciplinarily generalized discussion of composition's work is understandable, in large part because our attention has been deflected by the strong affective pull exerted by (a) the vivid place that classroom concerns occupy in our daily lives across institutional settings (no matter where) and (b) our desires to contribute to the equity and education of a democratic citizenry (everywhere). In supporting and constructing these focuses, composition has evolved a master narrative that works against a full institutional or spatial imagining of composition administration by drawing primarily on the continued predominance—pervasive in our intellectual approaches to the social, as Edward Soja notes in the quotation below—of a temporally focused historical narrative of ourselves:

> An essentially historical epistemology continues to pervade the critical consciousness of modern social theory. It still comprehends the world primarily through the dynamics arising from the emplacement of social being and becoming in the interpretive contexts of time. . . . This enduring epistemological presence has preserved a privileged place for the "historical imagination" in defining the very nature

of critical insight and interpretation. . . . [N]o hegemonic shift has yet occurred to allow the critical eye—or the critical I—to see spatiality with the same acute depth of vision that comes with a focus on *durée*. The critical hermeneutic is still enveloped in a temporal master-narrative, in a historical but not yet comparably geographical imagination. . . . Space still tends to be treated as fixed, dead, undialectical. (Soja, *Postmodern Geographies* 10–11)

Composition's disciplinary master narrative has certainly been forged through the retelling of a history centered on shifting social climates and political periods that have been inscribed on profiles of changing rhetorical theories or student bodies: the Civil War, Reconstruction, the Women's Movement (Waves one, two, etc.), the post–World War II era (the GI Bill), the Civil Rights era, and so forth. Indeed, the weight carried by issues associated with basic writing evidences how centrally these generalized political narratives of social change define composition, basic writing in particular being a course whose national and disciplinary history is synonymous with issues of access created by those shifting social climates and political movements in the United States. That composition's classroom scene in American higher education is so closely associated with changing times and accompanying student bodies creates a disciplinary ethos that is student-centered, politically conscious, and socially virtuous. It is no wonder that most compositionists feel passionate about—and protective of—this storytelling as an important characterization of—and justification for—our work in higher education. But there is no one-size-fits-all narrative of any composition course or class. In fact, this overarching master narrative of composition's ethos presumes the perspective of an institution with selective admissions or with a history of problems of access: how might the history and dynamics of basic writing differ at, say, a historically black college or university or a community, technical, or two-year college where institutional class and not access has played a more defining role?

And, as we discussed at greater length in the prologue, the actions of the South Carolina Commission on Higher Education (CHE) to remove basic writing and basic writers from four-year state-supported institutions in the early 1990s showed us that local (or, in this case, statewide) institutional politics, power, and economics certainly play as large a role as any more global, imported set of institutionally independent standards for success in and access to college writing classrooms. We also saw just how easily we compositionists can lose our classroom-based place for change, since the South Carolina CHE 1991 decision effectively shut us off from the classroom as a space/place or position from which to locate change, help, or access for a significant group of students. In our fall 1991 research seminar, formed to consider what we might do at the University of South Carolina to help students adjust to college writing demands, we saw that most solutions were classroom-based (as in the pedagogies proposed by Shaughnessy or Bartholomae and Petrosky). While our reviews of these approaches informed our comparative teaching of basic writing and regular first-year composition (FYC) courses at that time, we knew that basic writing was about to go. What we saw in research available in 1991 was how studies of student writers within educational settings—including Janet Emig's early *Composing Processes of Twelfth Graders*, Elizabeth Chiseri-Strater's *Academic Literacies*, Linda Miller Cleary's *From the Other Side of the Desk*, and Robert Brooke's *Writing and Sense of Self*—exemplified composition's increasing work to embed our disciplinary view of student writers within the network of localized relationships that contextualize students' development as college writers.

Given our position, our awakening, and what we were seeing in composition's growing qualitative-research work in 1991, it came to seem odd that, as Porter and colleagues note, even within a focus on the classroom as site of change, much research on basic writing erases the specific classroom (and even the institutional site) with the persuasive effect of creating a learning environment that seems amorphous and accessible from anywhere. For example, in *Rethinking Basic Writing*, Laura Gray-Rosendale questions her experiences with basic writers over the years so as to develop a better analytical model of the interactional phenomenon that gives rise to basic writers' social construction of identities. Her assumption is that with a better model for understanding basic writers as writers, teachers can design courses and assignments to use what basic writers *can* do rather than to focus on what they cannot do. But it is her use of a "best teacher and class" that is key to our point. She devotes a substantial section (pages 56–71) to discussion of the teacher and course with which she would work, praising this teacher's carefully developed approaches, assignments, and attitudes toward students. It seems that to access interactions between students in small groups, she had to be able to, in a sense, "control" the teacher's approach, the writing assignments, and even her own influence on the situation as participant-observer. Gray-Rosendale attempts, in essence, to neutralize the institutional setting as a noninterferring factor in order to observe these students' interactions and development.

Deborah Mutnick's *Writing in an Alien World* provides another example of our disciplinary tendency to bypass the influence of our institutional places/spaces, of the local and historical. Mutnick's work began at a "downtown university," where Bartholomae and Petrosky's acculturation model for a basic writing and reading program or course was being adapted to an urban, multicultural setting with many more basic writing students than at the University of Pittsburgh, where they developed the model. Mutnick's basic reading and writing course that focused on "how the self is constructed in and through history, language, and literature" was grounded in her "theoretical interest in the dialectic between individual consciousness and social systems in arenas like language and culture," and sought "a more social, dialogic interaction between teacher and student, among students and between readers and writers" than the Pittsburgh model (ix, xxiv, 13). In this case, Mutnick's multiple positionings tend to obscure the influence and dynamics of the particular institutional system in which she works, even though it is this system that largely constructs the everyday grounds on which the individual consciousness and social systems meet. As we read the case studies, we see that her institutional context as an important part of the "dialectic between individual conscious-ness and social systems" is in effect erased when we look from the perspective of good people doing good things in the program—and from the position of someone who occupies several of the available institutional roles: teacher, researcher, administrator.

Such evasions of space are particular to neither Gray-Rosendale nor Mutnick. Many teachers and administrators of writing can recognize this position. In fact, having been made forcefully aware on several occasions of our local powerlessness, we have felt that if we can't do anything else, at least we too can be "good people doing good things" in our small corners of the world. This position is a reality. But we need not limit our understanding of what has happened on local levels to analyses that ignore the role of institutional systems and power relations. Absenting institutional geography from our analyses (by neutralizing the classroom or institutional setting in our research, by operating from disciplinary master narratives that silently privilege certain institutional positionings) is holding composition back as disciplinary citizen of academe. By being so helpful, by working so hard to create our own world within the academic world, by continuing to locate student problems within the purview of our classrooms, by accepting the limitations and boundaries placed around our daily worlds (and, inevitably, around our ways of thinking about student writing), most of us ensure our roles as mitigators—and thereby as maintainers—of institutional invisibility. And we foster a concomitant lack of accountability and awareness of the role of higher education institutions in the construction of student writing "problems."

Basing our history on generalized concepts of national-level changes in student bodies sets up a nonreflexive approach that narrowly focuses composition's disciplinary attention on sites of work with students and writers—such as classrooms and labs—that are relatively easy to disembody (i.e., institutionally disengage) and thereby fosters a disciplinary rhetoric that disables and distances us from serious engagement with the complex dynamics, what Dobrin and Weisser might term the institutional "ecology," of our everyday work worlds. As a result, FYC programs today are most likely to regard student writing either through the microscopic lens of transcription error or through the macroscopic lens of social transformation. The institutional geography that lies somewhere between these views is one that Composition must explore, because it provides a perspective on student writing that we have also neglected.

Certainly, for many of us in composition and rhetoric, the "place" to introduce change is course content and assignments. But, even so, we acknowledge that not all of us have the luxury to take this approach, especially if we find ourselves in a small school or college where few others have composition training or interest and where the majority of faculty may well be adjunct or overworked (teaching many sections with many students), predisposing them and us to seek the path of least resistance: textbooks with ready-made assignments; handbooks with exercises, tests, and answer keys; and so forth. Or in an English department that has little regard or respect for the work of composition, because that work is associated with graduate student teaching assistants who are, at best, initiates. To assume that error is due to ignorance of rules is, after all, less time-consuming than to explore the more complex, politically charged dynamics at work—much less braving the "rudeness" or even danger of calling the institution's attention to itself.

Thus, current ways of addressing "error" (particularly in handbooks) assume the simplest (linguistic) cause of that error, when evidence suggests that simple ignorance of linguistic rules is not the cause, that there is a much more complex and complicated set of rhetorical triggers behind the writing "problems" that surface in student writers' work. (See the work of Charles Coleman, for one example.) We have not fully and rhetorically situated student writers' work within the educational contexts that produce it. We have not tackled the rhetorical exigency of "error" where the full scene of student writing in its particular institutional space/place has been examined. Identification of a "rhetorical grammar," while helpful in making connections between linguistic naming of language structures and the rhetorical purposes that those structures can and do serve, still does not move beyond internalized analyses to those that acknowledge the institutional setting, systems, and relationships in which student writing is produced.

That we have not made these moves is one more sign of how we create and support rhetorical distances that most truly—and still—work against access to college. Thus composition's focus on politically charged times in the general history of higher education institutions in the United States has blinded it to the institutionally charged *spaces* in which the work of composition in America has been and is being done. Or, at least, it has kept us from including critical perspectives on the spaces of our work in research and pedagogical approaches. It has promoted an unstated assumption (one favored by the academy) that academic structures, systems, and therefore spaces/places are (or should be) very much the same—virtually generic from institution to institution.

Such transparency of space disables the teacher or researcher from hearing students' questions about the mode of instruction (assignments, assessments, classrooms, placements, programs, etc.) as probings of underlying institutional, social, or academic cultural assumptions, as probings of conceptions of writing that inform the predominant institutional constructions of their everyday educational environments and relationships therein. It keeps us from seeing how students' questions and confusions might be a reaching for the "unvoiced" connections that our disciplinary positioning has placed outside the periphery of our vision. From seeing the ways in which the "problems" identified in student writing perhaps represent literacy practices that have been created and reinforced by years of institutionalized education—and how they (and their silencing) reproduce existing practices. This same transcendence or transparency of space also disables us as professionals from seeing the ways that our workplace differences potentially deconstruct our polite disciplinary pretenses of sameness or oneness as we gather at conferences over the reified body of student writing that is produced and reproduced over and over again, year after year.

In going along with this unstated assumption (so that we might universalize ourselves into a discipline), we compositionists have, even while resurrecting rhetorical theory and history, paradoxically instantiated ourselves as an essentially arhetorical discipline. This arhetorical treatment of ourselves parallels our similarly arhetorical treatment of students and their writing by ignoring the effects of local sites on the everyday lives and work of student writers and their teachers. In doing so, composition has created class systems and hierarchies that distance

those of us who do this work (often within the same institutional setting) from each other—and from our student writers.

This is one way of understanding James Sledd's pointed critique
of "boss compositionists" and of composition's "disciplining" of itself
within higher education's administrative (and accompanying "re-
wards") system. Sledd argued that in taking on the administrative
trappings and structures of a typical discipline, composition was forgetting its roots and its reason for being. He objected to this forgetting
as unethical; his sarcasm and satire—irritating to some, forceful to
others—sought to provoke compositionists to resist the ascendant
master narrative of institutionalized disciplinarity, with its attendant
job security for the few.

If our writing programs enact pedagogies that reputedly value the
highest levels of social consciousness but allow their own supporting
institutional cultures, structures, and mechanisms for maintaining
power to remain invisible, then we are not giving our students (or our
teachers or ourselves) the tools to negotiate the deadening distances that
institutional and organizational hierarchies and bureaucracies place
between their workers and their own everyday practices, distancing
strategies that students will most certainly face in institutional settings
outside higher education as well. What might it mean to ask for this
level of systemic self-reflexivity within higher education institutions?
What happens when critical consciousness begins at home?

Higher Education's Memorializing Hierarchies

To begin shifting our disciplinary gaze requires closer attention to
the nature of higher education's institutionalizing of academe, the
roots of the rhetorical stance that makes our avoidance of the institutional so pervasive/persuasive, so natural. Becoming more aware
of all our options for institutional critique requires that we be more
aware of institution as the place/space of our work as compositionists.
The problem with "work currently voiced as institutional critique,"
Porter and colleagues argue, is "that much of it equates 'institution'
with 'discipline'" (618), but that equation is not composition's invention: it is a tradition that in many ways has defined academic home

life and constructs the rhetorics through which academic disciplines universalize themselves.

Take, for example, compositionists' pervasive use of the idea of the social construction of knowledge (following Berger and Luckman's *Social Construction of Reality* and drawing heavily on Thomas Kuhn's notion of paradigms in *The Structure of Scientific Revolutions*). Part and parcel of our preference for egalitarian master narratives, this way of representing academe focuses on the collaborative building of knowledges and discourses through the participation of community members in an often democratically styled process of interaction and exchange of ideas, much like Burke's "parlor room," where new discussants continually come in the door, listen in on conversations around the room, join in discussions, and eventually move out of the room (*Philosophy of Literary Forms* 110–11). As people we are mortal, but the discussions are not—knowledge making goes on—and of course such a metaphorical parlor room never needs dusting, cleaning, or renovating, never calls attention to itself (except perhaps at retirement parties when the discussant's physical body is literally walking out the door), but simply provides a place where all can interact.

This preferred view conflicts with the critique by feminist and ethnographic researchers, both in and outside composition, of traditional research approaches and accompanying academic identities of neutrality. Feminists and ethnographers invite researchers to attend more closely to the particulars of everyday life, the relationships between researcher and the researched, and the differences between where the researcher and the researched live. So at some level we know that higher education is indeed a messy place. But compositionists, particularly those who live at research institutions, because we prefer to see academe as a space from which to do good things, are also apt to support the idea that academe is in some sense a neutral space. We are aware too that within most academic research, rendering the particulars of your own supporting institutional context as a visible influence on your work would put you at a disadvantage, would call attention perhaps to the fact that you might not be in the same intellectual or mental "parlor" as everyone else. At the disciplinary level, the goal is for research conducted by different researchers at different institutions to be able to speak the same language for a cumulative knowledge-building effect and to rely on the same master narratives of that work (no matter the differences in the institutional contexts of the researcher). Even at the institutional level, collective scholarly ethos rests on the value of work done by individuals, labs, teams, and so forth across different everyday contexts. The value placed on such work rests in good part on the invisibility of—or at least an appearance of sameness across—the specific institutional sites that actually house, clothe, feed, and otherwise sustain the academic bodies who populate any given discipline. If the specific institutional infrastructure or context of a researcher's project is visible, then it is seen to interfere with the researcher's work, rendering the results—at least in traditional ways of thinking about research—less useful because they are less generalizable to other contexts. Or such attention earns the work the label of "application," which is regarded as less valuable because it is removed from "original" research. In composition, for example, it is hard to persuade evaluators of tenure and promotion to recognize the work of setting up service-learning projects or other special writing programs as intellectual work equal in value to that of others. Such work renders the particulars of the institutional setting more visible and, furthermore, applies theory to those who live at lower or beginning levels of the institutional hierarchy; thus composition's prestige is dealt a double whammy.

This traditional and still powerful set of assumptions about the value of knowledges produced and work done within the academy affects those in lower positions in the hierarchy as well. It is a cliché that a college classroom is not the real world, where reality is the world of work outside academe. But neither is the work of student writers regarded as "real," in contrast to the work valued most *inside* academe, because of the hierarchy, or what cultural geographers might term "scale," that operationalizes our conception of higher-ed institutional life within the United States. Work accomplished (and texts produced) at or in proximity to positions in the upper reaches of this scale are assumed to be part of real participation in the social construction of knowledge; most others are considered merely practice along the way (though programs that involve undergraduates in real research with professors, particularly in the sciences, will cast the work of upper-level undergraduates as collaboration in an apprentice-type position more typical of graduate students). Overall, the typical conception of development and achievement is organized within U.S. academe—through its differing institutions, programs, curricula, and courses—along the lines of a scale of being/becoming that ignores institutional position/space by conflating it with the temporal development of certain abilities at different times in one's institutional life. It is the temporal master narrative of this developmental scale (a logical extension of that which is begun with basic writing) that still holds sway over our institutional lives:

- *Entering undergraduates* are required to master building blocks or basics such as critical thinking, reading, writing, quantitative literacy, technology literacy skills, and general education requirements in history, science, and the like.
- *Advanced undergraduates* move from initial survey courses, in which they learn content and terminology considered foundational to their field or discipline, into upper-level courses and labs in which they are exposed more and more to debate about the seminal texts, basic research methods, and content knowledge of their fields.
- *Graduate students* then take seminars and labs in which they move quickly beyond additional content knowledges to learn about, observe, practice, and then participate in the disciplinary processes and social relations that immediately surround the production of knowledge in their field, including taking a critical "insider" view of research methods, data collection and analysis, and eventually the politics of publication.
- Some of those who graduate with advanced degrees then enter into the *professoriate*, with its own hierarchy of adjunct and instructor teaching positions, non-tenure-track writing program administrative jobs (as in writing centers), and assistant, associate, and full professorships after institutionally designated periods.

- And a smaller number still from the professoriate enter into upper levels of *administration* within higher education institutions, becoming program administrators, department chairs, deans, provosts, and so forth.
- Note: The value ascribed to the last two positions on this scale is assigned not just by when such positions are achieved (the temporal aspect of this hierarchy) but by where they are achieved. Those who would wish to see higher education as an egalitarian social institution may deny it, but there is a definite class system among different types of U.S. higher education institutions, institutions with graduate programs that award doctoral degrees having more power because of their relative proximity to knowledge-producing functions of the academy, while those institutions farthest from knowledge production (and the daily experience and reminders that disciplinary knowledges are open systems) are more likely, by the nature of their daily work conditions, to present disciplinary knowledges as "closed" systems of knowledge-already-made.

Of course, despite the way this hierarchy focuses our attention on a temporal-developmental timeline, campus spaces too can be mapped according to this general academic geography of knowledge making: typically the nicest offices with the nicest views, furniture, and staffing belong to those at the uppermost (later) levels of the scale, and those at the beginning level have little permanent space at all, with graduate and undergraduate students often sharing the smallest spaces or partitions (such as cubicles or library carrels) or the even more generic public services and spaces of classrooms and labs.

And there is a parallel dynamic by which the value of academic "voices" coming from different positions is judged, by which academics (including, to some extent, compositionists) are constrained and guided in the time to be spent on analyzing the systems of relationships that inform the features of a writer's discourse and writing. As indicated in the above positional descriptions, primarily at the upper levels, particularly in graduate programs, are the complex personal and institutional social relations that construct knowledge-making activities that are disciplinarily legitimized for critical examination as influences on the research and writing produced there. Student writing at much lower levels in the hierarchy (as in composition classes) is typically not examined for rhetorical features related to the institutional relations of knowledge construction.

But, from feminist Doreen Massey's idea that social relations construct the places (physical locations) and spaces (organizational positions) in which we live and work, we see that such relations actually construct life and work at *every* physical place and corresponding position (space) on this scale. Exemplary qualitative studies of student writing from the 1990s mentioned earlier (Brooke; Cleary; and Chiseri-Strater) recognize the influence of general social relations, such as "identity negotiation" (Brooke), with which students look for and construct their places in society. But here we are trying to look squarely at institutionally constructed-and-constructing social relations that influence student writing. Scholarship on alternative discourses in the academy has begun to acknowledge such institutionally located relations of power and knowledge making. In "The Intellectual Work of 'Mixed' Forms of Academic Discourses," Patricia Bizzell points out that scholars have used other modes of communication because they provide ways of thinking not otherwise available in more traditional academic discourse. According to Bizzell, these alternative forms (such as the use of first-person point of view and experience in academic research articles) are not, however, limited to scholars: "The new forms are being used by everyone, not only by students and scholars from underrepresented social groups, and the reason is not far to seek . . . they make possible new forms of intellectual work" (5). These "new" forms have, in fact, been around in higher education for some time, and our lack of attention to institutional space/place has caused us to mislabel what are essentially differently positioned or located forms of intellectual work (and accompanying rhetorical features of spoken or written discourse) as work or writing of different inherent value. It is not coincidental that the new forms being used (particularly the more personal forms analyzed by Bizzell) tend to foreground the social relations, processes, and politics of the personal that in the traditional developmental trajectory of higher education (described above) are (or "should be") attended to only in later educational experiences and which in traditional academic discourse modes designed to contribute to "universalized" knowledge may never have appeared directly in professional, published academic research articles.

Bizzell's analyses help us see that students and faculty members carry with them, and interact within, a complex set of social relations that constructs their interactions with the physical places and positional spaces associated with *each* level and time on the higher education scale. But differences in attention allowed to such relations define not only different positions on higher education's institutional hierarchy but also the hegemonic inequality that lies at the core of academic life in higher education. Academe's own hierarchical temporal master narrative thus disfavors investigation of the institutional-rhetorical coherence of student writers' work and thus constructs student writers' frustrated responses to the truncated and conflated ways in which their work is assigned, responded to, and evaluated in the realm of the "affective" or "emotional"—not so much because their responses are illogical but because they ask for factors or features to be taken into account that lie beyond the realm of the system as it has defined itself. And the objectivity still generally prized by academic systems is thus defined not so much by what is logical or illogical, rational or irrational, male or female as it is by maintaining the positions in a hierarchy based on which the institution has organized itself to maintain a certain set of power relations.

Unfortunately but inevitably, this higher education organizational scale confers a kind of false authority (power that can be wielded by both administrators and teachers) resting on an objectivity that arises from the scale's self-professed lack of interest in the social relations that are a part of life at every place/space in academe. These social relations are institutionally acknowledged (or not) according to academe's preferred temporal master narrative, what Soja termed "historical epistemology" and what Doreen Massey points to as the negative affects/effects associated with academe's preference for temporal over more specifically and physically self-reflexive examinations of institutional spaces/places:

When we convene spatial differences into temporal sequence, as did/do so many modernist narratives, we are repressing the actuality of those differences. But there is another process also going on. . . . It is an act of distancing; the creation of a particular kind of gap. The primary aspect of this is that the process of becoming a producer of knowledge (and a definer and guardian of the kinds of things said to be knowledge) involves setting oneself apart from the things one is studying. . . . There has been a social geography of knowledge production (elite; historically largely male) which gained (and continues to gain) at least a part of its prestige from the cachet and exclusivity of its spatiality. (Massey, *For Space* 74–75)

Even at the top of the scale, the social relations that contextualize a field's "social construction of knowledge" are opened up for examination often *only* to the extent allowed by those who have positionally and *historically* dominated a field, or by those who are at institutions positioned (by "class") such that their voices can be better heard, as illustrated by Massey's analysis of the modern "science park"—the kind of large scientific research complexes built to both promote and attract large research projects and grants at modern universities:

The particular form of the proliferation of the division of labour within industry which resulted in that (so well known it seems natural) separation of "conception" from "execution" was propelled by forces both of class and of a particular notion of knowledge. Knowledge as removable from the shop floor, for instance. Knowledge as separable rather than tacit; distanced rather than embedded and embodied. . . . It is a recapitulation of an old story in Western history: the spatial seclusion of the desert for early Christian thinkers, the emergence of monasteries as elite places of knowledge production, the mediaeval universities. All of them places which crystallise through spatialisation a separation of Mind from Body, a notion of science as removal from the world. . . . That is one strand of the spatial histories these places ["science parks"] enfold. Another is that, through Western history, they have been part and parcel of the struggle around the creation of intelligible genders, of certain forms of "masculine" and "feminine." . . . The masculinity of the world's science parks today is not just a product of, nor can it be measured by, the fact of the overwhelming dominance on them of male employees. It is an outcome of a longer deeper history of gender construction which itself was/is spatially embedded within the making of defensive, specialised, "places of knowledge." (*For Space* 143–44)

Thus, the exigencies of the student writer (working, à la Massey, on the "shop floor" of higher education along with many compositionists) are quite different from those at the upper/advanced levels of academic culture. But these are spatial differences (and distancings) of power that rhetorical researchers across the disciplines have only begun to investigate, and often their investigations begin at those "advanced" positions on the higher education institutional scale (to illustrate the rhetorical evolution of genres important to academic culture, as in Charles Bazerman's *Shaping Written Knowledge*), where it is so easy to ignore issues of position/space/place.

The harmfulness of this system extends into every reach of our educational system. Teachers are led to identify themselves (and their authority) with disciplinary knowledges and approaches that are indifferent to varying institutional contexts. For K–12 teachers, disciplinary knowledges and approaches are increasingly embodied in state curriculum standards—and in the standardized testing that accompanies these standards, which are based on an appalling lack of systematic understanding of the effects of institutional space/place, position/location on the work of teachers and students therein. In South Carolina, for example, each school receives its own "report card" showing how that school's student population has fared in basic subjects on these standardized tests. College teachers typically base their authority on disciplinary affiliation that supersedes the need to know much about their particular institutional contexts or even about the history of disciplinary knowledge construction, research methods, and pedagogies: their focus, like that of researchers, can be reserved for the content knowledge that constructs the body of their discipline and is embedded in the textbooks that typically guide courses and testing. The "what" of content knowledge, rather than how that knowledge comes or came to be produced, generally takes precedence. And the farther one moves away from participation in graduate programs in any given discipline, the greater the distance from research of the kind sponsored by graduate programs in a discipline—and the greater the reliance on a general and temporally focused narrative of the content knowledge in that discipline as the basis for authority (which is then co-opted by standardized testing in K–12 and by assessment systems in undergraduate education).

Though researchers will view the discipline as an open system of knowledge to be added to, constructed, reconstructed, et cetera, the position of teacher—and of undergraduate courses and classrooms in the educational hierarchy—largely requires teaching faculty to act as if the discipline encompasses a closed system of knowledge: textbooks and programs of study, curriculum standards and standardized testing all encourage teachers to construct their authority on just such per-spectives. The accountability movement in K–12 schools, along with the assessment movement in higher education, places emphasis on an accounting of "value-added," though we have yet to understand the complex dynamics at any given school, to fine-tune our understand-ing of the different starting points embodied by the complex relations among students, institutional infrastructure, and community history at any given educational site.

And, for many college-level academics, our discipline is, in a very real sense, our home. We may move from institution to institution of higher education, but our disciplinary affiliations keep us feeling "one of the family." As compositionists, if we find ourselves in a smaller college or university as one of only a few compositionists (or the only one in sight), our disciplinarity gives us a sense of familiarity, pro-vides our safe harbor wherein we can speak from a sense of shared background and understanding of relationships and history—and we can do so as if there are others of us, even if we find ourselves alone at that particular space/place. When we speak from our disciplinary knowledge base in a meeting with non-comp-rhet faculty, we can invoke our disciplinary family (research, professional associations, and standards) to stand with us in support of our positions. Disciplinarity supports us as we make it through the sometimes hostile particulars of any given institutional space/place. We can arm ourselves and gird our loins with disciplinary research and histories of theory and practice. And in today's world of higher education, where budgets are typically tight and upper-level administrators may be managers drawn increasingly from the business community, our disciplines become an even more beloved home for many academics.

Given the pressures of academic culture to rise above local circumstances within any specific institution, why is it important to examine local contexts, to engage in institutional critique, at all? Because our disciplinarily created home life is an idealized landscape. This is an important issue for those of us in composition in particular, since failing to address local concerns and issues—where *local* refers to our own campuses and our own programs—means unwittingly adopting an arhetorical stance that runs counter to the very historical foundations we have claimed for ourselves. Administrators, teachers, and other professionals in writing programs at institutions where the problems of their institutional contexts are not so easily discounted, risen above, universalized, or neutralized, may well leave conferences and finish journal articles feeling a gap between what they have heard or read and what they experience in their everyday institutional contexts. Back home, such problems as resources, workloads, history, and survival (of the institution, of students, of programs) permeate their struggles to apply disciplinary knowledges and to enact commensurate pedagogical approaches generated often by, and certainly for, the situations of those at more privileged institutions or programs therein.

Critics such as Sharon Crowley and Susan Miller have described the dysfunctional systems in which many compositionists find themselves "back home," systems fed by what they and others have termed composition's feminized position within higher education. In fact, one of the qualities that differentiates composition from other disciplines in higher education is that our discipline has at times called on institutional sites and other disciplines to be more self-aware: institutions through focusing attention on issues of access and admissions (basic writing), and disciplines (writing in the disciplines, writing across the curriculum) through research on their social construction and rhetoricity. So even if composition is not such a safe place in higher education, our embattled position makes this home all the more dear to us, makes us all the more fierce in defense of what we do, even though we face distinct differences in the conditions of our home institutions. Porter et al.'s criticism remains; as a discipline, we compositionists have spoken about our specific home spaces/places primarily in general terms, assuming that most of us operate within generally similar sites and systems. Though we articulate our feminized position, we essentialize it, generalizing that position to all compositionists, as if all of us experience oppression in the same ways despite differences in the nexus of individual, disciplinary, and institutional histories at any given site. We thereby continue to adopt the same arhetorical stance on the specific contexts of our work.

We would do well to recollect the stance on "home" exemplified in the work of writers bell hooks, Marilynne Robinson, and Toni Morrison, as well as feminist cultural geographer Doreen Massey. They and other feminists remind us that the places we are taught to consider home are constructed as "safe places" by the same master narratives that maintain society's ignorance of the everyday lived realities (and struggles) of women (or any minority) within those spaces. In Robinson's *Housekeeping*, the leaves that drift into corners are emblematic of the details that gather force as Sylvie and Ruth are increasingly unable to maintain the standard of normalcy held up for them by the sheriff and townspeople. For bell hooks, relationships within the "home" sustain and are sustained by a strong Southern black womanhood, even while maintaining the tradition of silence in public spaces/places for that same group of women. In Morrison's *Beloved*, "124" signals from the first utterance of the novel the missing, the absent presence, the ghosts of "rememories" engendered by relationships and horrendous events tied to the "old home" plantation, ghosts now manifesting themselves in the new home site. We both are and are not safe at home. Either perspective exerts its own potentially paralyzing force.

As compositionists, we are stuck between the institutional and disciplinary horns (homes?) of a dilemma. It is not that we have not considered our home spaces/places but that, as Porter et al. point out, we have not theorized our institutional spaces/places in ways that allow us to connect where we are (institutional settings) with what we are doing (discipline)—to connect our sense of what is wrong with how we are positioned as a discipline in higher education's institutional hierarchy with our everyday work with student writers in our specific local contexts. The gap between our theoretical and pedagogical perspectives, on the one hand, and what we actually do and where we are in our everyday institutional work, on the other, remains a problematic sign of our overreliance on an overgeneralized disciplinarity.

Those gaps—between institutional positioning, disciplinary depictions, and our work in actual spaces/places constructed through our everyday relationships with teaching colleagues and students—maintain a rhetorical distance that holds us back, that keeps us looking at the work of student writers in ways that only reify attitudes about what "nontraditional" students bring (or do not bring) to the academy, attitudes that we like to believe have been left behind but that remain embedded in higher education's memorializing hierarchies.

Interactional Inquiry and Feminist Rememories of Emotion

The admittedly initial analyses, above, of academe and of composition's institutional and spatial positioning therein introduce several themes that are and will be key to the work presented both in this section and in later chapters: (a) that spatial awareness and accompanying reinterpretation of our disciplinary narratives and preferences (for temporal sequencing) are sorely needed; (b) that such reinterpretation will call on us to interrogate current positional and power differences that writing research and pedagogies establish between the roles of teacher, researcher, student, and administrator and across different institutional sites; (c) that such reinterpretation will require that we ferret out those distancing mechanisms by which we have unconsciously learned to ignore institutional differences as negligible (or nonexistent) influences on teachers and students of writing; and

(d) that methods (such as interactional inquiry) are needed to facilitate institutional critique in academe at all levels and, again, across different institutional sites.

Porter and colleagues argue that institutional critique proceeds by noticing "gaps and fissures" (like those noted in Massey's and Soja's analyses of the privileging of the temporal and ignoring of the spatial) and applying those analyses to higher education and composition's master narratives of self. We agree, even while arguing for a way of organizing as many participants as possible to operationalize and realize the goal of rhetorical actions responsive to the institutional space/place. Our experiences in Studio programs have shown us the value of a more specific methodology for facilitating sustained interactions between participants (and awareness of their positional perspectives) that builds, over time, more complex analyses of the institutional power relations and positionings that affect all higher education participants—and in languages and forms that better express the value of the different kinds of intellectual work that occur at different institutions and different positions therein. To these ends, we introduce our work with the methodology that we term *interactional inquiry*.

Because of our early positioning within our state- and national-level struggles over basic writing, we turned, in that fall 1991 research seminar, not only to those researchers and theorists mentioned earlier but also to the then very recent work of Marie Wilson Nelson in *At the Point of Need*. Nelson focused on a tangibly different institutional space—the writing center—for working with basic (and English-as-a-second-language) writers. Her work from the everyday position allowed by the writing center reminded us that Mike Rose's questioning of the concept of remediation also emerged from a similar writing-centered point of view, in combination with his own working-class background. For Nelson, working "at the point of need" in student groups led by writing center personnel opened up errors by locating them within the contexts of actual production. Her work was unique not because it was located in a writing center but because she used research approaches to structure a support system for that work.

Through staff meetings and collaborative inquiry teams, the writing center, in Nelson's vision and practice, became a center of research on student writing, far removed from the "fix-it shop" stereotype. Though Nelson, like Shaughnessy, focused on reseeing error, she did so by locating the scene for student writing much more in the everyday affective world of the production of writing, as that world was opened up within the qualitative research she and her assistants conducted in the writing center. She and her staff focused student writers' attention on discovering the patterns in their own writing "errors," patterns that rested as much in the affective and attitudinal approaches of student writers as in their knowledge of basic sentence structures. Also, Nelson's cooperative, qualitative inquiry approach (one that she has further developed in her work at National Louis University since that time) with her staff group appealed to us and turned us toward important work done in our own field with the use of groups inside the classroom not only for workshopping writing but also for promoting greater awareness of and attention to writing process and real-time response to written products (Elbow; Brooke, Mirtz, and Evans), as well as the long history of writing groups outside academe (Gere).

What came together in our minds and discussions was a program that would combine our own field's movements toward "the social," toward small groups, toward workshopping, toward qualitative inquiry, and (as we will show shortly) toward feminist focuses on the interactional nature of knowledge production as a "rememorying" of institutional space. But because our own field was so inwardly focused, we had to go outside our field for models of ways to support interactions across levels and layers of groups as research, to resee composition's space in ways that Doreen Massey would have us see space (even though our awareness of space was, at that time, just beginning to develop through our experiences):

- "as the product of interrelations; as constituted through interactions, from the immensity of the global to the intimately tiny";
- "as the sphere of the possibility of the existence of multiplicity in the sense of contemporaneous plurality; as the sphere in which distinct trajectories coexist";
- "as the sphere therefore of coexisting heterogeneity. . . . a product of relations-between, relations which are nec-

essarily embedded material practices which have to be
carried out, it is always in the process of being made."
(Massey, *For Space* 9)

What we found lay outside the bounds of U.S. higher education
altogether, much less tied to those disciplinary imaginings of self most
familiar to our institutional settings. Human inquiry approaches forged
by Peter Reason and John Rowan of the Postgraduate Research Group
at the University of Bath (Reason and Rowan; Reason) seek to effect
change within local institutional settings by organizing small groups
of people who work or live at a site (hospitals, city hall, prisons, etc.)
to meet regularly for activities and discussions that bring out issues
and problems particular to the site. Over time, the group *cooperatively*
moves through cycles of *inquiry* (discussion, role-playing, storytelling,
writing, etc.) and *action* (trying out approaches, actions, or changes
discussed within the inquiry group in their daily lives at the site): the
results of actions are discussed back in the inquiry group meeting,
and further plans are made; the "script" of life at that site, including
power relations, is thus externalized, worked on, negotiated. Early on
we coined our own term—*interactional inquiry*—to signal our belief in
the importance of highlighting and attending to the lateral interactions
across previously existing institutional hierarchies or boundaries.

Basing the Writing Studio program on human inquiry approaches
meant seeing each student group not just as a writing group but
as part of an overall program of regular, active inquiry into writing
processes and products within the courses, program, and college in
which these students and we were located. In addition to leading student groups, Studio group leaders also meet regularly; bring writing
to share; discuss observations, interactions, and patterns; and look
within individual scenarios and events at student writing as work
embedded in the dynamic interaction of individual, course, disciplinary, and institutional contexts. What impressed us about this research
approach is how exploring often intimate interactions—what Patricia
Mann refers to as "micropolitics"—brings participants greater understanding of the larger workings of organizations—and vice versa. We
saw human inquiry as a research approach that (a) acknowledges the
presence and influences of what Bourdieu terms "habituated practice,"

(b) proposes that people can organize themselves in a way that raises awareness and effects change in the organizational contexts for their work and lives, that their collective collaboration might gain them a voice that an organization could "hear" or that could reshape their position therein, and (c) operates from an assumption that the power dynamics, history, and physical space/place of the setting permeate the work of those within at all levels, including the everyday.

Reason and Rowan's use of small groups of people meeting regularly and engaging with each other through discourse (though primarily in oral, story-telling forms) of course resonated with Peter Elbow's *Writing without Teachers* and *Writing with Power*, as well as the writing workshop pedagogy outlined in Elbow and Pat Belanoff's *A Community of Writers*, a text with which the two of us were familiar from our composition teaching. Likewise, Reason and Rowan's focus on a community of inquiry that works toward action for social and civic change resonated with the growing literature at that time on Freirean approaches, on critical consciousness, and pedagogies thereof (Shor). But Reason and Rowan's "new paradigm" research was also interesting because it deconstructed traditional research roles and broke down boundaries between where research and education were (temporally) thought to be in a traditional institutional hierarchy:

> The simplest description of co-operative inquiry is that it is a way of doing research in which all those involved contribute both to the creative thinking that goes into the enterprise—deciding on what is to be looked at, the methods of the inquiry, and making sense of what is found out—and *also* to the action which is the subject of the research. . . . Thus in its fullest form the distinction between researcher and subject disappears, and all who participate are both co-researchers and co-subjects. *Co-operative inquiry is therefore also a form of education, personal development, and social action.* (Reason 1, ending emphasis added)

That the distinction between researcher and subject can be dissolved is, of course, debatable, particularly when we, our graduate student

staff and group leaders, and students occupy such definite positions
in the university hierarchy. But nonetheless we believed that striving
for cooperative inquiry and talking as openly as possible about our
various positionings were part of what we wanted to put on the table
at our weekly Studio student sessions and in our weekly staff meetings. The distinctions among us instantiated by our positions in the
university are not so much dissolved as made open for discussion
rather than silently or politely ignored. For example, when students in
Studio sessions wanted to talk about their teachers in personal ways
("she doesn't like me," etc.), it was part of the group leader's job to
steer discussion away from blind conjecture about a teacher's personal
preferences. The group leader could take a view of the teacher based
on the role he or she was working to fulfill in the program, to look
at the teacher's responses as constructed by a number of interrelated
local factors (ranging from the teaching assistant's own educational
background, interests, and level of experiences in the classroom to
the institutional resources of time, materials, and equipment that
were or were not available, to where he or she might be in the general
first-year composition course outline and what topics, readings, or
assignments are being worked on or toward), to explore the kind of
relations that these factors set up in the classroom, and to encourage
students to ask their teachers questions or to visit them during office
hours so that they might gain greater insights of their own into their
teachers' perceptions of their work.

Likewise, in our staff meetings, as we discussed different student
groups and their interactions with their classroom teachers and assignments, the two of us worked together and with our group leaders
to look at how the assignments and approaches of different teachers
(seen in their Studio student groups on a weekly basis) were connected
to the institutional and disciplinary conditions, backgrounds, and
interests of those same teachers—and to do the same when looking at
the assumptions that underpinned our own practices and interactions
with student writers and their work. In both student and staff Studio
groups, what was key was the comparison across the participants in
the program, comparisons made possible by having students in Studio
groups who had different first-year composition course teachers, and

by our staff having students in their groups from several different teachers as well.

Our look at alternative research approaches along the lines of Reason and Rowan's cooperative or participatory inquiry was also heavily informed by our joint interest in feminist theory and research methods. Our own prior attractions to feminist thought informed our understanding of the action research methodology on which Studio is based—Nancy through her work with the fictional forms and relationships between women in the work of New Zealand artist, writer, and teacher Sylvia Ashton-Warner and Rhonda through her work tracing the concept of "recollection" from classical rhetoric into the work of twentieth-century feminists such as Mary Daly. In fact, our first attempt to "theorize" Studio work in *WPA* and *CCC* articles for composition audiences drew heavily on the feminist theory that was then (and is now) informing important work in composition. We were particularly interested in work that was reflexive about the "spaces" for "other" in the academy, including feminist writings in our own and other disciplines, primarily sociology (Belenky et al.; Flynn; hooks; Kirsch; Mann; Susan Miller; Ritchie; Smith; and others). In conference presentations when we attempted to enact Studio staff sessions and explore specific stories of our work with student writers in Studio, we were looking to compile the details of "other" lives and to locate patterns in these details that did not fit the master narrative of what causes or leads to writing problems, a master narrative that we saw guiding most handbooks, course curricula, assignments, and the grading of student writing. One such presentation was "Pedagogy as Institutional/Institutionalized Practice: Bringing a Program for Mainstreaming Basic Writers into Being" at the 1994 Conference on College Composition and Communication in Nashville. Each of us, along with seven of our graduate student staff members (from staff groups for two years), wrote one-pagers to read in the session and thus brought to the conference stories of our Studio students and our own experiences as staff members in the Studio endeavor, generating material for and demonstrating the process of "theorizing the cross-section."

Cited as a background source for Reason and Rowan's concept of participatory inquiry, the SPUJJ collective's (an acronym made from the initial letters of the authors' first names) approach to "memory work" provided us with a specific model of how the work of many such small groups might be a powerful basis for effecting change in larger master narratives (Crawford, Kippax, Onyx, Gault, and Benton). "SPUJJ collective" names a group of women psychology researchers in Australia who collected thousands of "memory stories" from groups all around their country and then "theorized the cross-section" of these stories, contributing to work on the social psychology of emotion and gender. Dissatisfied with the state of 1990s psychological theory about women, these Australian women researchers—Susan Kippax, Pam Benton, Una Gault, Jenny Onyx, and June Crawford—used small groups composed of coresearchers and a cycle of writing and reflective activities as a way to supply modern psychological theories with better understandings of the social nature and construction of emotion. They drew on the work of German sociologist Frigga Haug with what she termed "memory work": groups of coresearchers wrote from prompts designed to elicit early memories associated with specific emotions and then shared their stories with others in their group, arriving at commonalities or differences across stories on the basis of gender:

> The underlying theory is that subjectively significant events, events which are remembered, and the way they are subsequently constructed, play an important part in the construction of self. Because self is socially constructed through reflection, Haug's theory dictates memory-work as method. The initial data of the method, memory-work, are memories, which are reappraised collectively to uncover and document the social nature of their production. (Crawford, Kippax, Onyx, Gault, and Benton 37)

SPUJJ termed this collective reappraisal "theorizing the cross-section." And if the distinction between researcher and subject, or the power hierarchies between ourselves and students, are an unavoidable feature of institutional life in higher education spaces, we nonetheless found immense value in the way that the comparisons made available within Studio student and staff groups—using writing and reading assignments from within our academic institution and the attendant attitudes, feelings, and writings or reflections thereon within student and staff groups as "prompts"—also made visible the complex social construction of people and ideas in the academic culture particular to our home institution. Though SPUJJ's work does not attend to specific institutional space or place, their methodology applied on a local scale did give us a useful framework for thinking about and capturing local insights. What is brought to the table at each week's Studio staff meetings are stories both from group leaders' observations of students in the Studio groups and from the students themselves about their work/writing. A Studio program's goal is to theorize the cross-section of these stories, looking each week for themes, patterns, possibilities, linkages, and connections that make sense of perceptions, actions, and attitudes toward writing and language use in their institutional setting.

This search for the larger lessons within our weekly work allowed and allows us to challenge each other in our weekly meetings, to ask about alternative readings and interpretations of what staff and our students see and experience. Theorizing the cross-section also created a space for critiquing and revising the program itself, bringing us the knowledge base from which to better understand the systems within which we live and work as we seek change therein. We saw how inquiry-based research methods and program designs can provide a way for higher education institutions to become more reflexive, to address the effects of themselves as contexts for learning and to resee their work with FYC as research opportunity instead of remedial drag.

The remembering and reconstruction of identity across and despite socially and institutionally constructed and maintained distances is a theme we recognized from the work of feminist novelists and writers—including Robinson's *Housekeeping*, which we used as a fictional frame for our 1996 *CCC* article on Writing Studio work. Feminist writers and thinkers often focus on the importance of space/place in their work of recovery, and this focus resonated in our work with Studio staff groups in various locations and in other institutional spaces to which we were invited to try out adaptations of the USC Studio program.

Connections between memory and location in the work of modern feminists and in classical rhetoric provided important (back)grounding for our early thinking about Studio principles and practice. In spring and summer 1992, as the two of us were writing our Studio proposal and struggling with departmental politics for its initial acceptance, Rhonda was also hurrying to complete a book manuscript, tentatively titled *Recollection and Its Return* (before giving birth to her second daughter, Emily, in late July), that would trace the connection between ideas about the social construction of memory and rhetorical theory. Arising from her dissertation work, which traced the influence of classical Greek (and earlier Egyptian) theories of memory on classical rhetorical theory, Rhonda had added chapters showing how twentieth-century feminist thinkers and writers such as bell hooks and Mary Daly were linking memory, location, and "the politics of the personal" (Grego, *Textual Nature of Memory*).

These twentieth-century feminists were interested in how the surfacing of emotions in connection to specific places calls attention to the undeniable realities experienced by "others" in a society that has constructed its master narratives to "absent" those experiences. Thus, in Toni Morrison's novel *Beloved* (recall that the subtitle of *Phaedrus* is *To My Beloved*), the connection between memory and place is used to deconstruct social rhetorics of race. From the perspective of the social institution of motherhood, society sees Sethe as a monster—a mother who brutally murdered her own children. But Morrison unfolds the story from the perspective of Sethe's daily interactions with her family and community, and as she does so, both Sethe and we as readers travel across the distances constructed by institutionalized racism (including that found most ominously in "school" for Sethe) into a deeper understanding of the details and the complexities of everyday life and lack of agency behind the thinness of the scene as it was depicted in that original newspaper account of her children's deaths. As the story unfolds, those forgotten, ignored, or unknown pieces of her life surface in what Sethe coins "rememories" that linger in the places of their commission, that live an unsanctioned life. These distanced events and experiences, the unacknowledged and at times horrific scenes of daily existence (such as pregnant Sethe's rape by the

School Master and his sons) live in places because in these spaces their realness cannot be denied and their presence there is strong enough to transcend their studied absence in society's preferred narratives of itself and its institutions.

This located and spatialized view of emotion and its connection with a rhetorical psychology and sociology was useful as we encountered the emotional landscapes of students, staff, and ourselves within the new territory of interactional inquiry during the early years of Studio work. In our 1995 *WPA* article on Studio, we hypothesized that the conflicts (and silences) between student writers' everyday perceived realities and what current "languages" for talking about writing do and do not allow one to easily express account for much student frustration. Putting issues, thoughts, ideas, attitudes, and feelings "on the table" (something we talk about in both student and staff Studio sessions) continues to be a key coinage, naming the only process that we know by which to explore this terrain.

We believed that the positioning of Studio—outside-but-alongside first-year composition courses—and the insights engendered about everyday practice within a writing program at a large university could help us see past what feminists might call the "master narrative" or what feminist sociologist Dorothy Smith in *The Everyday World as Problematic: A Feminist Sociology* terms a "ruling apparatus":

> The ruling apparatus is that familiar complex of management, government administration, professions, and intelligentsia, as well as the textually mediated discourses that coordinate and interpenetrate it. Its special capacity is the organization of particular actual places, persons, and events into generalized and abstracted modes vested in categorical systems, rules, laws, and conceptual practices. The former thereby become subject to an abstracted and universalized system of ruling mediated by texts. (108)

By engaging the particulars of everyday writing and practice within a specific setting in Studio sessions, we felt able to move beyond the "abstracted and universalized" ideas about composition that are inevitably a part of any writing program's pedagogical approach, no matter how critically conscious that approach may be—and in this sense Studio throws into contrastive relief institutionalized, disciplinary ideas about writing versus local, felt realities. The past fifteen years of work across our respective Studio programs have convinced us that higher education has not taken a full account of the rhetorical exigencies encountered by students and teachers as they travel between cultures/worlds; we have not attended as fully as necessary to the historical, institutional, and individual dynamics and logics of difference (and the linguistic and rhetorical expressions thereof) that construct those cultures/worlds. The relations that construct everyday life and work in any institutional or organizational setting—including higher education—create the complex rhetorical exigencies that inform writing, as opposed to the spatially thin, temporally focused narratives we have constructed about student writing and the at times embarrassingly glib ways of acting and talking about our work with student writers that these narratives allow because they can rest on what is already known, believed, or just presumed about student writing.

As we have worked to reconstruct the "other" logics of student work in the uneasiness and tensions that surfaced through our program's weekly contextualizing of student writers' work (and their teachers' responses thereto), we came to see how Studio is what Smith terms "an exploration rather than an account of a destination" (106), that Studio seeks what Patricia Mann (*Micro-Politics: Agency in a Postfeminist Era*) terms "interpersonal agency"—a rearticulation of "individual agency within particular institutional frameworks" (23). Thus, one of our most important disciplinary goals must be to forge writing program structures that can provide support for students and their teachers as they explore and negotiate the institutional spaces/places that influence their everyday work. To this end, we believe Writing Studio's interactional inquiry highlights composition's a/rhetorical situation and supports the institutional critique called for by Porter and colleagues systematically and systemically, in ways that the following chapters will further articulate and interrogate.

2 / Institutional Critique and Studio as Thirdspace

This chapter pursues further understandings of institutional critique and thirdspace, both of which are gaining in popularity in composition and, in the case of thirdspace, in general culture. First, we use Kenneth Burke's pentadic analysis to highlight an attitude in higher education institutions that is responsible for many of the "gaps and fissures" Porter et al. claim as a starting point for rhetorical action aimed at productive change. Second, we explicate the ways in which this attitude is responsible for the devaluing of emotion and the recasting of it as a label applied to those behaviors outside institutional norms. Third, we turn to the work of specific educational researchers, critical theorists, postmodern cultural geographers, and feminists to further explore the concept of "thirdspace," with which we would equate actions taken within those gaps and fissures. We use this theoretical explication of thirdspace to introduce key assumptions and some of our practices and observations as we discuss those programs we term "Studio," preparing for more explicit examination of specific institutional locations and examples in chapters 3 and 4.

Shifting the Circumference of Our Analysis

In *Geographies of Writing*, Nedra Reynolds introduces compositionists to geographers' concept of "spatial scale," explaining that "[m]ost nonspecialists also understand spatial scale in the way that Adrienne Rich did as a girl [reminiscent also of a scene in Thornton Wilder's *Our Town*] preparing to send a letter to a pen pal":

    Adrienne Rich
    14 Edgevale Road
    Baltimore, Maryland

> The United States of America
> The Continent of North America
> The Western Hemisphere
> The Earth
> The Solar System
> The Universe (qtd. in Reynolds 54)

Reynolds explains that "[h]uman geographers also rely upon this nontechnical but powerful form of spatial scale to demonstrate how the social production of space stretches out from individual bodies to the home, neighborhood, city, region, nation, and world" (54–55). Even closer to home, we find an explication of this same basic idea of scale, but with a rhetorical twist—and a distinction key to institutional critique—in the work of Kenneth Burke.

In *A Grammar of Motives*, Burke proposes the dramatistic pentad as a means to discover what he calls the "motives" of discourse:

> In a rounded statement about motives, you must have some word that names the *act* (names what took place, in thought or deed), and another that names the *scene* (the background of the act, the situation in which it occurred); also you must indicate what person or kind of person (*agent*) performed the act, what means or instruments he used (*agency*), and the *purpose*. (xv, emphasis in the original)

Central to the use of Burke's pentad is the element of "scene." Burke begins his discussion of the pentad with a first chapter titled "Container and Thing Contained" and with this statement: "Using 'scene' in the sense of setting, or background, and 'act' in the sense of action, one could say that 'the scene contains the act.' And using 'agents' in the sense of actors, or acters, one could say that 'the scene contains the agents'" (3). Though Burke does not argue for the importance of any one pentadic element over another, parallels between "scene" (the way one names the "place" of action) and the importance of which-ever term is chosen to be the "container" in exercising the pentadic ratios to critically probe different perspectives on any given action or situation makes "scene" feel like a kind of master trope. Certainly the social production of space—and the consequences of how we choose to name space/place—is embedded in Burke's conception of scene, as examples and discussion by rhetorical critics Foss, Foss, and Trapp (drawing on Burke's *A Grammar of Motives*) illustrate:

> "Scene" is the ground, location, or situation in which the act takes place. Terms for scene include such labels as, "it is 12:20 P.M.," historical epochs such as the "Elizabethan period" or the "Depression," or "in Florida in January." A scenic statement might even be as broad as "in a period following the invention of the atomic bomb but prior to a soft landing of electronic instruments on the surface of the moon."
>
> How the scene is designated is important because this label indicates the scope of the analysis. A variety of circumstances are available to select as characterizations of a scene: "For a man is not only in the situation peculiar to his era or to his particular place in that era (even if we could agree on the traits that characterize his era). He is also in a situation extending through centuries; he is in a 'generically human' situation; and he is in a 'universal' situation." The scene in which the artist is painting, then, could be described as "a studio," "New York City," "midnight on February 3, 1984," "the United States," "the post-modern era in art," or "the planet earth." The scene selected has an impact on the selection of the other terms in the pentad and establishes the circumference of the analysis. No particular description of the setting is the correct one; Burke simply points out that how scene is labeled affects the scope of the critic's interpretation of motivation. (Foss, Foss, and Trapp 169)

Given Soja's contention that intellectuals have privileged temporal master narratives to the neglect of the spatial, and Massey's argument that this privileging has masked exclusions of "other" perspectives (see chapter 1), most of Burke's examples for "scene" are fairly traditional to temporal-based master narratives favored by modernist intellectuals—"Elizabethan period" or "Depression" or "era"—though Burke's insistence on the full consideration of all pentadic elements indicates a thoroughly social understanding of "rhetorical situation."

Foss, Foss, and Trapp note that

> Burke intended the pentad to be used *internally*—within a rhetorical transaction such as a speech—so that the pentadic elements are selected from the actual content of the discourse. The act, then, would be the act discussed by the rhetor, the scene would be where the rhetor says the act occurs, and the agent would be the person or persons the rhetor sees as engaging in the act. (168, emphasis added)

Such rhetorical analysis is the kind that most college writing courses promote for student writers (rhetors) as they approach an assignment. It typically creates a sense of audience and purpose that are internal to the texts being read, studied, and discussed so that student writers come to some understanding of the intellectual scene in which their words, too, will live, from which their words, too, should draw motivation. College courses thus immerse student writers as rhetors in the intellectual scene internal to the texts studied and those to be produced, typically either through a kind of "case" approach that presents some organizational (as in technical writing classes) or social or disciplinary issue or texts for discussion, reflection, or debate or through a liberatory pedagogical approach that presents community or social issues for the same (sometimes including service-learning experiences and projects as well). In either of these cases, student writers are helped by teacher, texts, and experiences to enact and understand the pentadic elements internal to the situation or issue for rhetorical analysis and action. Because the actor/rhetor in such cases is the student writer, it is possible that the rhetor could designate the scene as the classroom (and thereby call attention to the institutional or material setting in which he or she is working). It is possible but unlikely, since the point of most assignments is to show awareness of scene in terms of the time, place, and setting inherent in the real world (or at least the disciplinary conception thereof) of the texts being studied.

By virtue of positioning and structure, most college courses enact internal pentadic analysis of the texts being read or written, thereby maintaining the transparency of the institutional setting. Even in a course directed by the goals of liberatory pedagogy, the scene is shifted from the course section itself to one that defines the civic problem or situation within which the students are studying and communicating. Bruce Horner notes, "More recent strategies which identify the social *with* the classroom, such as collaborative and contact-zone pedagogies, despite their difference from each other and from expressivist and process pedagogies, nonetheless also imagine the classroom as . . . a privileged, dematerialized location from which to act on the social" (43, emphasis in original). In moving from "classroom" to "social," the institutional location that would materialize composition's work is ignored.

Though Burke's pentadic analysis was to be used to discern motivations internal to a group of texts, Foss, Foss, and Trapp point out,

> The pentad has been extended, however, to apply as well to the larger context in which the rhetoric studied is seen as the act, with the other elements selected to correspond to it. In this case, a speech would be viewed as the act, the scene would be the place where the speech was delivered, the agent would be the rhetor delivering the speech, and so on. (168–69)

Applied to the work of students, student-writing-as-assignment would be the act; student writer the actor; the particular course the scene; curriculum, teachers, physical and monetary resources, program of study, et cetera, the agents; and so on.

In external analysis, the particular course and classroom as a local scene exist in the spatial scale that includes in its larger reaches the particular higher education institution. Attending to the scenes of student writing (and therefore our analyses of student-writing acts, actors, agents, and purposes) within an external pentadic analysis encourages us to attend not only to the complexity and influence of the classroom with its variety of people, programs, and points of connection to worlds both inside and outside academe but also to the complexity and influence of the institutional location as a scene with a variety of people, programs, material and economic conditions, buildings, history, and points of connection to worlds both inside and outside academe as well.

However, if a key ingredient of Porter and colleagues' "institutional critique" is to locate gaps and fissures (wherein they believe change is possible), then just such gaps are going to be found for some time yet in the tension between internal and external analytical approaches as regarded by the academy: academic disciplines prefer and privilege internal pentadic approaches to its defining texts, for one reason because the scenes internal to disciplinarily privileged texts are easily located within the temporal master narratives that guide intellectual work therein. External pentadic approaches, on the other hand, either are ignored altogether or are recognized only to establish a benchmark for determining the difference between "original" intellectual work, as opposed to the less valued work of either education or application, particularly when the application is particular to a specific institutional space/place.

Though a consistent use of external pentadic analysis could constitute a rhetorical act with immense consequences for composition, our use, much less recognition, of external pentadic perspectives is patchy at best, relegated to areas of our work that do not fit easily within academe's preferred temporal master narratives of its internally focused interpretations, as the following examples of the above instances indicate: (a) To the extent that they attend to (or at least identify) institutional scenes and their influence on student writing, liberatory pedagogy, professional and technical writing, and more recently, service-learning approaches manifest in part our field's impulses toward external pentadic analyses of student writing and the teaching of writing. But the institutional scene typically identified with these approaches as an influence on student writing is some civic or corporate organization and not the particular higher education organization that houses teachers and students itself. (b) Composition has enacted and does enact external pentadic analysis of higher education as an organizational setting for student writing so as to look at and talk about writing program administration with the hope of making it seem part of our disciplinary intellectual work. In reality this ploy is unconvincing when composition is housed within a department where others carry out more internally focused disciplinary work (as in literature, linguistics, critical theory, cultural studies, etc.) because the contrast between the internally and externally focused work is seen as that between subject matter and education areas.

Thus, though Porter and colleagues point to the development of rhetoric and composition doctoral programs and undergraduate writing majors as rhetorical actions taken within institutional spaces available for change, we believe that such programs are effective only insofar as they are able to resist a retrenchment into internal pentadic analyses of composition's work, and only insofar as such programs can insist on external pentadic awareness of the institutional influences of higher education on academic writing and can bring that awareness into arenas and areas of higher education life typically reserved for the intellectual work of disciplines that rests on internal pentadic analysis. And, we must ask, what about the many institutions where there is no chance for a doctoral program or even for an undergraduate writing major? Where there may not even be the infrastructures for writing program administration, as those of us who have lived at four-year state-supported (or well-endowed private) colleges assume? Where there may be, at best, only one or two faculty with professional training or interest specifically in composition or rhetoric, where most faculty's professional area is one of those internally focused disciplines?

Must the possibility of institutional critique rest on structural possibilities found only in certain types or classes of institutions? Let's hope not.

Indeed, we believe that Studio programs, operating outside but alongside student writers' participation in other college courses and making use of interactional inquiry methodology, take rhetorical advantage of the tension created by just that gap between internally and externally focused pentadic analyses (a tension and gap felt by both students and teachers of writing) that we have presented here and which we will explore in further detail in the section on thirdspace. We believe that thirdspaces like Studios open up space for externally focused pentadic analyses in higher education institutions and that systematically pursuing spatialized analyses of student writing and the teaching of writing within these spaces will blur the lines between internally and externally focused analyses and can effect change in the valuing or devaluing of particular kinds of work (specifically that of composition) in higher education that ensue from this undoubtedly false binary.

Metarhetorical Awareness and a Spatial Understanding of Emotion

Before our survey of thirdspace theories, we stop to give an example of a devalued area of composition's work that can now be recast. Though higher education's understanding of the significance of *emotion* within academic work is still blinded by its own institutional transparency, compositionists have long noted its importance without being able to effect any overall change in academe's view. Among compositionists most recently attentive to this problem, Dobrin and Weisser note in *Natural Discourse* (2002),

> While emotion has existed in some contexts in Western thinking, it has been mostly relegated to the creative arts. As such it stands in sharp opposition to the rationalistic thinking that long dominated the sciences. In a sense, scientific rationality has been defined as that which "gets things done in the world," while emotion and the arts are seen as something superfluous and, at best, life enhancing. (160–61)

In arguing for the value of refocusing composition's attention on space/place in general—under the aegis of "ecology," "environment," and "ecocomposition"—Dobrin and Weisser spend considerable time in their last forecasting chapter on the need to shift composition's view of emotion: "Ecocomposition recasts the personal and emotional as a dialectic, highlighting the importance of 'particular' perspectives in order to avoid totalizing narratives and meta-narratives" (161); without naming it as such, they connect to Porter et al.'s project of institutional critique, contending, "A move to include emotive response as integrally crucial to understanding issues of environment is a move to resist the control wielded over natural bodies, landscapes, and environments" (164). Still, the difficulty, they acknowledge (particularly in their chapter 2), in separating "ecocriticism" (as *interpretation* of texts) from ecocomposition (as *production* of texts) indicates the difficulty anyone in academe will have in trying to use a disciplinary concept evolved for internally focused pentadic analyses (in the case of "ecocriticism" as an interpretive approach to literary texts) to generate an externally focused counterpart ("ecocomposition"). Such a direction for change will be incomprehensible to academic privileging of internally focused pentadic analyses, and the institutionalized discipline will certainly prove resistant to the separation, as Dobrin and Weisser make clear has been the case in their attempt not only to separate from their beginnings in literary critical theory but also to distinguish between nature (nature writing) and environment as a broader, ecological metaphor for space/place and material conditions therein.

Like Dobrin and Weisser, we too draw on feminist research to effect a recasting of emotion (see chapter 1). Unlike ecocomposition, however, interactional inquiry in Studio student and staff groups provides a methodology for working from within "particular" perspectives toward a view of what "emotion" signifies in the higher education spaces where students and teachers of writing work. Studio began from a moment and place where the field of composition failed to protect or convincingly articulate its territory: the South Carolina Commission on Higher Education removed basic writing courses from a certain class of institution for reasons of expediency and efficiency, about as far as you can get from any disciplinarily valued, internal pentadic analysis of a set of definitional texts. Nonetheless, we too have found "emotion" to be a central intellectual concept.

Our experiences in Studio programs, as well as our experiences as teachers and writers, have shown us that it is in engagements with the external pentadic elements that student rhetors (and their teachers) feel and express many emotions, uncertainties, and attitudes about their work. For a conference presentation at the Southeast Regional Writing Center Association Conference held in Charleston, South Carolina, in February 1999, Ruby Blair (a teacher and Studio staff group leader in the Bridges Writing Program version of Studio at Benedict College) produced a one-page of graphics, titled "The Realities of the Student Writer." It illustrates student writers' feelings about their work with academic writing in their first-year composition courses, emotions that she had seen expressed in her Studio sessions.

Student realities, a one-page of graphics created by Ruby Blair.

Though we know that student writers also become passionate about beliefs, experiences, and concerns internal to the issues and texts about which they are writing in college courses, Studio's third-space provides an opening for expression of those emotions and of their location and position in a particular institutional space. We know that these emotions often motivate perseverance (or not) with college (writing), particularly for students whose backgrounds, family, and friends are not very familiar or comfortable with college and the academic environments and literacy practices therein.

Rounds of student groups and staff meetings (our theorizing the cross-section) have helped us see that the academy's positioning of these critical emotions of engagement—within external pentadic elements operating outside preferred disciplinary internal pentadic work—contributes to the continued view of such emotions as outside that which academic systems designate as "rationality" and as outside that with which academic faculty—particularly those who live in that upper class of institutions that focus on disciplinary research—need to be concerned. From a spatial viewpoint, *emotion* names not merely a personal response or even just a feminized and devalued response, or as Dobrin and Weisser argue, "a constructed response" (161): from an interactional inquiry view of higher education institutional space, *emotion* names a space/place of exclusion that will manifest itself in different ways, depending on the class, discipline, structure, and hierarchy of the specific institutional site from within which Studio interactional inquiry is being used (as chapter 3 examples will show).

Studio student groups and their "outside but alongside" position, with students from different course sections and different instructors, thus provide a way of organizing the work of ordinary, everyday teachers, lab specialists, graduate teaching assistants, and students so that we can productively work with the everyday complex mix of scenes from within which students and teachers daily negotiate academe at any specific institutional site. What we have seen in Studio student and staff sessions where we regularly engage in overlapping internal and external rhetorical analysis of student writing in our encounters with academic texts is that our disciplinary and institutionally preferred narratives of the motivations behind teaching college writing courses tend to gloss over this scenic complexity of student writing, what Doreen Massey would term a "meeting-up of histories" (*For Space* 4). Student writers who do not as readily mimic or feel comfortable with an internal pentadic analysis, perhaps because they have difficulty ignoring the complexities and contradictions inherent in the rhetorical acts, scenes, agency, and so forth that are external to their assignments, are those often designated as nontraditional or basic writers, not because of what they lack but by virtue of what they bring to their academic experiences. And though we long ago stopped seeing Studio only as a replacement for basic writing courses, we believe that to help those student writers who tend to be thus designated (by the same academic system that has so efficiently misunderstood emotion as irrational), we must provide writing program space in which to acknowledge the academic institution, course, and classroom as everyday scenes for student writing—to broaden the circumference of our analysis of and our work with student writing.

Whenever we depict scene in such a way as to distract from the immediate situation or complexity of scene within which student rhetors operate, whenever we teach, assign, or evaluate writing in ways that do not acknowledge the complexities of their work within the course, class, program, and institution (thus ignoring these spaces/ places as a "meeting-up of histories"), then we participate in hegemonic systems that tacitly encourage these students to drop out, to stop trying, to fail. We adopt an institutional control over their work and the way in which it is evaluated. We disempower students.

Technically speaking, we place rhetorical distance between students and their work whenever we ignore or devalue students' "metarhetorical awareness": awareness not only of those external pentadic factors that influence their academic writing but also of the deficiencies and pretenses of the purely internal pentadic analysis that typically constitutes a "rhetorical" approach to writing in their college (composition) courses. Whenever we deny or ignore the validity of an external pentadic analysis of student writing, or belittle it by failing to understand its influence on features of student writing, attitude, and behavior, then we place rhetorical distance between students-rhetors and their discourse. Reinforcing or increasing such felt distances between students and educational discourse (even unconsciously) tends to place physical distances between students and higher education institutions. Doing so is the opposite of the rhetorical action for change that compositionists want to promote. Depicting the scene for student writing in a way that focuses only on engagements internal to the discipline or texts studied and neglecting the agents associated with the external (institutional) scenes that also shape and motivate student writing make it easy to call student writing problems and errors "deficiencies" attributable to a dematerialized linguistic ignorance that parallels composition's treatment of the classroom as a "dematerialized" location (Horner)—a kind of unconscious (and infantilizing) motivation reserved for those students who bring different awarenesses and sensitivities to their work because they operate from an external pentadic analysis of their work as student writers, from a metarhetorical awareness.

Thirdspace Reformulations

Over the years of our work in Studio programs, we have explored different ways of understanding and articulating students' "metarhetorical" awarenesses of their higher education institutional scene, turning particularly to the work of feminists in academe who often examine assumptions about those areas of human experience—such as emotion—that have been ignored or discounted within academic research and most disciplinary formulations because they have been seen as falling outside the purview of (patriarchally defined) knowledge production (or transmission) in academe. In recent years, our search for ways to articulate a positive view of our engagement with students' metarhetorical perspectives on their work as student writers via interactional inquiry within Studio groups has brought us to "thirdspace."

As a concept explicated in the work of Edward Soja, Homi Bhabha, Doreen Massey, and Kris Gutierrez, thirdspace has helped us as compositionists working not to transcend our institutional circumstances, operating within institutional life to understand the interactions between internal and external pentadic perspectives on student writing.

Both a physical and metaphysical identification of space, thirdspace exists in the interstices—between outside and inside—on the border; it is like the beach: the space between ocean and land that is sometimes ocean and sometimes land, a space that is both/and. These theorists provide a language and perspective from which to look at the institutionalization of students and teachers of writing and their life in the margins, at the ways in which our institutions of higher education are invested in modernist structures and approaches that instantiate those margins and whose complicity in maintaining boundaries must be more fully acknowledged if we hope to understand the local spaces/places of our work in higher education institutions well enough to engage in institutional critique.

Keep in mind that these theorists and researchers have one major impulse in common: they each have used a greater attention to space/place (if not always the specific space/place of institutional life) to turn their professional eye critically on their own positioning and space/place in their respective higher education disciplines, if not their specific institutions. We contend that this "spatial" turn toward greater disciplinary self-awareness is the same move that informs examples given by Bizzell ("Intellectual Work") of the use of I in a professional historian's academically published discourse. In other words, alternative discourses at more "advanced" levels of higher education's institutional hierarchy are the result of a metarhetorical impulse that is the same as or similar to those often designated too simply as "deficient" discourses at the "beginning" levels of the same hierarchy. In this section we show how each researcher's ideas about thirdspace reverberate with several of our preceding analyses to further situate composition's institutional positioning of teachers and students, while along the way we introduce a few Studio-gleaned observations about student writers and differences across institutional locations, observations that will be expanded with more specific examples and discussions in chapters 3 and 4.

Gutierrez, Rymes, and Larson: Unscripted Improvisation

Our first encounter with thirdspace was in the urban-classroom work of Kris Gutierrez and her research associates Betsy Rymes and Joanne

Larson. Their work was particularly interesting to us, since they began with thick description of classroom discourse, a qualitative research practice familiar to and valued by compositionists, and because they treat conflict in the classroom (another concept familiar to and favored by compositionists) as a starting point that makes evident the social spaces of the classroom.

> We identified the thirdspace by observing the competing dis-
> courses, the epistemologies, the script, and the counterscript
> of the various social worlds in the classroom, and the resulting
> tension and conflict between groups in this diverse classroom
> community. We observed how sociocultural tensions emerged
> as participants struggled for intersubjectivity and created the
> potential for the third space. From this perspective, conflict
> was redefined as a positive response that bridged the multiple
> and varied social spaces in the classroom. . . . Here, "What
> counts as knowledge" (Freebody, Luke, & Gilbert, 1991,
> p. 454) is negotiated between student and teacher, and the
> possibility of contesting a larger societal, or transcendent,
> script emerges. By departing from their own scripts, teacher
> and students let go, slightly, of their defensive hold on their
> exclusive cultures, and the interaction between their scripts
> creates a third space for unscripted improvisation, where the
> traditionally binary nature of the student and teacher script
> is disrupted. (452–53)

Gutierrez and colleagues' "script and counterscript" seem similar to the conflict between internal pentadic analysis (seen as the script of answers and behaviors expected by the teacher as the subject matter authority) and external pentadic analysis as the counterscript of pop-culture (or "underlife") examples that, in their countering nature, evidence students' awareness of the institutional scene of the classroom setting. Though located firmly in classroom settings, Gutierrez et al.'s research reverberated with what we had seen in Studio student groups, where we certainly have seen student writers struggling to understand teacher-scripts for how their writing "should" be, or juggling several inherited or tacitly gained, often vague, ideas about the elements that "good writing" should contain. When student writers cannot discern the reasons or worlds that inform the rationality of teachers' scripts, they counter them in Studio student groups less with underlife behaviors and more with questions, observations, and speculations about their education, their teachers, and the intellectual reasoning behind the writing instruction with which they were and still are being presented in their first-year composition classrooms.

Gutierrez describes how difficult it is to sustain, or even to take advantage of, the thirdspace moments as they occur in the classroom observations; in contrast, the "outside-but-alongside" positioning of Studio groups means that they can be a kind of "safe house" for risk taking on the part of both students and teachers. Studio small group sessions may be a more supportive space/place from which to enter into such risky moments, because interactional inquiry in Studio groups provides openness to student concerns and determination of the group's agenda on the basis of student concerns and needs. Studio groups are not held by a curriculum or program of study to any sense of *script* that must cover content (subject matter) that is the result or imitation of internal pentadic analyses typically applied to the material being taught.

In their classroom ethnographies, Gutierrez et al. attended to the intrusions of underlife, or the "range of activities people develop to distance themselves from surrounding institution" (451), as defined by Goffman, and to "those behaviors that undercut the roles expected of participants in a situation" (451), as defined by Brooke ("Underlife"). Such distancing activities and undercutting behaviors may well be brought into Studio student group sessions as well as classrooms, but interactional inquiry (a) assumes that the institution has also set up ways in classrooms to rhetorically distance students (see discussion above) and, in response, (b) sets up the power and authority relations in Studio groups quite differently from those relations in a classroom. Thus, some activities and behaviors that students use to distance themselves from the educational institution do not "fit" or will not be as successful or comfortable in the greater intimacy of a small group setting and are more likely to be abandoned. In addition, Studio's opening up of different writing courses, teachers, and assignments for weekly discussion can put those distancing activities on the table for discussion, as the script (and thereby the counterscript) enacted across more than one classroom is more openly examined by students and group leaders in Studio groups as they meet to discuss not just the students' writing but the contexts in which the writing is being assigned and assessed.

Homi Bhabha: Changing Our View of the Problems to Be Solved

Postcolonial theorist Homi Bhabha also uses thirdspace as a way of talking about the relationship between a master narrative, or script, and alternative approaches to social problems. His thirdspace is an imaginary space that exists "in-between [the] political polarities" of the right and left through which traditional and oppressive power relations are maintained—the term he uses is *hegemony*. To imagine, seek out, or work within this space is a political act, because moving to this space and speaking/acting as usual therein changes "the statement's conditions of use" (22).

In other words, in a thirdspace like Studio groups, the usual scripted responses on which teachers base their authority, as well as students' counterscripting moves, don't quite fit, because in this space teacher-student power relationships are not as rigidly determined by institutional scripts as in the typical classroom. This "reinvestment" or "alteration in its [any statement's] field of experience or verification, or indeed any difference in the problems to be solved, can lead to the emergence of a new statement" (Bhabha 22). Speaking from within a thirdspace changes the standards against which we verify a statement's meaning and changes our view of the "problems to be solved." For example, when Studio groups examine a teacher's comments on a student's writing, the student writer is able to contextualize those comments by examining and explaining what he or she was attending to in the passage being labeled (as fragmented, as incoherent, or as needing "more details"). Such continual recontextualizations of student writings change our Studio sense of the problem to be solved from one of plain ignorance of rules (solvable by recourse to handbook chapters on writing problems) to perhaps the way the student was representing the task to himself or herself, differences in genre conventions, or the teacher's own ignorance of generational differences in frame of reference, understanding of an issue, and so on.

Bhabha notes that such a change is always political (22). Our experiences in composition certainly provide evidence for this assertion. Because institutional and systemic structures are invested (often heavily in terms of historical decisions tying up personnel, time, space, equipment, and monetary resources) in former standards and former views of the problems to be solved (such as a view of grammar and mechanics as the major problems in student writing), they will not wish to abandon those investments (textbooks, handbooks, exercise books, course outlines and syllabi, assessment instruments, teacher training, job descriptions, organizational hierarchies, habituated practice, etc.). The persuasive force of scripted experience cannot be easily overridden by attempts to preach or provoke people from modernist, traditional, or comfortable positions. What is required, in Bhabha's terms, is a way to involve former "right" or "left" players in the thirdspace experience so they can see how old investments do not address the current reality of problems.

For example, composition as a discipline has been heavily invested in the construct of basic writing, though increasingly our higher education institutions are not. How can we provide experiences that would counter our own field's disciplinary tendency to define "disadvantaged" student writers in ways that make it easy for the institution to divest itself of them? The solution (or, as Porter et al. would say, rhetorical action) that we devised in the early 1990s was to provide or articulate experiences in thirdspace places with those labeled "basic writers," experiences that would generate their own persuasive force about the unrecognized intelligences of these students and a redefinition of the work of basic writing and composition (if not also a greater awareness of the impact of external pentadic agents and scenes on students in higher education). Other rhetorical actions could certainly also be possible; we simply worked from our disciplinary knowledges and ethics and from within the situation and the possibilities available to us in the English Department at the

University of South Carolina (USC) and later at Benedict College and USC's College of Engineering.

Bhabha's point is that we must all move from our current positions, because binaries—even those such as "script" and "counterscript" or "internal" and "external" pentadic analyses—finally serve and maintain hegemony. Thus Bhabha speaks of negotiation (rather than negation) in a space of "discursive temporality" (25). We contend that such a negotiation space is operationalized in Studio interactional inquiry small groups involving both students and teaching staff at a particular institutional site. Theorizing is an imagining that seeks a negotiation between "contradictory and antagonistic instances" that can "destroy those negative polarities between knowledge and its objects" (25). After all, our institutional hierarchy, presented in chapter 1, illustrates that we all negotiate higher education's institutional spaces by daily movement through coexisting internal and external pentads and the spaces that provide the scenes for these coexistences, though we do so in institutions that mimic the socioeconomic class status of its students in the physical places and resources that it does and does not provide for life in the external pentadic scene. Thus, as Johnathon Mauk notes, students at the community college where he teaches squeeze into stairwells and hallways, spend time between classes in their cars. For Bhabha, these "negative polarities between knowledge and its objects" correspond to a right-left binary positioning that is the essence of all others: on the right is "knowledge" represented as extrahuman, and on the left, the "objects of knowledge," as in those people about whom knowledge is made through their exclusion (25). Thus, for example, we have assumptions about students' behavior and actions and (writing) abilities founded on knowledges made "about them" (through internal pentadic analysis of texts) without, largely, consulting them and working with the more complex dynamic and matrix of factors that affect their work, their processes, their products. Acknowledging these (dis)affecting factors in a thirdspace (like Studio small groups) forges bonds (between students and teachers via group leaders and their communication from that thirdspace) that can break hegemonic holds, can reorder our disciplinarily universalized work that allows the institution to distance itself from "other" students.

Edward Soja: The Collapse of First- and Secondspace

Like Bhabha's work, the postmodern cultural geography of Edward Soja examines closely the particularities of place and context as a way to move beyond hegemonic and institutional tendencies to pit those particulars (and the people involved) against each other by ascribing them to the predetermined (i.e., scripted) oppositional positions of "teacher" and "student," for example, or any positions segregated by association with "internal" versus "external" pentadic perspectives on life in higher-ed institutions. Instead of classrooms, Soja works with cities. Urban planning strategies and policies based on a model of the industrially centralized city did not fit the realities of life in newer cities like Los Angeles in the 1990s. Unlike older models of the Chicago school—"a commercial core anchoring concentric rings of industry and settlement" (D. W. Miller, A15)—today's archetypal city is sprawling and decentralized, qualities that foster hybridity (A16) and different forms of activism. Older political structures don't work in these new, fragmented settings, giving rise to new forms of unionizing and organization around social issues of work and life. The academic field of urban studies has thus been rejuvenated through self-conscious examination of the single, monolithic "place" or landscape (Chicago) that was being used as the basis for describing and future planning of all urban development, as well as rejuvenated through a consequent move toward ways of describing social spaces that reflect more current realities of the ways people organize their lives and work.

The realization that different spatial arrangements indicate changes in social relationships among the people who live and work therein is important for composition's turn toward institutional critique. Several important scholars in our field have already advanced critiques that call attention to the politics of work in first-year composition college programs for those who do not occupy positions of power across different types of institutions. Crowley and many others have shown us composition's twentieth-century history and the university's use of large numbers of low-paid adjuncts in ways clearly analogous to the reindustrialization and use of inexpensive labor for new craft industries in Los Angeles. The problem in both L.A. and in composition is a widening of the gap between haves and have-nots. Like city services such as water and sewage, institutional services (such as benefits, tenure, and office space) have been made available to some but not to others in composition's current higher education institutional spaces.

Like the needs and commensurate new social activism spawned by the changing cityscape of L.A., composition periodically attempts to mitigate the injustices of inequality forged by the often different institutional locations and positions occupied by those of us who generally call ourselves compositionists. As Porter et al. point out, our professional organizations have met, produced, and published professional standards for the everyday manifestations of our inequality, such as class sizes and teaching loads, or the discounting of administration as intellectual work by the academy. These statements recognize that composition researchers and theorists working for programmatic and pedagogical change may act as if we are all living in "Chicago" (as in "University of"), when a majority of composition's workers exist in very different, often fragmented, places.

Studio interactional inquiry cannot avoid sensitivity to just such differences in institutional sites and the power relations enjoyed (or suffered) by composition teachers and students therein. Leading a staff made up of mostly literature graduate teaching assistants in USC's first-year composition (FYC) Studio presents quite different issues from the Bridges Writing Program staff of seasoned faculty members and teachers at Benedict College. Though both groups bring expertise, their expertise and career positions are quite different. In a graduate teacher-training program in an English department, a composition and rhetoric graduate program may work toward a unified FYC, seeking to unify TAs by teaching them a particular disciplinary (internally focused) approach to instructing students in how to read and produce texts. Most such programs at four-year graduate-degree-producing institutions thus strive for a modernist, Chicago-like structure, while the faculty members in Benedict's FYC area bring together a much more varied set of graduate training, degrees, disciplinary interests, and experiences and will necessarily exist much more like the fragmented development of a postmodern L.A.

This contrast between Chicago and L.A., between modernist and postmodernist structures, is a productive spatial metaphor. In her 2004 4Cs chair's address, Kathleen Yancey in essence argued that compositionists should study L.A. rather than continuing to work, unawares, to instantiate or institutionalize Chicago. She provided an overview of the varied technological literacies that many students engage in—outside academe and unassigned by teachers, in a space (the Internet) that is already generally thought of as a thirdspace of tremendous importance to the continuance and spread of a democratic and open culture—and asked us to think about how and why our composition and writing program approaches are so distant from the nonacademic communication media (such as instant messaging and other forms of Internet communication), such that English departments are on the decline and our traditional approaches may render us obsolete. She urged compositionists to find ways to make our pedagogies and our programs engage with these new media and mixes. But without a broad-based theoretical and practical understanding of how our local institutions, as well as higher education, as general institutional settings for academe are invested in having us maintain Chicago, without understanding the social construction of composition's current space/place within the academy, without ways of acknowledging and articulating how institutional structures maintain traditional structures and systems therein (including composition's own predilection for traditional approaches), such self-examination will not likely produce changes that can have long-lasting (or even desired) effects. It is not just that composition is failing to engage with the new techno-city of L.A. that can render us obsolete: the ways the academy and its higher education institutional hierarchy construct relations within have placed many of us who work primarily at the "beginning" levels in that hierarchy in a very differently imagined space from those more fluid and less hegemonic electronic and Web spaces. And not even just a differently imagined space: Rhonda recalls listening to Yancey's speech and thinking about her department's struggle to keep a single overhead projector working and accessible to faculty as the only instructional technology available, about the Internet-capable computer classroom on campus that had been turned into a lab for the exclusive use of the math and sciences areas, and wondering whether her institution's claims of one computer for every ten students meant computers that actually work.

According to Soja and theorists of the new urban studies, modernist urban planning models grew from observation of an actual city, Chicago, but the instantiation of those models within schools, departments, city planning offices, computer programs, and publishing paradigms brought about or signaled their institutional co-option. Thus postmodern cultural geography and urban studies are as much about institutional and disciplinary self-awareness as they are about a paradigm shift from Chicago to a Los Angeles–based model for the field. In "Planning in/for Postmodernity," Soja discusses the identity crisis faced by those working in the traditional modernist field of geography and even more so by those in the more practice-oriented field of urban planning in ways that echo our Studio-guided observations of our work in composition.

> In many ways, urban and regional planning, and planning theory in particular, have been even more resistant to post-modernization than Modern Geography, largely because their practical foundations and philosophy, their insistent call for "the translation of knowledge into action in the public domain," have been more explicitly and consciously rooted in the emancipatory projects of post-Enlightenment modernism. In their more inherently pragmatic reactions to postmodernity, planners have had fewer opportunities than geographers or cultural critics to retreat into purely theoretical debate and discourse, or into the warm confines of established traditions, far from the madding and demanding crowds of civil society. (237)

Soja's description cannot help but call to mind the same "life on the edge"—neither a part of the "warm traditions" nor "theoretical debate" (both luxuries allowed by the life of the upper-class academic)—that everyday work in college writing programs brings.

Soja uses this difference in positioning within his own discipline to define the corresponding "first" and "second" spaces within which his discipline has in effect been trapped. In his much cited book, *Thirdspace: Journeys to Los Angeles and Other Real-and-Imagined Places*, Soja outlines how thirdspace is, according to Lefebvre, "a remembrance-rethinking-recovery of spaces lost . . . or never sighted at all" (81), bringing attention to that which Soja argues is neglected by both first- and secondspace epistemologies. For Soja, thirdspace is just one position within the "trialectics of space" with which he brings ideas about the spatial relations into mainstream social life as well as to that life "on the margins" in which we compositionists have been so interested and engaged. According to Soja, "Firstspace" is "perceived space" wherein knowledge is empirical, observable, our life-worlds "concrete" and "mappable" (*Thirdspace* 74–75). But analysis and attempts to understand the "production of Firstspace" have focused on "how Firstspace is socially produced" with little attention to "how material geographies and spatial practices shape and affect subjectivity, consciousness, rationality, historicality, and sociality" (77). The parallel firstspace for student writers would be their everyday work to produce their assignments, their written work. But without attention to how local institutional geographies have shaped and affected students' work, we have relied on versions of current-traditional pedagogies and stereotyped views of student writing problems manifested still in drill-and-skill handbooks, exercise books, and labs to structure that work. We have often assumed a narrow, linguistic (internal pentadic) source for student writing problems and successes because we have not attended to larger spatial and material dynamics and their influences on students' work.

Secondspace is the contrasting "conceived space" of the artist, of the theorist, who looks beyond the "concrete and mappable" to what might be or what could be or what is—but has been ignored. Postmodern composition's focus on the cultural and social construction of knowledges, or Bartholomae's focus on students' invention of the university, or any particular disciplinary theory and accompanying model for student writing would provide an example of composition's various secondspaces. But, according to Soja, in his home field of geography, there have been problems with analyses found in secondspace as well.

Often, some very interesting insights about human spatiality were produced. But equally often the interpretation abruptly ended with naïve categorical idealizations, such as "men's mental maps are extensive, detailed, and relatively accurate" while women's were "domicentric" (centered on the home), more compact, and less accurate in terms of urban details; or, the poor have highly localized mental maps in contrast to the wealthy, whose mental maps come close to reproducing a good road map from the gas station. Readers were left with the impression that the conceived space defined an urban reality on its own terms, the mental defined and indeed produced and explained the material and social worlds better than precise empirical descriptions. In such illusions of transparency, as Lefebvre called them, Firstspace collapses entirely into Secondspace. The difference between them disappears. Even more significantly, also lost in the transparency of space are its fundamental historicality and sociality, any real sense of how these cognitive imageries are themselves socially produced and implicated in the relations between space, power, and knowledge. (*Thirdspace* 80)

Our work with Studio models across different academic institutional landscapes has brought us to see that composition must acknowledge and push past our own tendency in the secondspace of our conferences and journals to maintain a similar transparency of space: we tend not to look very closely at the influence of specific institutional arrangements for the assessing and teaching of writing as mechanisms for the production of basic writers and basic writing. We tend to ignore what Soja terms the "causal flow in the other direction" (*Thirdspace* 77): typically our institutionalized discipline acts as if writing produces the institutional label (and corresponding position) "basic," but proceeding from the other direction would mean looking at how the label produces the writing.

   In contrast, thirdspace "can be described as a creative recombination and extension, one that builds on a Firstspace perspective that is focused on the 'real' material world and a Secondspace perspective that interprets this reality through 'imagined' representations of spatiality" (Soja, *Thirdspace* 6). The focus is brought to the space itself, with historicity and sociality important in the analysis. But it is the space itself that determines the shape of the analysis. It is the shape—what Burke would term the "scene"—that contains the history and social interactions. Thus, when someone is interested in moving from a basic writing course to a thirdspace perspective, it is that particular group of people in their particular institutional setting, in relation to the other local elements of curriculum and program development, that must be included in the shaping of a thirdspace program like Studio. Studio names a very broad concept that can be applied in many different ways. What one program in one department in one university does with the concept might be very different from what another does or can do within the pentadic elements and ratios of another particular institutional setting.

For instance, at the University of Arizona, an English department chair who is amenable to breaking out of the traditional English department structure provides a friendly opening to encourage the exploration of a small-group supplement to the first-year English course. This administrator is able to stretch the institutional reward system to cover this work and give teachers full-time equivalent credit for supplemental instruction. At Miami University–Middletown, faculty found a defunct course similar to a Studio arrangement and shifted Studio credit to that catalogue description. At USC and Benedict College, the credit for supplementary group work is factored into the course grade through the cooperation of course instructors. In the Research Communications Studio (RCS) at USC, students receive independent study credit (one hour each semester for three semesters) with their research advisor, and a grant from the National Science Foundation pays the students a small stipend to "work" in Studio on their communications about their research. In yet another configuration, the Opportunity Scholars Program (a U.S. Department of Education student support services program) at USC employs undergraduates who have participated in the program from previous years to work as near-peer tutors for incoming freshmen. Studio programs cannot be adopted wholly by another institution (or even by another program in the same institution), because the shapes of the spaces in which they can be developed are different from one institution (or program) to another. Studio thirdspace is flexible, and according to Soja, thirdspace must be so. Studio is not a destination that can be adopted; it is instead a process to be adapted to the particular institutional or programmatic conditions—of the history of that place and the people who are creating it within the space available. Limiting the concept of thirdspace, even or especially in terms of what we can imagine at any given moment in time, would limit the heuristic power of the concept.

According to Soja, it is the "intentional ambiguity that keeps thirdspace open and inclusive rather than confined and securely bounded by authoritative protocols" (*Thirdspace* 162). Lefebvre saw the "intellectual project as a series of heuristic 'approximations,' never as permanent dogma to be defended against all non-believers" (qtd. in Soja, *Thirdspace* 9). As the shape of an institution changes, new possibilities arise, new fissures between spaces and places in the university can be identified for opening up new thirdspaces, and some previously sighted spaces close up. For instance, as the USC Writing Studio space was in the throes of closing (more on this situation later), Libby Alford, from her perspective in the College of Engineering and Information Technology, read a one-time call for proposals from the National Science Foundation that, in an unusual and open manner, asked for creative new engineering education programs. It was this call for proposals along with previous work by a university-wide committee that studied and made recommendations for supplemental writing spaces (such as satellite writing centers) that provided the opening for a new program in engineering based in part on the idea of a writing center but more specifically on the original FYC Writing Studio and the use of interactional inquiry within student and staff small groups. It is necessary to keep attuned to the fluidly changing shape of the institution and opportunities that open up therein. Thus composition and rhetoric at USC moves from the modernist centralization of knowledge in a roped-off area (historically in departments of English that privilege their own internally focused pentadic analyses) to a more postmodern position across the university, to new spaces wherever the topography opens up crevices that can be occupied. Moving to writing (or communications) within the disciplines requires the study of and experience in working within not only different disciplines but the accompanying different geographical and cultural areas of the institution. With that move comes the necessity to "dwell therein," in the manner of Heidegger, becoming, as much as possible, a part of the culture in those different spaces, though living in a different academic "field" of experience necessarily creates its own hybrid space and accompanying heightened awarenesses. Thus, like L.A. as a postmodern, decentralized city, the RCS represents one way that the discipline of composition and rhetoric decentralizes to open up other thirdspaces within different areas of the institution.

Postmodern geographers' realization of the nuances of space is a clear parallel for composition and rhetoric as a postmodern discipline that moves across disciplinary boundaries to decentralize its work and re-create itself in different disciplinary cultures. Soja concludes his chapter on "heterotopologies" "*with the assertion that an alternative envisioning of spatiality (as illustrated in the heterotopologies of Foucault, the trialectics and thirdings of Lefebvre, the marginality and radical openness of bell hooks, the hybridities of Homi Bhabha) directly challenges (and is intended to challengingly deconstruct) all conventional modes of spatial thinking*" (*Thirdspace* 163; Soja's emphasis). Through the theoretical lens of thirdspace cultural geography, we can gain a view of the landscape that stretches beyond the borders of our limited space in English courses and programs or beyond the borders of any disciplinary insistence on internal pentadic perspectives.

Doreen Massey: The Social Construction of Space

The problem, pointed out by Porter et al., of equating "institution" with "discipline" that we have explored (*a*) as a problem created by the dominance of time and our accompanying failure to acknowledge spatial relations or (*b*) as a problem created by academe's preference for internal versus external pentadic perspectives can now also be seen as resulting from what Soja refers to as the collapsing of firstspace into secondspace: firstspace being the particular institutional setting or site and secondspace being our disciplinary conception thereof, a conception that guides general curriculum, courses, textbooks, and so on. This collapse creates the arhetorical foundation of our work in college writing programs with student writers. Porter and colleagues suggest that we move away from first-year composition altogether and into more discipline-specific rhetorics, as Studio has done in USC's RCS, but we have to recognize that those disciplines have also been founded largely on the basis of the same collapse. They are no less (perhaps even less) self-reflexive and thus perhaps even more arhetorical in their denial of external pentadic influences on student writers and learners. Through calls by the National Science Foundation, like the one answered by Libby Alford and Nancy, we can see that some disciplines—particularly those in the sciences, where minority participation is historically low—are aware of the need to work against disciplinary perspectives that exclude by virtue of what they do not recognize about themselves.

The collapse of first- and secondspace creates what we would term a spatial amnesia that is at the heart of why higher education institutions are not inclusive—though they have in some cases rather superficially adopted the rhetorics of access. Disciplinarity encourages an internal rhetorical analysis of a discipline's discourse and thereby diverts attention from the external analyses that would refuse to ignore the self-defining by self-denying collapse of first- and secondspaces within higher education institutions. And thus, disciplines become institutionalized.

Without acknowledging the need for systematic spaces within which to acknowledge, discuss, and explore the "external" scenes for student writing, writing programs thus limit the scope of their interpretations of the complex motivations behind the work of student writers-rhetors. As Horner makes clear in *Terms of Work*, compositionists must address the "other" identities and internal conflicts on the local, state, national, and international levels that construct and permeate everyday life in academic institutions of higher education. And, as Doreen Massey would have us see, these levels "cross-cut" each other and influence the most immediate political and rhetorical grounds on which anything we do (whether writing or teaching) in our individual classrooms or labs, writing centers or Studio groups, is based.

Massey's redefinition of the social makeup of the spatial is important, because in so redefining (and in her attention to higher education as an institution that produces knowledge) she provides a way
to move beyond the internal and external binary that we have used
thus far to examine composition's institutional position. Her work has
particularly helped us better understand some of our central observations from Studio student sessions about student writing and development across institutional sites. As Brandt and others in composition
have made clear, "writing is social action," but it is by clarifying the
spatial character of writing (including the roles, positionings, and
"reasons why" that contextualize writing in a particular space/place)
that we can reconnect the dis-connect that many of our students feel
between themselves and the "academic writing" that their courses
demand. Better understanding of the social dynamic of the particular
space/place that influences writing—or what we refer to above as the
metarhetorical aspects of student writing—provides us with a different
way of seeing and approaching student writing.

Massey's work particularly helped us as we moved from our early
focus in Studio work on developing student writers' "metadiscourse"
to our growing understanding and exploration of the metarhetorical
needs and abilities of student writers. In other words, instead of "talk
about writing" (where the *discourse* in *metadiscourse* is often used to
refer to the text itself, however mistakenly narrow a conception that
might be), Studio moves to encourage realization of and talk about
the larger rhetorical situation (inclusive of both external and internal
pentadic approaches) that surrounds and motivates the writing (in
this case, student writing) itself. Massey's work helps us see that
when we step out of the internal rhetorical situation set up by a writing class within its writing assignments, we enter a world in which
the social relations among those who occupy the various spaces of
student writing are no longer transparent, a world in which we must
acknowledge issues of power.

Specifically, ideas from Massey that inform or explain Studio
thirdspace practices that we will discuss here include (*a*) drawing on
the "simultaneous multiplicity of spaces," (*b*) recognizing issues of
mobility and power, (*c*) externalizing internal differences and con-

flicts, (*d*) exploring accumulated history, and (*e*) encouraging an "extra-verted sense of place."

Drawing on the simultaneous multiplicity of spaces. Massey's redefinition of the spatial focuses on complexity and power: she views the spatial as "an ever-shifting social geometry of power and signification" that

> implies the existence in the lived world of a simultaneous multiplicity of spaces: cross-cutting, intersecting, aligning with one another, or existing in relations of paradox or antagonism. Most evidently this is so because the social relations of space are experienced differently, and variously interpreted, by those holding different positions as part of it. (*Space* 3)

Studio student group practices, along with the outside-but-alongside positioning, help make Studio groups self-conscious about their containment of what Massey refers to as "a simultaneous multiplicity of spaces." Students from different sections of a course bring different classroom lessons, topics, readings, and assignments. Or, even if two instructors are giving essentially the same assignment (i.e., an argumentation paper), the different instructors' interpretations, details, and expectations regarding the assignment might be quite different from one another. A graduate student instructor writing a dissertation on a literary figure might handle a reading assignment or comments on a draft quite differently from another graduate student writing a dissertation in linguistics or comp-rhet. Likewise, students with different writing histories bring experiences with writing and language use informed by a varied collection of different institutional, academic, social, cultural, and home-life spaces/places and the power relations encountered therein. These issues (and the way that their experiences inform underlying assumptions about writing and about writing in college) emerge as students are encouraged by the group leader to explain their assignments, to "teach" the other group members the terms and concepts taught to them by their teachers, to recall class discussions of readings or issues for writing (and to engage in such discussions in the Studio student groups), to brainstorm in front of the group and with the group about their topics, to read their drafts, to write pieces of drafts, to revise parts and wholes of drafts, to figure out their teachers' grades and comments on their papers, and to make decisions about research and writing processes (next steps) with their group members.

Recognizing issues of mobility and power. The existence of a "simultaneous multiplicity of spaces" and the "ever-shifting geometry of power," according to Massey, places

> different social groups and different individuals . . . in very distinct ways in relation to these flows and interconnections. This point concerns not merely the issue of who moves and who doesn't, although that is an important element of it; it is also about power in relation *to* the flows and the movement. Different social groups have distinct relationships to this anyway-differentiated mobility: some are more in charge of it than others; some initiate flows and movement, others don't; some are more on the receiving end of it than others; some are effectively imprisoned by it. ("Power Geometry" 61; Massey's emphasis)

Here there are several important connections relevant to composition, basic writing, and our Studio work. First, student writers' interest in the metarhetoric of their work as student writers—as well as their emotions of frustration, anger, and so forth—are often motivated by their recognition of the ways in which they are, somehow (and for different reasons), part of a social group that is less "in charge of it" than others—where "it" refers to the flow and movement of, for example, who gets good grades, who was in college preparatory courses in high school, and who was not. Such determinations have very real consequences in the "movement" of students to the next grade level, to a different class, to a certain kind of college, and so on. This flow or movement is controlled by many institutional mechanisms that instantiate existing socioeconomic and racial or cultural stratifications in our public school systems.

Thus, when students initially come to Studio, as when they are placed into basic writing courses, they can be resistant to additional work, because this requirement and placement signal to them that they are in the social group that is "imprisoned" and not that which wields power in the academic system (or in society). Such a placement does not mean, however, that Studio is the same as basic writing courses, and this is a key point. Numerous times when we have discussed our movement away from basic writing because of student resistance—whether at conferences or during consultations on a campus—we have heard the response "Well, students are always resistant to extra work" with the clear implication that they do not always know "what's good for them" and that Studio is, in this sense, just like basic writing courses because there "we know what's good for them." On the contrary, Studio works to understand students' resistance itself as a metarhetorical response and issue, in a variety of ways appropriate to the institutional site and the background and experience of the group leader: Studio groups may begin by discussing or writing (and reading each others' writing) about previous educational, English, or writing experiences, or about students' own perceptions of their strengths and weaknesses as writers, with an emphasis on encouraging students to talk about the specific kinds of help that they believe they do and do not need, or just about their general concerns relative to entering college, the writing they face in their college courses, and so forth. Such practices allow resistance to be voiced in a nonclassroom setting, where it becomes clear to student writers that their statements' "conditions of use" are very different from those they may be used to in classroom settings. We assume student writers' resistance may well grow out of their own perception of (or emotional reaction to) Soja's collapse of first- and secondspace. Such assumptions and accompanying actions help students see that Studio is a different educational approach than any separate basic writing course that they may have imagined.

Externalizing internal differences and conflicts. Because of their institutionally located diversity, Studio student groups make particular use of the ways in which "the social relations of space are experienced

differently, and variously interpreted, by those holding different positions as part of it" (Massey, *Space* 3). As Massey notes, "places do not
have single, unique 'identities'; they are full of internal differences and
conflicts" ("Power Geometry" 67), internal differences and conflicts
that Studio practices and group leaders seek to *externalize* in every
Studio group meeting through the presence of different students who
have different teachers who give different assignments and who comment on student writing differently.

By focusing attention on these differences across teachers and
sections and everyday lives, Studio group sessions help students to
resist attributing difference to personal idiosyncrasies and, instead,
help them (with the group leader's presence and knowledge of the
program and of different instructors' backgrounds) to "locate" those
differences in a particular context or set of circumstances, to better
understand their assignment, their course, their teacher, even academic writing itself as part of what Massey later terms "the coeval
multiplicity of other trajectories," always engaging student writers (and
Studio staff and group leaders) in "the necessary outward-looking-
ness of a spatialised subjectivity" (*For Space* 59). Studio work to thus
institutionally locate (rather than exclude) a student's attitude or reaction or confusion may then suggest a certain action or set of actions
that might be taken to negotiate a change in the writing, a question
to ask the teacher, another way to approach a reading assignment or
discussion question, or another way to understand some "error" in
the student's writing as difficulty in transitioning among (in writing)
the "multiple trajectories" of everyday life and history within which
the student writer is enmeshed.

When awareness of such multiplicity, differences, and conflicts
rises to the surface of an interaction between two or more people,
then there is a thirdspace. We have come to see that such a thirdspace
(wherein, as Soja and others note, new relations can be negotiated and
come into being) is the larger goal that encompasses and surpasses
our initial desire to help students be more fluent with metadiscourse.
After all, our original intent that students be better able to talk about
writing in general and their own writing specifically was to ensure
that students would be able not only to understand and discuss future

course content but also to engage in the actions necessary to attain that understanding and to enact it within their writing. Studio student groups present a space/place in which (a) avoiding the differences and conflicts would be difficult and (b) the risk of bringing out these conflicts and negotiating them is reduced: there is no grade at stake, and the conflicts that a student may feel between him- or herself and his or her teacher can be played out and explored in a way that respects what these emotions represent in terms of the student writer's institutional location. Massey notes, "Further yet, within this dynamic simultaneity which is space, phenomena may be placed in relationship to one another in such a way that new social effects are provoked" (*Space* 4), and what we argue here is that Studio groups place the "phenomena" of writing within academic institutional settings in relationships that can create just such "new social effects."

Exploring accumulated history. As a Studio student group gains momentum and its members gain lived experience with each other, the group gains in the depth of its explorations. Massey refers to the role that such accumulated history plays in a specific location: "all these relations interact with and take a further element of specificity from the accumulated history of a place, with that history itself conceptualized as the product of layer upon layer of different sets of linkages both local and to the wider world" ("Power Geometry" 68). And certainly our work in Studio groups has made us increasingly aware over the years of the accumulated history of educational experiences with writing (and with other language arts such as reading, literature, and oral communication) that students bring with them and how this history influences their writing specifically. In Studio observation of student writers' "moves," we have seen that many of what initially are labeled variously as student writing problems, errors, or deficiencies can be located in the students' accumulated history, can be interpreted as meaningful and often inventive or creative rhetorical responses to students' encounters and struggles with the multiple and conflicting identities found in their previous writing instruction, delivered by teachers who themselves are pushed and pulled by differing approaches to and sources for writing standards: State, national, and professional organizations all have their standards, with varying languages and histories and debates therein; thus the metarhetorical worlds of writing multiply!

When Bartholomae speaks of "inventing the university," he seems to refer to what Massey would call the "long internalized history" of academe, a view of the heart of academic culture as the disciplinary and philosophical debates found in texts whose authors are so distanced from each other in time and space that often students read and debate the ideas found in these texts with little attention to the specific contexts and circumstances of the authors and their ideas at the time of their writing. Other pedagogical approaches attempt to "teach the conflicts" and to reduce the distance between readings and texts that are important to academic culture by looking at the contexts and circumstances (often those that can be recaptured from intellectual or social history of the general time) that influenced the conflicting ideas found in texts—or found in a classroom when two or more students disagree about the ideas in those texts. But neither of these approaches necessarily "locates" the instruction itself—as a position among many within that institutional setting—as part of the student writer's "rhetorical exigency" in the sustained way that Studio interactional inquiry facilitates.

An extra-verted sense of place. In acknowledging the scenes in which student writing takes place (and their rhetorical effects), we construct a better position from which to change both our students' and our own sense of place for our supplemental work with student writers—from a place of imprisonment or a kind of purgatory into a sense of possibility and potential empowerment. Massey calls this possibility an "extra-verted" sense of place, using terminology parallel to our own previous discussion of the need to take an external pentadic view of student writing.

> [W]hat gives a place its specificity is not some long internalized history but the fact that it is constructed out of a particular constellation of relations, articulated together at a particular locus. . . . The uniqueness of a place, or a locality, in other words is constructed out of particular interactions and mutual articulations of social relations, social processes,

experiences and understandings, in a situation of co-presence, but where a large proportion of those relations, experiences, and understandings are actually constructed on a far larger scale than what we happen to define for that moment as the place itself. . . . And this in turn allows a sense of place which is extra-verted, which includes a consciousness of its links to the wider world, which integrates in a positive way the global and the local. ("Power Geometry" 66)

Studio group leaders foster this extra-verted sense of place by explicating assignments not only in terms located within the assignment itself (examining internal pentadic elements found in its prompt, reading, and history of conversations about the topic or reading on which it is based, etc.) but also by simultaneously opening up the external pentadic analysis of such assignments in the field-discipline of composition and rhetoric (or in other disciplines), in terms of the history of the course at that institution, in terms of what the leader knows about the disciplinary background of the students' teachers, in terms of the history of such courses overall, and, sometimes most important, in terms of his or her own experiences as a writer who has negotiated similar assignments or teachers in his or her academic career. Students likewise participate in this opening up as they recount and connect to their own past experiences with writing, as they too engage in bell hooks's "struggle for memory."

But, as we hope these first two chapters have made clear, it is as a discipline that composition has the most recollecting to do. We began our first Studio program at USC with the goal of developing students' abilities to talk about their writing (metadiscourse), but what we found is that the implications and consequences of the simultaneous "outside-but-alongside/inside" positioning of Studio small groups were larger than we realized; we found that our initially forced spatial and institutional relocation of supplemental instruction through writing resonated with our original goals in such a way that our very understanding of student writing development itself has been affected, has significantly shifted. We begin to see how students' metarhetorical preoccupations—their best guesses and observations, their patterns for dealing with their own best analyses of their writing assignments—influence their writing style, organization, development, and sentencing. This shift has made us wish for a similar shift in the terminology our discipline typically uses for talking about student writing—our own disciplinary metadiscourse for responding to student writing.

With a few exceptions, our field has tended to take terms for talking about writing from fields with different intentions from our own and has used this terminology to focus on (often generically enacted) internal pentadic analyses of student writing. We use our courses to turn student writers' attention to civic, social, and political scenes that typically lie outside the academy, that are internal to the life and texts of a particular discipline, or internal to the life and mind of the student writer himself or herself, believing that attention to these external-to-the-institution or internal-to-the-student-or-discipline spaces/places can put ourselves and our students back in touch with the "social construction" of writing. Yet in doing so, we effect an arhetorical view of student writing. We capture only a part of the social and spatial scenes that influence student writing processes and products, a part that often leaves out anything but superficial attention to the local and rhetorical exigencies of students' work. As the chapters that follow will show, Studio work illustrates how the differences inherent in composition's "home" institutions, disciplines, programs, courses, and classrooms and the secondspace conceptions of writing that they assume do matter, both in affect and effect on student writing—and that when we recognize these differences and the accompanying multiplicities, we engage in a different set of relations with student writers and their work, we develop a different sense of the problems to be solved.

3 / Higher Education's Geographies of Student Writing

Turning from abstract explorations in the previous two chapters to concrete examples and practices of interactional inquiry among both student and staff groups in the next two, we ask questions suggested by the theoretical frameworks developed thus far: What has living in Studio thirdspaces with students and staff shown about the ways that student writers are aware of and influenced by the institutional geographies and relationships that surround their work? In what ways do Studio thirdspaces help us realize and negotiate the intersections (sometimes collisions) between the internal pentadic focuses of classroom and course assignments and the external pentadic contexts for that work?

Locating Student Writers

To begin to answer these questions, we will describe the three institutional sites within which the two of us have worked with Studio programs and from which we draw the examples in this chapter and the next, paying attention not only to student writers' location and positioning but also to the kinds of documents that were collected at each Studio site. In this chapter we focus on interactional inquiry within Studio student groups, so here we look at each of these three sites in terms of how student writers were and are located and positioned, defining the institutional geographies of these sites in terms of not only the physical and material realities of place and location but also their position and space within the higher education hierarchy outlined in chapter 1. (In chapter 4 we focus on interactional inquiry within Studio staff groups, and in both that chapter and the concluding epilogue we focus more on the institutional location and positioning of staff and program administration.)

The three sites are

- the original first-year composition (FYC) Writing Studio at the University of South Carolina (USC) in full operation in the English Department, from 1992 to 1996 under our joint direction and then from 1996 to 2001 under the direction of Nancy Thompson and graduate instructors Mike Barnes, Chris Fosen, and Mark Sutton, and with other staff members named in the acknowledgments (because we have described in detail in the prologue the origin of the first FYC Writing Studio at USC, in this chapter we will emphasize details of institutional location and position and comment on institutional relationships that played a role in the history of this original Studio program);
- the FYC Bridges Writing Program at Benedict College, a FIPSE (Fund for the Improvement of Postsecondary Education)-sponsored version of Studio that was in full operation from 1997 to 2000 and in partial operation from 2000 to 2002, under Rhonda's direction, with Nancy serving as outside assessment consultant and Cheryl Jackson as administrative specialist (during the three years of FIPSE funding), as well as other staff members named in the acknowledgments;
- an offshoot of the original Writing Studio at USC called the Research Communications Studio (RCS), an NSF (National Science Foundation)-funded project that worked with undergraduate student researchers conducting research with faculty in the College of Engineering and Information Technology, in operation from 2002 to 2006 under the leadership of Libby Alford and Nancy Thompson, along with chemical engineering faculty member Mike Matthews and staff members named in the acknowledgments.

What stands out at each of these sites are the ways in which the intersections of social and institutional histories reinforce in different ways the distances placed between student writers and the knowledge construction and research at the upper levels of the idealized institutional hierarchy outlined in chapter 1. As we discussed there, at advanced levels of undergraduate and graduate studies, knowledge is admitted to be an "open system," in which the relationships between researchers and subjects and the relative rawness of data are issues for discussion and debate. In other words, at the upper levels, we notice the boundaries between the pentadic elements internal to a discipline's debate/texts and those external, material scenes in which the researchers themselves are working. In so noticing, we see the issues of data collection, bias, and so forth arising as "fuzzy," or lacking clear definition and, therefore, debatable. But students who enter the university at "lower levels" (or who are associated with those of a race, gender, or class more typically found at such levels) are positioned such that their encounters with the external pentadic elements of institutional scene—and the fuzziness of boundaries between the internal and external pentadic elements—are depicted and interpreted as evidence of their lack of academic expertise. Thus, instead of offering something parallel to initial seminars in research methods or "introduction to topics in . . ." that explore the academic and higher educational history of such gray areas as we do for entering graduate students, higher education puts basic writers (and often FYC writers and even some upper-level writers) into courses or categories that assume that what is needed is to pare down skills to the basics (further distancing student writers from discussion of those institutional rhetorical contexts that have influenced their writing development and that continue to influence their writing choices) or, as we have seen in some FYC composition pedagogies, courses that focus on discourses outside the academy altogether. It is as though our higher education institutional hierarchy can admit that the boundaries between internal and external pentadic analyses of life within higher education are less than clear in front of only those most advanced student-participants (by then winnowed down and homogenized) over whom the discipline has more specific control. For students elsewhere in the institutional hierarchy—and for those who work more as teachers with those less advanced students than they do as more traditionally defined researchers—higher education has constructed institutional sites that present quite different histories and infrastructures, as illustrated below.

The FYC Writing Studio at USC

As a four-year, state-supported institution of higher education, USC is the state flagship institution, housing numerous graduate programs that bestow master's and doctoral degrees, including the state's only long-standing Ph.D. programs in English or American literature and MFA in creative writing, as well as more recent master's and Ph.D. programs in linguistics, comparative literature, and (most recent of all) an emphasis in composition and rhetoric. Through the 1990s, composition and rhetoric had a difficult history in the department, with the usual suspicions of composition as a nondiscipline because of heavily service-related activities and a privileging of scholarship in rhetoric that leans toward the classical or literary side (both in the expertise of faculty hires and in the publications favored for promotion). "Writing process" was brought to the department most obviously by Erica Lindemann in the late 1970s, with a summer workshop funded by the National Endowment for the Humanities (DiMedio) that was attended by several higher education faculty in the area (including some Benedict College faculty at the time). Lindemann's work resulted in the establishment of USC's Writing Center, originally envisioned as a place for upper-level undergraduate and graduate students to obtain help with the researched-writing projects typical of those in more advanced levels of higher education's institutional hierarchy. Unfortunately, this positioning of the Writing Center for greater acceptance by those who would define the university in terms of its support for the research-related activity of its graduate degree programs and faculty was not entirely successful: By the 1990s the Writing Center director was often not a full-time faculty member but an advanced graduate student, and in the wake of mid-1990s budget cuts the English Department would use the Writing Center budget line item as its buffer zone for enacting as much as a 12 percent budget cut within a single year.

USC has a long history as an elite and elitist institution, originally founded to train the sons of the South's leading (white) families to be community leaders. Like most such universities in the nineteenth-century United States, courses in rhetoric and then, later, stylistics and literature were offered in the program of study. Officially, basic writing courses for those considered less prepared for advanced academic study (and writing) at USC were born in the 1940s, about the time of the GI Bill, pretty much in line with the general master narrative of composition's service to the country's changing student bodies. But there had been another time, in the more distant and yet vividly recalled past, when "underprepared" students found themselves in "precollege" courses: During the Reconstruction era, a time called the "Radical Reconstruction" in South Carolina between 1873 and 1876, African American students were admitted to USC, where they were taught by a faculty that included the University's first African American faculty member, Richard Theodore Greener, who was also the first African American graduate of Harvard University. In this first year, these students were placed in special sections of courses and met more regularly with faculty outside the classroom for additional tutorials. The 1960 USC catalog, perhaps in anticipation of impending desegregation, included a short reference to the Radical Reconstruction era in recounting the institution's history, calling it "an experiment in the co-education of the races that ended in disaster." Actually, it ended with the election of Wade Hampton and the "Redeemers" to the governor's office in 1877; the subsequent establishment of South Carolina State University in Orangeburg as the higher education institution for the separate education of African American men and, later, women illustrates the policies of appeasement and segregation that subsequently defined the Jim Crow era in the South (Hollis; Grego, "Rhetorics of Tradition," "Recollecting Student Ethos").

We mention this more "ancient" history for a reason. Postprocess pedagogues like to teach texts that raise awareness of the histories and rhetorics of race, class, and gender that are embedded in our larger society and are at the heart of many contemporary controversies. But those same histories and rhetorics are embedded also within our institutional geographies in higher education. Specifically, courses that focus on composition and writing instead of rhetoric and literature at the university, for example, have been historically associated not just with a group of war veterans but moreso with an "unwelcome" group of students and "an experiment in the co-education of the races" associated with the end of the Civil War. Though Nancy arrived at a time and in a program that sought to promote and support social change and justice in the state during the desegregation of the university in the 1960s, the university's English department nonetheless maintained a traditional profile through the middle to late 1990s: Until a spate of new hires in literature and critical theory that began after several retirements in the mid-1990s, the department's power base was in bibliographic studies, Southern literature and traditional-period literary studies, creative writing, and linguistics. Women's studies and African American studies programs were and still are separate divisions with separate directors and faculty drawn from several different departments.

What this meant for "basic writing" at the university is that, as described in the prologue, there was little institutional support for keeping basic writing courses when the Commission on Higher Education proposed their removal from four-year state-supported higher education institutions in the early 1990s. And what this larger history meant for FYC student writers at USC is that the institutional positioning of composition at the beginning and lower levels of academic work (wherein knowledge is to be presented as a closed system and where student writers find themselves institutionally distanced from their own perception of the overlapping internal and external pentadic spaces of their work) was further compounded by the institution's historical association of social groups seen as less prepared with composition and writing courses at beginning levels of college matriculation. Minus any systemic self-reflection on the way that institutional and disciplinary hierarchies and geographies of knowledge construction embed a kind of de facto segregation with this kind of (often buried but nonetheless real) historical association and assumption, desegregating higher education at the minimal level of initial "access," as at USC, is likely to be far too little an adjustment.

This institutional positioning of student writers at the beginning levels of this university carries with it several realities of both geographic and hierarchical institutional location for those who work with these students. Geographically, USC's teaching assistants (TAs) shared offices and cubicles tucked away in corners and between the individually held offices of faculty in the Welsh Humanities Building. The Writing Center, where they also worked, is in a few cramped rooms in the adjacent Humanities Classroom Building. Hierarchically, the position of those TAs primarily responsible for the education of entering student writers was no more spacious: USC's English Department uses its surplus of graduate students, particularly those in literature programs, as TAs who carry the load of FYC course instruction. Often when these graduate students begin their work as composition teachers, they are new to their advanced levels of graduate study, having only recently been admitted to the ranks at which they will "rediscover" their discipline as an open system of knowledge in which they are now expected to begin constructing knowledge themselves. Taking on such tremendous challenges to their own previous approach to "being" in their discipline, TAs would seem to be more open to understanding the ways in which the external and internal pentadic scenes intermingle and confuse their FYC students—and we have seen it work this way for some. But for many, their lack of experience precludes such an openness: Whenever the definitional boundaries of knowledge and the activities of the knower are shifted, as they are for entering graduate students, there is likely to be a vulnerability that, when coupled with yet another new responsibility such as teaching a class (or two), makes it more likely the TA will hold to and enforce even more strongly on his or her FYC students the strictures of behavior reserved for those in the "beginning" institutional positions.

In *Academic Discourse*, Pierre Bourdieu, Jean-Claude Passeron, and Monique de Saint Martin explore misunderstandings between college professors and their students as a sociolinguistic phenomenon. They contend that not only is there vocabulary specific to university education but that there also exists a code that goes beyond the denotations of words. According to Bourdieu et al., many instructors, especially inexperienced teachers, lack awareness of the code they are using and thus fail to define it, while the students believe they should understand the language being used by the instructor and therefore will not risk looking ignorant by questioning it. Thus this code is often difficult for uninitiated students to break through. From what we have seen in our Studio sessions over the years, a significant part of this code identified by Bourdieu et al. is in the institutional geography of a student writer's FYC experiences that we describe below, in the internal and external pentadic disciplinary and institutional scenes for student writing at USC.

A seemingly simple instance from our Studio experiences illustrates these complexities: Carson, a nontraditional-aged African American male student who participated in an early Studio group in FYC at USC, made us aware of the frustration aroused when an instructor seems unaware of the differences in understandings brought into a classroom. When assigned to buy a notebook for his class, Carson had no way of knowing exactly what kind of notebook the teacher meant: whether it should be a spiral notebook or a ring binder or something else. But he bought a notebook and then came to his Studio group angry and frustrated after the TA informed him that it was the wrong kind. Though this example may seem trivial, cracked open it reveals the instructor's assumption that she, Carson, and all students in the class inhabit the same linguistic and cultural worlds, that the "histories" that meet up in the classroom are all pretty much the same. It also reminds us of the kinds of "form" rules that beginning teachers will often enact and the way that beginning students, like Carson, will attach more weight than necessary to the successful (or unsuccessful) fulfillment of such rules. Carson's frustration at his failure to correctly interpret the "code" of expectations in this instance was likely also amplified by his awareness that in terms of both his age and race, he was not "like" the majority of students in his class—students who, it must have seemed to Carson, just knew "automatically" or "naturally" what kind of notebook to buy.

Studio's use of interactional inquiry in the thirdspace of its "outside-but-alongside" small groups with an experienced group leader allows insight into the effect on students like Carson of dealing with (often years of) just such layers of institutional positioning. It also allows insight into the ways that our institutional settings, where relations between people are systematized and abstracted into the roles of "teacher" and "student" by the classroom environment, course materials, and so on, carry and mask not only those assumptions that inform the work required but also those brought to that required work by students. In the comments and problems (like Carson's) that came out in Studio sessions, we heard questions and saw situations that made us more aware of the connections that student writers make between (*a*) the internal pentadic elements of the subject under disciplinary discussion and (*b*) the external pentadic elements of the institutional situation and geography that surround their particular class's activity or exploration of a topic or text.

In the original FYC Studio at USC, we saw how Studio groups were able to respond to students and their ongoing work "at the point of need" (Nelson), which is not to say that the group leader could come in with the "right" answer but that Studio space and time helped us use the moments and awarenesses and anxieties and angst that present themselves to open up the various histories and relationships that come together at that place and time to construct how student writing will be read—and to access insights that can inform student writers' choices and their larger metarhetorical awarenesses. Examples follow:

- A Studio group leader turns to a handbook or other reference tool to point a group of students to information that they need, but this move is not just "fixing" a "deficiency" or an "ignorance." The group leader uses that specific movement and moment to talk about when a certain sentencing strategy would be considered helpful or appropriate (in terms of genre or rhetorical situation) and by whom not only in terms of global readers who are a part of the internal pentadic context but also in external pentadic terms of teachers at that institution and their backgrounds, which inform the various attitudes that students may encounter toward, for example, the use of fragments or dashes or commas in their writing.
- Often we heard students bring up in a Studio session the "writing rules" they had been taught, such as being told not to begin a sentence with *and* or *because*, not to use *I* in an academic essay, and to use a certain number of sentences in a paragraph. Such moments, when students trade the "rules" they have been taught, minus any understanding

of why teachers may have given them those guidelines, provide an especially rich interactional inquiry. They make all participants aware of the ways in which the external pentadic situation, that is, the kind of class they were in, the background of the teacher, the teacher's purpose (to prepare students for timed writing tests, for exit exams?), and so forth, is influencing their education. Such inquiry allows everyone to acknowledge that which we all experience in higher education settings: the influence of a particular institutional context on teaching and learning.

Such discussions bring the student writers and their texts out of arhetorical isolation as the territory of mere "error" and open their work up as a rhetorical context for discussion not only of internal pentadic elements but also of external pentadic realities, such as the negotiation of terrain that is the work of writing in any case. Studio thus resists the tremendously seductive nature of looking at writing and talking about it as if the collapsed first- and secondspace perspectives on "good student writing"—to which we have been so schooled that they seem natural—are sufficient.

Interactional inquiry will not typically happen in an institutional geography such as FYC at USC because (as in the case of Carson) it is unlikely that the less experienced TA course instructor will have the time or the awareness to work with such moments. The curriculum may be unable to respect (or point less experienced instructors to) such moments as ripe for metarhetorical treatment in the classroom, where focus is typically much more on the internal rhetorical analysis and production of texts. At USC, as at other four-year state institutions where graduate students teach the majority of FYC courses, there was a theory-based rationale behind the plans given to TAs for teaching FYC courses: in the 1990s, English 101 introduced students to the writing process and to academic argumentation, while English 102 focused on response to literature by introducing students to various styles of literary criticism. Contacts between teachers and students in classrooms are structured, controlled in a sense by the need to enact these programs. When they occur, contacts are relatively brief, without time to discuss, compare, and question so as to acknowledge the local rhetorical contexts out of which all the conflicting "rules" and guidelines may have arisen. There is usually time only for keeping the focus on arhetorical disciplinary knowledges and contents, which are often distant from the actual frustrations and concerns of student writers. It is just not "efficient" for teachers to ask why the majority of a student's sentences are not fragments when those that are can be dealt with quickly and "easily" by referring the student to a handbook chapter or, increasingly, a helpful Internet Web page with a handy self-grading quiz to test the student's knowledge at the end. Handbooks and their electronic equivalents are valuable reference tools; they refer student writers to the accepted and assumed master narrative of grammar instruction but also use student writers' lack of linguistic knowledge to justify the referral and thus reify the arhetorical treatment of student writing on a daily basis.

It was within an institutional geography that predisposed FYC instructors to enact just such an arhetorical treatment of student writing that the original FYC Writing Studio thus operated. This positioning also influenced the kind of documents that the program used, produced, and was able to collect for our use in drawing examples for this chapter and the next. Because USC's FYC Studio was seen in part as a training adjunct to support new instructors and to further develop the teaching skills of more advanced graduate TAs, the documents produced and used by the program were related to communications, consisting primarily of dialogue sheets or memos by which Studio group leaders provided weekly reports to each TA on each of their students' work in that week's Studio meeting. These were prepared first in hard copy and, later, electronically via departmental e-mail. These dialogue sheets were, necessarily, brief, since each group leader had up to twenty Studio students about which to write each week. Our hope was that the dialogue sheets would prompt responses back and forth between group leaders and TAs, though in reality they often simply prompted the usual hallway conversations about a student's work and attendance in Studio.

Studio group leaders composed weekly "one-pagers" (one-page write-ups about whatever Studio or teaching experiences staff members wanted to discuss that week) for our staff interactional inquiry meetings. These sheets often contained references to questions, problems, and events within the staff member's student groups. Other data about the original Studio program came from those graduate students (in comp-rhet and linguistics) who not only served as Studio group leaders but also conducted research that led to dissertations. At least two Ph.D. students in comp-rhet and one in linguistics conducted research on Studio, including Anita Guynn, Michael Barnes, and Sonja Launspach. Their studies provide transcripts of Studio interactions, many of which are too detailed to include in their entirety here but which we drew on as we reviewed the records of Studio work for this book.

The FYC Bridges Writing Program at Benedict College

Just a mile down the road from USC in Columbia is Benedict College, an HBCU (historically black college or university) across the street from another HBCU, Allen University, in the heart of several of Columbia's historically black neighborhoods. Established in 1870 by the American Baptist Mission (Allen University is AME-based) and Northern benefactor Mrs. Bathsheba Benedict, Benedict College is an open-admissions college. In the mid-1990s its enrollment was around one thousand undergraduates, a figure that rose to between twenty-five hundred and three thousand in the early years of the twenty-first century. Like many historically black colleges, Benedict College provided, before the desegregation years, many educational programs at the bachelor's level and below. During its first two decades, when it was called Benedict Institute, the school provided a range of options for students of many kinds and levels: classical-collegiate study in theology for preachers, normal school education for teachers, precollege high school courses, and programs in trade skills such as printmaking, carpentry, brickmaking and -laying, and sewing. Thus Benedict College covered all bases by providing both DuBois- and Washington-style educational opportunities. Before desegregation, even through the 1940s and 1950s, Benedict housed an elementary school on its campus as well, filling the gaps in the then very poor state-provided primary education for African Americans in the neighborhoods and communities immediately surrounding Benedict. College catalogs reveal that Benedict hired many of its own as teachers in the early years of its history. They include John R. Wilson, an 1891 graduate who returned to the school in 1902, when he was listed in the catalog (then called "Bulletin") as an instructor in mental science, rhetoric, and history (Grego "Rhetorics of Tradition").

What this history means is that, in essential ways, the teaching of writing at Benedict College existed on several undergraduate and precollege levels for decades and that teachers (always in short supply) were teaching across several levels at once long before state "standards" outlined the exact skills to be gained at each grade-level, as we have now in South Carolina. Course designations like "basic writing" arrived in the catalog in the 1940s (e.g., "Functional English" and, later, "Remedial English"), along with other course titles clearly imitating curriculum developments at USC. It is just as clear, however, that such courses must have been enacted quite differently from the similarly named course at the much better staffed and resourced university just down the road and in another world entirely. In fact, Benedict College catalogs show from very early in its twentieth-century history the existence of supplemental instruction through "labs" operating alongside students' participation in catalog-described writing, reading, and speech courses. In fact, Bridges Writing Program (BWP) staff member and Benedict College FYC instructor Ruby Blair called Rhonda's attention to the fact that separate writing, speech, and reading labs (each staffed with learning specialists) were—into the 1970s and early 1980s—located in small offices that adjoined the actual classrooms in which writing, speech, and reading courses were taught. Teachers of those courses would, during a class meeting, consult with these learning specialists and send individuals or groups of students into the labs to work on the spot with particular problem areas. In fact, these small adjoining rooms are still to be found in the Fine Arts Building, complete with signs outside each classroom indicating the lab that used to be housed there. This kind of immediate, hands-on attention to and intervention in student learning processes makes sense in a small community where the needs of students at many different levels must be attended to. Benedict College's history, its institutional geography, and its enactment of higher education's hierarchy suggest that, by necessity, there was less distance between the internal and external pentadic lives of students and instructors.

Social changes, however, affected both the college's institutional geography and its learning environments. Well into the 1960s and 1970s, the African American communities, schools, and business districts that surrounded Benedict College provided Columbia's African Americans with self-sufficiency and the means to help each other survive the difficulties of living in the heart of the old Confederacy. Unfortunately, several factors contributed to the decline of this area. In post-Civil Rights and post-desegregation Columbia, high-achieving African American students were recruited by larger, majority white institutions and then drifted to live in other areas. As the population in the Waverly, Oak-Reid, and Martin Luther King Jr. neighborhoods aged, the residents were not replaced by younger African Americans looking for permanent homes. Instead homes were rented by more transient populations, and a general decline in neighborhoods surrounding the college set in. Social connections and ties that used to bind residents were stretched and broken by changing times. With increased racial integration came calls for reduction in a perceived "duplication of services," as when the Commission on Higher Education and other state government officials periodically call for reducing the number of higher education institutions in the small state. Centralization of services is more efficient, more cost-effective, they say.

Centralization of services also led to the decline of Benedict College's own original "outside-but-inside" learning labs. In the 1970s, federal grant monies became available and were used by the college to set up an intensive five-days-per-week English course that encompassed writing, reading, and speech, though the program was apparently too expensive to be sustained once grant monies ran out. In the 1980s, federal grant monies were again obtained to create the BCCARES (Benedict College Center for Academic Reinforcement, Enhancement, and Support) area as a central location for all learning labs (writing, foreign language, math), as well as counseling and testing services. These monies also provided for the hiring of two English learning specialists who would be housed in a different building from the classrooms and to which students would either be referred or voluntarily come for help in all English areas. When Rhonda arrived at Benedict College in the mid-1990s, this physical separation of labs and lab activities from the classrooms, along with the separation of the lab learning specialists from the course teachers, had resulted in a lack of communication and layers of misunderstanding. Learning specialists felt that they were having to "teach the course," and teachers were suspicious that the specialists were undermining their instruction. Course syllabi were structured as lists of which handbook chapters would be covered in any given week, and no rhetoric or reader was being used, though several good collections of writings of African American authors and essayists had been used in the past. (Rhonda found copies buried in the English lab room cabinets.) Internal pentadic elements were being reduced to issues of sentence-level correctness, grammar, and punctuation (at a time when rising concern was being expressed even by African American political leaders and celebrities over the prevalence of Ebonics), while rising numbers of students in each composition class, combined with the more centralized attention to external pentadic factors that influenced these students' success in the BCCARES area, were draining the two FYC courses and classrooms of their programmatic coherence and attention to rhetorical content and context.

Faculty and (increasingly) adjuncts hired to teach FYC courses were of widely differing ages and educational backgrounds, and, unlike at USC, they were already full-fledged professionals, not impressionable "learners." Thus, the ways in which the "beginning" levels of incoming students were defined might vary widely from teacher to teacher. However, these students were getting the benefit of course teachers who were often alumni of an HBCU, if not Benedict College itself, and who understood the intersections of external and internal pentadic factors in these students' early encounters with academic culture.

The Research Communications Studio in Engineering at USC

USC's initial Writing Center began as a centralized service (as opposed to similar services at Benedict College, which were formerly tied to specific institutional sites for actual work), and this centralization seemed to be problematic for several reasons. Too much distance between service and need makes it harder for institutional participants to value the service. At the same time, having the service and the need in close proximity may also make it more difficult to be aware not only of the larger institutional context and geography but also of academic and disciplinary cultures manifest in those external pentadic elements (though proximity with the department in which the communications instruction works provides the opportunity for more familiarity with the expectations of communication in that environment). Thus, the Research Communications Studio (RCS) located the service close to the need, but some engineering faculty sometimes devalue this type of work as "service" and may not feel compelled to overcome the stereotypes within their assumptions about who is and is not a "natural" at engineering.

Also, it is harder for both faculty and students in engineering to be self-reflexive, because these students are doing work that is more "advanced" in the institutional and disciplinary hierarchy, and according to that institutional hierarchy, everyone should be at the same "level" of internal pentadic education. Of course, at this level of success, those external pentadic factors are not supposed to present obstacles or differences among participants, in the sense that higher education's idealized hierarchy sees itself as color-blind, gender-blind, and so on. The numbers of minority graduates in the sciences, of course, belie this idealization. To what extent can RCS's help all student participants, as well as those who encounter obstacles and differences? (To what extent do RCS's help advanced undergraduate disciplinary faculty become aware of the role played by these factors is a question for the next chapter.)

During the thirty-five years Nancy has been at USC, there have been several writing-across-the-curriculum initiatives, usually built around attempts to move the Writing Center to a more centralized location within the university. (One of the reasons the Writing Center has always been a target of budget cutting is that the English Department has resented having to continue funding a service for the whole university community.) The most recent initiative began in the mid-1990s with a Writing Center task force committee appointed by the provost and chaired by Nancy to study the feasibility of enlarging the purview of the writing center. A program of satellite writing centers was proposed and encouraged by the provost, who, unfortunately, abruptly left the university before the program could be put in place. The one surviving outcome of the initiative resulted from Writing Center director Jennie Ariail's previous working relationship with the chair of the Department of Electrical and Computer Engineering, Robert Pettus, who had an abiding interest in language and communication. He and his assistant chair, Jerry Hudgins, began a collaboration with Jennie (a comp-rhet graduate student at the time) and Nancy (supervisor of the graduate student Writing Center directorship), out of which came the initiative for the Electrical and Computer Engineering (ECE) Writing Center. With the help of these engineering professors, Nancy and Jennie wrote a grant proposal to use some of the money from a Gateway Engineering Coalition (NSF) grant program already in place in the College of Engineering and were awarded fifty thousand dollars to start up this satellite writing center, which Libby Alford, a recent comp-rhet Ph.D. graduate, was hired to direct. After working with funding from the Gateway Coalition until that project ended, the dean of the College of Engineering funded the initiative for the whole college, and the program became the Professional Communications Center (PCC). When that dean left, the funding for the PCC was endangered, and Libby was "encouraged" to find grant funding, which is the normal expectation for faculty in engineering. That's when Libby came upon the NSF open call for innovative programs in engineering education. Libby and Nancy, with the help of three engineering professors in three different engineering departments (Electrical/Computer, Chemical, and Mechanical), wrote the NSF proposal that funded the RCS to work with undergraduate research students in those three departments. After the four years of funding through that NSF grant ended, the RCS program continued for one more year within the grants of other engineering professors' summer Research Experience for Undergraduates, also funded by NSF. Thus, grants have always been the source of funding for this initiative, in an environment where grant funding is expected.

Though grant funding might provide the means to create and open a thirdspace program, it raises issues of control by granting agencies, and only if the initiative closely matches the guidelines of the agency is it a feasible source. And, of course, such funding usually comes to an end, because funding agencies want good programs to be integrated into the institution's structure. The engineering college has been urged to hire a communications faculty or staff member to head up its communications initiative, but it is difficult for the college to commit itself. Such hiring remains a possibility, though, because the accrediting agency for engineering has in place a list of objectives for engineering education, one of which concerns the development of students' communication abilities. It was this disciplinary requirement that provided an opening for the original RCS proposal.

Basic Interactional Inquiry Practices in Studio Student Groups

While Studio thirdspaces can thus be located in quite different institutional sites, with institutional geographies that locate and position student writers quite differently, as previous discussions illustrate, there are specific practices useful across Studio programs at different sites, practices that facilitate the spatial reimagining of student writing and of student writers in both internal and external pentadic contexts. These practices will be useful particularly to those who want to foster interactional inquiry into the external and internal pentadic experiences of student writers. The practices we discuss and provide examples of here include

- beginning a Studio group by collecting and discussing student-writing (i.e., educational or literacy) histories;
- having students check in at the beginning of each Studio group session by writing or telling what they have brought to the group in terms of drafts, assignments, problems, and so forth;
- asking students to bring actual writing, copies, and artifacts (including textbooks, assignment sheets, graded work, etc.) to share with the group and with which we

can focus discussion about the larger patterns, theories, and landscapes of their education and courses;

- encouraging students to teach each other what they have learned or heard in their composition classes; and
- helping students to interpret and contextualize their assignments and teachers' comments on their writing or work.

Beginning with History

Given previous chapters' discussions of the need to bring spatial analyses to our work with student writers, it may seem odd that our first "basic practice" makes reference to the temporal issue of history. But, as we hope that the above discussions of our three institutional sites illustrate, a large part of the spatial deadening of different institutional sites in higher education has occurred because of the assumptions that one higher education hierarchy has determined the institutional geographies of all and that the specific institutional history is moot. But in fact the specific institutional history and geographies of writing, both past and present, constitute the external pentadic rhetorical context, or "scene," within which compositionists work with student writers at a specific site. While the social history of the site (and of composition at that site) is key to understanding those external pentadic elements of purpose, attitude, agent, and scene that student writers will encounter, the attitude that student writers will bring to these encounters has been shaped by their educational history. Beginning with this educational history is a way to demonstrate to student writers that they and their writing will not be regarded arhetorically, that the FYC program regards them as located and historied human beings who have reasons for thinking, behaving, and writing the way that they do.

Thus, at both USC and Benedict College, a "writing history" assignment was created and described in detail for FYC instructors' use as a beginning in either the classroom or the student groups. At USC, the TAs' orientation program included a session to explain the Studio program and instruct TAs in how to use this assignment during the first week of class. First, a heuristic exercise led students to make a timeline of reading and writing experiences by thinking back and noting those that come to mind. The exercise helps students consider the distance between their present writing ability and memories of their learning to write. This and further informal development (conducted in their composition class) of one of the experiences leads to the students' writing of a focused essay that describes themselves as writers, including their strengths and weaknesses, attitudes toward writing, and ways they go about producing their writing. The results of this assignment were collected, along with a portfolio of writing from high school that students were asked in their admissions materials to bring. Usually about half the students brought a portfolio, and there was no penalty for not having one. TAs then used both the writing history assignment, as well as high school portfolio writings, to get to know the student writers in their classes and to identify those they wanted to recommend for the limited number of spaces available in any given semester's Studio groups.

We asked these TAs to consider not just (*a*) the student writer's command of sentence grammar and form—which was often their first thought about how to identify potential Studio students for "remediation"—but also (*b*) the content and (*c*) what student writers were saying about their previous writing and educational experiences. One of the major criteria used to identify students who might benefit from Studio groups was (*d*) students' previous experiences with writing, especially those who indicated an attitude toward writing that inhibits their writing ability, as well as those who stated outright that they wanted the help of Studio. What kinds of writing (genres, audiences, purposes) had the students worked with in their prior education? To what degree did the student writer seem aware of his or her writing strengths and weaknesses? Had the student writer developed strongly negative attitudes toward writing that might hinder her or him from negotiating the demands of USC's FYC course sequence? To what degree did the student writer seem to be merely parroting very narrowly conceived ways of talking about his or her writing gained from poor or poorly understood previous experiences (e.g., "I have poor grammar," "I can't spell")? And finally, we also encouraged and helped TAs to think about (*e*) their own teaching development and to look for student writers whose writing exhibited features or concerns that they themselves would welcome the help and partnership of Studio in working with.

At Benedict College, where placement decisions were already determined by Freshman Placement Testing conducted in another area, the writing-history development process and assignment was used in introductory group sessions with students (*a*) to self-consciously model both writing and small-group processes as a way of introducing student writers to the essential structure of the Studio-modeled BWP, (*b*) to introduce student writers to their group leaders and teachers, who then were able to look at and discuss with each other patterns in students' prior educational experiences that may have resulted in their placement in our lab program, (*c*) to surface and place "on the table" students' attitudes toward writing, writing teachers, and their lab requirement in context with their larger educational experiences, (*d*) to provide the perceived history of each group member as a starting point for building further understandings and making connections, and (*e*) to make available a further writing sample for the classroom teacher, if she or he was interested. In addition, at Benedict College the social histories of the institution and of those teaching there, as discussed above, were often so intimately intertwined that beginning with the educational history of students placed student writers in harmony with the values of this particular institutional site—and thus made sense to the BWP staff.

Benedict College's open admissions recruitment in the mid to late 1990s was primarily among traditional-college-aged African American students from rural South Carolina or urban areas in the Northeast and Southeast who were not in college preparatory courses and may have a low high school GPA (some lower than 2.0). Many of the students who scored low on the holistically graded essay and multiple-choice editing test that made up the Freshman Placement Testing in English either expressed strongly negative attitudes toward academic writing in general or specific past experiences or teachers in particular or were unable or reluctant to say much at all about their past academic writing experiences in terms of specific people, influential relationships, actions, products, places, and so on. The number one "weakness" that these student writers were able to comment on seemed to be poor grammar, and we noted that, even when asked, most were unable to differentiate their problems with the mechanics of standard written English in any more specific way. Awareness of or metadiscourse for identifying rhetorical aspects of writing typical of internal pentadic analysis (including genre, audience, or purpose) was most noticeably absent. And though students' strong attitudes about previous educational experiences indicated metarhetorical awareness of the influence of educational settings, these student writers often lacked a productive way to deal with or understand the mechanics of those influences. Familiar with the impoverished or inattentive education these students may have received in poor, rural South Carolina schools, as well as in overcrowded urban areas, we knew that many of our students' educations had focused narrowly on decontextualized mechanics of writing and that their exposure to ways of talking about internal, much less external, pentadic rhetorical elements and concerns was likely to have been minimal.

It was not only socioeconomics that influenced the narrowness of some of our BWP students' previous education in writing. Early in her work at Benedict College, Rhonda was observing an English education student, in the field at a prominent and well-regarded area high school, working with eleventh graders on a reading of *Hamlet*. Rhonda saw in the "regular" (non-college preparatory) English class a young African American man sitting in the back of the room with his head on the desk. As other students took turns reading parts in various scenes, this young man would raise his head, chuckling to himself at moments of irony and wordplay either embedded in the text itself or created by his classmates' mispronunciations or stumblings over slightly risqué parts. In her conference afterward, she talked with the young teacher about introducing irony, tropes, and some history of drama to enrich class discussions and perhaps to draw this young man more "into" the class through language that would name and make a part of class discussion the intelligence of his reactions. This young teacher agreed and cited similar experiences that supported students' need for context and vocabulary with which to name their intelligences and thereby feel connected to and a part of the academic world. But, as Rhonda and the young teacher looked at the difference between "regular" and "advanced" English according to state standards, they saw that the absence of such "extra" contextualizing information and materials was exactly what differentiated these two levels in the mandated curriculum. "Advanced" English curriculum dictated introduction of contextualizing information about the history of drama and the vocabulary for naming wordplay. "Regular" English did not.

Neglect, ignorance, or inattention to the history of a topic or discipline, we have noted, makes it even less likely that a course or teacher will be able to draw in those external pentadic elements, since history of a topic or discipline would raise issues and discussion about what people did and why they did it in their past settings, times, and scenes. Such discussion allows for the comparison of past with present situations and responses, allows for acknowledgment of the overlap of internal and external pentadic factors. Of course, such extras could be presented, but increased attention to testing of standards and increased state legislation of accountability measures (including school report cards in South Carolina) mean that it is increasingly unlikely that the students who need the social contexts that enrichment materials often carry with them will get such exposure.

Higher education is not without blame in the setting of state standards such as these. Geographies of knowledge in higher education institutions are traditionally defined by a curriculum that is structured analytically rather than experientially, that is, according to how experts analyze, or break down, the parts of an education and a discipline upon examination of its current terrain and state of knowledge (looking at knowledge as a closed system), rather than according to the ways that those students from different cultural and social backgrounds are likely to first encounter the differences between themselves and the makers and presenters of knowledge. Undergraduate education assumes the importance of starting with "the basics" (building blocks such as critical thinking and writing skills), moves to introduce and immerse undergraduates in the analytical content of their disciplines later on, and generally saves debates over research methods and interpretations of evidence, as well as awareness of competing schools of thought and the lives of researchers, for graduate-level work. This depersonalizing or stripping of immediate social contexts, as well as larger social histories, from academic culture, coupled with the often complete absence of discussion of the relationship between knowledge production (internal pentad) and institutional contexts in which that production lives (external pentad), represents another kind of impoverishment of student writers at both the high school and beginning-college levels.

Studio group work with students and our staff inquiries at both USC and Benedict College have made us aware of the difficulties that this system presents to students who already feel unwelcome in higher education, who need to understand the social contexts and motivations for academic work, and who need someone to acknowledge the frustration they feel as they interact everyday within academe's complex social contexts for knowledge production and learning–even as higher education institutions work so systemically to ignore these same contexts.

Just because Studio offers a place and an approach for surfacing these contexts with students does not mean that students are not resistant. Resistance to participating in what is, after all, still an extra hour's work each week (even with differing ways of giving their work "credit" tried at USC and Benedict College) does not disappear. But we start each Studio semester by placing both the Studio program and the student's experiences in larger contexts of program and in-dividual-institutional histories where that resistance can be better negotiated, taken out of the realm of merely individual negativity or personal feelings to which such resistance is typically attributed. In typical classroom settings, students' unexamined resistance might sometimes be used to shame such students or to isolate them as a bad element in such a way that only further contributes to the alienation that some students bring into their college English courses. We have found that beginning Studio sessions with an open examination and frank discussion of students' writing histories—putting their histories in context of those of their classmates or fellow group members, shar-ing stories and seeing common patterns (why do so many students report that they enjoyed writing in elementary school but began to dislike it in middle school?), discussing possible reasons for a past teacher's behavior or response to an assignment, and so forth—begins to reinvest students with a sense of greater understanding and possible partnership in their further writing development. In this way, as Doreen Massey says,

> we recognise space as always under construction. Precisely because space on this reading is a product of relations-between, relations which are necessarily embedded material practices which have to be carried out, it is always in the process of being made. It is never finished; never closed. Perhaps we could imagine space as a simultaneity of stories-so-far. (*For Space* 9)

In the space of the RCS, the relations that end up in an assignment to attend Studio groups include self-nomination in addition to nomination by the student's research advisor, typically a faculty member conducting research to which a beginning or advanced undergraduate is apprenticed. The general "wisdom" in engineering is that young engineers are abysmally poor communicators and, thus, even the best of students need instruction in technical writing. At USC, they are not required to take a technical writing course because the curriculum is already so full, so RCS moved into that space to provide help in the form of small groups in which students work on the communications assignments they have to produce for an independent study with their research advisor (i.e., writing detailed records of research for later use in more formal communications, writing professional papers, producing posters and PowerPoint presentations for conferences). Resistance is countered by the awarding of one hour of credit (for each of three semesters) and payment to the students of a small stipend provided by the NSF grant.

Several versions of student histories come into play in the nomination of engineering undergraduates for the program. Generally, most engineering students are seen to need help with communication: the difficulty often lies in communicating complex technical information to a lay audience or even other technology-minded researchers outside engineering. Thus, all engineering researchers can benefit from a supportive communications environment. Professors recommend students for RCS (and students nominate themselves) for different reasons. Some students are known to have difficulty with communication in their humanities courses and so are referred to the University Writing Center and the RCS for development. Some are nominated by professors because they are the star students who will be expected to write their research for inclusion in professors' scientific articles. Others might be nominated as beginning engineering students to give them the experience of working in a group of undergraduates (with graduate student mentors) as an apprenticeship for becoming a researcher. All will be expected to communicate effectively, and engineering professors feel unsure about teaching the communication skills well enough themselves, though these professors are often quite proficient in writing and speaking about their research.

The first writing assignment for RCS students is to explain in a paragraph their research project and to articulate their role in the research. Sometimes it takes most of the first semester (of three semesters of involvement) for undergraduates to understand what they are doing and how it relates to the overall project and, further, to application in the world. For instance, Luke's mechanical engineering research on nastic structures was highly mathematical in nature. (As he learned to explain, nastic structures are plant cells that cause motion, as in the closing of the Venus flytrap.) The research project concerned development of a synthetic nastic structure composed of "hydraulic microactuators modeled after biological nastic motor cells" (Matthews). His role in the research was to present the mathematical details to be used to cause hydraulic actuation. In his explanations, he learned to connect with audiences by beginning a presentation with the point that this research was to be applied to making airplane wings that can change shape as necessary and that the process was developed from the biological ability of the Venus flytrap to move spontaneously when stimulated. Often, his introduction to presentations was a picture of a Venus flytrap.

Albena, an electrical engineering student, was assigned to a research project with the technical goal "to build an optimum configuration of solar cell links that results in an enhanced power generation capability without additional components that increase the cost" (Iotova). Her specific project was comparing two solar cell configurations to determine their power in different sun and shade environments. She learned to explain that the technical details, as shown on her Web page, feed into the development of solar battery arrays that soldiers can wear to power their electronic equipment in the field.

For these students, getting to know the history and objectives of the research project they are hired to work on is one of the first steps in a process of learning to communicate about that research. Exploring and coming to understand the history of their work is, for student writers at advanced levels in the institutional hierarchy, part of the essential spatializing of their work, placing the abstract research projects into the real time and places and people of their labs and activities therein. For RCS groups, patient listening and asking questions of novice researchers finally results in understandings on the part of group members that can be fed back to undergraduate students as they figure out how to communicate about their technical projects.

Checking In

After students are identified or nominated by their instructors for RCS, accepted by Studio, or placed into BWP and scheduled into groups (all of which occur in the first two or three weeks of the semester), they begin coming to weekly meetings. After the first meeting, which welcomes them to the program and lets the group members get to know a little about not only one another but also the staff group leader, group procedures, and their own role in the groups, students begin bringing work to the weekly sessions. Every weekly small-group session begins as students walk into the Studio room or area and, after initial greetings and chitchat, each communicates with the entire group about what they have brought to the group that week.

Students "check in"—either by writing on a check-in sheet or on a board, both in common sight of all group members—noting what assignment they are working on, where they are in the process, and what help they would like to have from the group. Below is a sample "whiteboard sign-in" for TA staff members associated with the original FYC Writing Studio program.

Studio Sign-In

Writer	Assignment	Due	Status
Laverne	Persuasion (letter to editor)	Mon.	Almost finished (copies)
Brendon	Persuasion	Tomorrow	Free writing that needs developing
Lindy	Argument (to be revision of persuasion paper)	Tue.	Beginning (copies)
Kobe	Persuasion (gun control)	Fri.	Almost finished (copies)

This check-in procedure is an initial way to tell students that this time is theirs, that the agenda for the meeting and supplemental instruction arises solely from their needs and brings out the meta-discursive and metarhetorical aspects of Studio by requiring students to be more proactive in presenting and talking about their work and by compelling them to articulate their needs in accomplishing the writing or other task associated with a writing assignment. This activity also becomes an exercise in students' use and interpretation of the metadiscourse typical of talk about writing. Students will use the language they hear from their teachers to generally indicate what they have brought and what they need that week ("I've brought a draft, and I need help with revision" "I'm drafting a paper, and I'm stuck" "I need help with my introduction" "I need to edit for comma splices"), but as the group leader and other students prompt the student writer for specifics about the assignment and learn about the context of the problems or feedback that the student writer wants, we move beyond the general labels for process and product "parts" and into the greater variety of metarhetorical circumstances that inform the student writer's work. And as the group moves through the semester together, both students and group leader build an understanding of the patterns that arise in each student writer's work and in his or her reactions to and interactions with the curriculum, teacher, and institutional setting. Thus they create a concrete sense of Studio "space as a product of interrelations" and of academe as a place of "coexisting heterogeneity" (Massey, *For Space* 9).

From this check-in, the Studio leader formulates a quick agenda: assessing which student work or works might first claim the group's time and attention that week (depending perhaps on who didn't get as much time as the others the previous week or which students have the most pressing needs, such as due dates or the student's own feeling of urgency or frustration) or which students' work might be grouped and discussed together so that commonalities (and cross-comparisons of the differences within discussion of the same writing issue) can help to get more mileage out of the time spent on a particular topic. This process can be demanding, as Rhonda's one-pager illustrates below:

Rhonda Grego, 1-pager, November 6, 1998

Tuesday at my 1 P.M. BWP meeting I worked with Larry and Ryan on agreement while Kevin and David drafted papers and then with Kevin and David on brainstorming/overcoming writer's block (Kevin) and development/organization (David) while Larry and Ryan helped each other with an agreement exercise (PHEW!)—all in one short hour.

In the whiteboard sign-in illustrated previously, all the students are working on persuasion or its revision into argumentation, so a discussion of principles of persuasion and audience analysis that grows out of the contents of one student's writing can be applied to others' writing during the meeting. Concepts can be more expansively illustrated by the different applications that arise in the students' work. The students' comments about their different teachers' presentation of persuasion concepts and assignments also help students "theorize the cross-section" of instruction about persuasive writing. As well, the array of "statuses" that exists in this check-in, all the way from free writing and beginning drafts to almost finished essays, illustrates the different stages of writing processes and gives students new options for managing their own writing process. In looking across assignments and classrooms and teachers at the ways in which concepts like these manifest themselves in the particular places at that institutional site, metarhetorical awarenesses are articulated and developed. Students are able to see writing development from the multiple perspectives represented, perspectives that come from student writers just like themselves working self-consciously within academic culture but from different specific places, perspectives they can add to their own repertoire of ways to approach academic writing. The reporting and projection procedures in weekly Studio sessions bridge the spaces of unknowns between students and the work they must produce. As another example, in the RCS two or three students might be working to produce poster presentations for a competition during Discovery Day, which occurs each spring semester at USC. Working together, staff members and students study the guidelines for entries, as well as previous posters that are hanging on the wall or have been saved in the shared electronic space. Some students may be entering the competition for a second time, so they share their experience from the previous year, once again bridging the distance between students and the work they must produce.

Bringing Writing—or Artifacts Thereof—to Share

One of the most critical principles of the Studio model is that participants must be working on a piece of writing, a related task (such as a reading with generative questions), or some other communication, and they must bring that writing or other artifact with which they are involved to share with group members. Focusing on the work students are in the process of producing, as projected in the sign-in process at the beginning of the studio session, is what determines the flow of the Studio session, not any additional curriculum that directs group activity and attention (and would add another level or layer of "histories" to an already complex situation being negotiated by student writers). This kind of participation, or embeddedness, is what makes Studio groups work: the students all need to embrace the risk of making their work public and the ownership that ensues from group participation. When student writers are in the flow of writing work, they are better positioned to engage with the metadiscursive generalities and labels applied to writing and the process of producing it. Equally important, they are in the midst of the complex metarhetorical relations that construct their writing "space," relations between

- teachers and administrators involved in the immediate writing assignment and its conformity to secondspace conceptions about writing currently valued by the discipline and by society at large (as, for example, in the RCS assignments that reflect the changing nature of requirements for effective presentation, as professionals learn new ways to use electronic presentations and earlier conventions become outmoded; in the changing nature of assignments given in first-year English classes, reflecting new program approaches in larger research institutions such as USC; or in changing approaches to assignments at the HBCU that include service-learning activities);
- those institutional figures who played a part in students' past educational experiences with writing and whose positions students recall and draw on as they write (i.e., the belief students bring to college courses that they must use language that is not transparent in order to sound professional and intelligent); and
- those people, places, and events that form the student writer's experiences that he or she is drawing on to inform the content and style of the current writing.

Our use of the term *artifact* comes, of course, from previous background in feminist research methods and from composition's own lively interest in adapting the methods of cultural anthropology and ethnography to research on writing, writing pedagogy, and teacher research, including the work of Eleanor Kutz and Hephzibah Roskelly; Eleanor Kutz, Suzy W. Groden, and Vivian Zamel; Linda Miller Cleary; Bonnie Sunstein and Elizabeth Chiseri-Strater; Ruth Ray; and others. The artifacts students bring might be a draft of an assignment—a whole draft, a rough draft, a piece of draft, a free-writing piece that could be a first step toward a draft, a visual or graphic image that fits into the assignment or helps generate ideas, an essay assignment sheet from a writing class, an article to summarize for their history class, notes from research, a list of articles or Internet sites related to a topic they are researching, et cetera. These adjuncts to the student writer's development, when seen as cultural artifacts, can be discussed, interpreted, and used by the group to enter into and discuss the social relations, processes, and assumptions that construct a different sense of academic writing in that institutional setting and that are part of each instructor's own disciplinary history as well. This too is the metarhetorical work of recontextualizing ideas about the form and format of writing by placing them within the social history, institutional relations, disciplinary values, and classroom exigencies that construct those ideas. For example, when students are doing work that requires some visual or graphic material, they benefit from bringing the material to the group and leading a brainstorming discussion to bring out others' understandings of the work, which can then enhance their writing. Studio sessions that provide opportunities to hear the variety of approaches group members take in "reading" visuals have worked well for students who are, for example, analyzing print advertisements. The presentation of graphic print advertisements also allows the group leader to engage students in discussions about the relationships between visuals and text, about the different conventions of genre and form in such popular texts versus those in academic writing, essays, reports, and so forth, and about sharing their considerable knowledge of these other genres and experiences in the process. Mark Sutton's one-pager for a Studio staff meeting provides an illustration:

> *Mark Sutton's one-pager, October 8, 2001*
>
> *Last week, one of my Studio students showed the group two ads for watches. She had to come up with an analytical thesis for them and didn't know where to start. Her peers immediately began to rattle off things they noticed about the ads: the backgrounds, the size of the watches, their position relative to everything else in the ad, the colors, the text, the people in the ads. They pointed to specific details and suggested the effects the advertiser was attempting to evoke. I didn't have a chance to talk.*

After they stopped, the writer tied their comments to a thesis on the different target audiences for the ads, which she wrote down. She said it was too abstract, so the group helped her, over about five minutes, make it more concrete. I put in my bit here, mostly to remind them of what a thesis should do and to tie what they said together. The student ended up with a functional thesis that she could refine later.

One of the other group members said, "You've still got to write the paper, and it's going to be hard to get three pages." The others agreed.

I replied, "Why? You two just came up with at least five pages worth of analysis."

They all looked at me like I was crazy, just like a student two hours earlier who I said gave a good explanation of completing an analysis that she swore she couldn't understand on her own.

This expectation of having to produce or bring something concrete can be the impetus for writers to move their process along. If students don't bring work or artifacts, the leader can use the check-in procedure to find out what assignment a student is working on and, at least, lead the group in a brainstorming discussion to generate ideas or a discussion about the assignment to check understanding, to get the thinking process started, and to open up any metarhetorical concerns or issues that are blocking a writer. Often students need extra help in developing a workable image of what an assignment is asking for, and, as the example below shows, they often can help one another better than the instructor who has created the assignment, or even the experienced Studio leader who bridges between instructor and student.

Terry Carter, one-pager, October 4, 2000

My students do have ideas and can see things in their writing that I do not see; each of us has a lens focused in a certain way that allows us to see only so much at one time. Last week, Karen was able to explain a concept to Lee in a way that made sense to them; she helped me out, as I was trying to get him to see this

*concept in the way that I saw it. She sort of jumped in and added
her view of the idea, and these clicked for Lee. I praised her for
explaining it in her own way and reminded them all that each of
them did have strengths that I may or may not have. I encouraged
them to step up to the plate and share them when one of us was
in need.*

Inevitably, Studio contextualizing of writing assignments and classroom experiences through examination and discussion of particular artifacts of student work means that group members will give more in-depth feedback and discussion of an issue than what any student initially "asks" for. Though the student might want the group to focus in a particular way, that is, to clarify an idea, it is counterproductive to even try to disallow comments that bubble up regarding other qualities of the writing, such as convoluted sentence structures that might prevent clarity. Students enter Studio sessions with the classroom-enforced secondspace conceptions of writing on the tips of their tongues, use this language (metadiscourse) to identify and articulate the difficulties a piece of writing might be causing for them or to check how a piece of writing is received by an audience. Then, however, ensuing discussion can and often does go beyond this initial terminology into a thirdspace. That thirdspace is opened up when the firstspace of their perceptions (drawn out by discussion and probing) and the secondspace of composition's current terminology for talking about writing interact, creating incipient awareness of the gaps, of what is absent from the secondspace conceptions. Then the group works together to forge deeper understandings and a fuller awareness of metarhetorical complexity, and finally to arrive at possible actions that the student writer can use to negotiate the situation in her own writing, in the writing assignment, with his writing instructor, et cetera. In this way, Studio helps each student expand his or her metarhetorical sense of the different meanings carried by the phrases used in their composition classrooms and in rhetorics and readers for talking about different aspects of writing process and product—and acts as an advocate for student writers in the process.

Encouraging Participation: Students Teaching Students

The Studio model's use of small-group sessions takes advantage of near-peer and peer-peer instruction (Lave 81–82). Working from a less-distanced position than the course instructor, the Studio group leaders, the staff leaders in the BWP, or the graduate student staff leaders in the RCS stand on a border that allows them to look one way into the mind-set of undergraduate students (where they have recently been themselves) or the other way into the added perspective and experience of an instructor or even a more advanced undergraduate. One of the most important roles of the Studio group leader is to foster conditions that encourage the active participation of all at whatever level of participation is available and accessible in that group. That means students must know they are expected to bring work or artifacts, that the other group members will actively respond to the work they bring, that those responses will be offered in the productive manner of inquiry, and that they, too, are expected to give feedback and to respond to others. Even if students cannot bring a piece of their own writing to the Studio, they can be led by the group leader to talk about the assignments they are working on, as the following one-pager illustrates.

> *Mark Sutton, one-pager, November 7, 2001*
>
> *A couple of weeks ago, one of the group members said he didn't have anything to work on. I didn't buy this, and the student knew it. Instead of ordering him to pull out his syllabus or badgering him about not participating, I started asking how his English class was going in general, a topic which tends to come up in my groups. After a minute of explaining some class activity, he admitted that he had to write [a] topic proposal for an evaluative essay. He hadn't brought it up because he already had a thesis: USC's rules for flag football were stupid. Another group member, who plays on Patterson's team, immediately agreed, and the two started sharing their experiences. As I am wont to do, I listened for a bit. Once I heard enough to understand the rules, I started raising counterarguments. For example, they thought forbidding*

the defensive line from raising their arms was too limited. I said it sounded like a way to keep people from getting hurt. Light people, I said, rarely play defensive line. Since I've tried to create a supportive atmosphere, the students didn't feel the pressure to agree with me just because I was the group leader. They challenged my ideas, which made me develop my own points more. Then they developed their own responses.

When we finished, I pointed out that we had constructed a fairly well-developed argument that he could shape in the paper he'd bring next week.

To an outside observer, this experience may have seemed like a waste of time. No one was taking official brainstorming notes, and I didn't use any rhetorical terms. We didn't even pull out a text. Still, I think the group members left with a pretty good idea about how to write an evaluative argument. In addition, the guy who had nothing hopefully left with the pattern for a paper. I don't think I would've been able to do this if I ran the sessions too businesslike. Like I wrote last time, Studio is supposed to be a place where everyone's opinions matter, and this means all opinions, not just those that deal with writing better papers.

With or without the instructor's written description of the assignment (which students are encouraged to bring to Studio or which group leaders can get directly from instructors), students' explanations of their assignments open up their understandings, or lack of understanding, of what the instructor is asking them to do. Questions from the group leader and other students help the student specify the details of the assignment and the approaches he or she will take in responding to it. This kind of conversation can lead to a brainstorming session that will help the student interpret the assignment and begin a draft to take back to his or her class.

As in other groups, no one group member can be allowed either to dominate or sit quietly all the time (though of course differences in personality and style must be taken into account). If one group member does not participate, other group members are likely to feel uncomfortable, as illustrated in the one-pager below, because they

don't know what that person is thinking, particularly early in a semester when group members are just getting to know each other.

Daniel Robinson, one-pager, November 13, 1995

*I do have one group that really brings me down, and this is
because I have one student in the group who refuses to participate. All semester I've been trying to determine whether this
young woman is shy or surly—perhaps both—but her reti-
cence and unpreparedness really kill the group's enthusiasm.
She simply does not communicate with the group; she does not
contribute to the discussion of either her own work or others'.
Frankly, the group works better when she does not show up,
which is fairly frequent.*

In initial group meetings (and even later in the semester, as in
Daniel's group), a number of factors can contribute to student nonpar-
ticipation. It takes some students a while to trust that the group session
is for their own use and help. Their own educational experiences lead
them to suspect that a "real" curriculum will emerge to control and
structure the group before long, and some will sit back looking for
signs of it to justify their continued inaction. It takes others a while
to shift from a passive stance toward their own education—they are
so used to having teachers control the agenda—to the more active
stance encouraged by Studio. Other students are either so unfamiliar
with "teacher language" for talking about writing or so alienated by
the ways that such language has been used to talk only negatively
about their writing that they too are reticent. Some students just
cannot seem to find connection between academic metadiscourses
on writing and their own experience of writing, particularly since
standard metadiscourse for talking about writing abstracts out the
social relations and expectations that most preoccupy them about
their work in and for college classes. We have worked through our
years of Studio experience to understand student resistance in these
contextualized ways—rather than labeling reluctant students as bad
elements. This attitude of looking for contextualized explanations is
communicated among group leaders and to students in Studio groups

through patience, persistence, and the kind of informed caring about contexts displayed by group leaders toward student writers.

As Studio group leaders and staff, we persist in our conviction that students benefit from teaching one another about not only the responses of an audience to one's communication but also their perceptions of classroom contexts and social relations that permeate their firstspace experiences as student writers. And, as all teachers know, we have often learned our subject best through our attempts to teach it to others. Studio shows us that often what we learn in attempting to teach others is where the gaps are in the secondspace conceptions that have been taught to us. Thus, group leaders attempt to do less of the talking and to engage other student group members in teaching concepts, explaining an assignment, passing on helpful hints or ideas from their own struggles, and so forth. In an RCS session, students are enlisted to explain to one another an outline of the kind of points that should be covered in an abstract, and thus instead of a textbook explanation or teacher lecture, a discussion ensues that covers different views of the genre. And for this reason it is helpful, though not always possible, to have students from different teachers, course sections, and engineering research groups in the same Studio group. Again, the focus is not on either a Studio curriculum or mere supplementation of any one teacher's weekly class design or topics; instead, we are working to move into a thirdspace of negotiation of first- and secondspace conceptions of writing. Having one predominant secondspace conception of writing (from one classroom teacher) can diminish students' opportunities to learn from and teach each other.

An Extended Example of an RCS Participant

In the RCS, undergraduate participants from different research projects in different engineering fields with different faculty advisors provide a great variety of approaches and intelligences. These circumstances make for a rich learning environment when managed so as to make space for each member to contribute to the education of another. One of the metarhetorical activities of RCS sessions is analysis of the expectations of different research advisors: some want the student to take initiative, even to the point of not asking questions and instead figuring out the answers for themselves, while others might offer the student detailed instructions. In Studio sessions, we work to read the research advisors' expectations, helping each student ask questions of, react to, understand, and otherwise interact effectively with her or his particular advisor. We attempt to deconstruct how the advisor is socially constructed himself (the research advisors having all been men, though sometimes a male professor's female graduate student works directly with the student) and the reasons and backgrounds for particular assignments, such as assigned research reports. This kind of analysis is especially helpful for students, because the research assignments for RCS are rarely written down, and bringing the analysis to the table helps to lessen the hierarchical distance between the student and the professor.

In one case, a research advisor was to guide the student Lavinia in the activities of a funded research project. He brought into the academic environment his extensive experience in the corporate world as a research writer. In an appointment with him a few weeks earlier, the staff members learned that the advisor wanted Lavinia to take more ownership of her research task and to take more initiative, with less direct guidance from him. He compared her negatively with a male graduate student who "takes to" research and said he expected that level of "commitment" from her as well. Back in the group session with Lavinia, the staff members led a discussion about taking initiative with a research project and being proactive in communicating with the research advisor. At the beginning of the next semester, when Lavinia was starting a new round of her research experience, she wrote in her reflection (written after each weekly session) to RCS staff: "I will try a new procedure that I discovered. . . . I am now in the process of forming the procedure that is a combination of previous works." In her report to her research advisor, with an awakened awareness of him as audience, she said, "I have recently become aware of a new procedure that might allow the preparation . . . with fewer steps in the process. . . . Before resuming my work with the [previous procedure], I will investigate the use of [. . .] as an alternative."

One specific question that Lavinia brought to the RCS concerned format. Early in the semester, she wrote in her reflection about seeing the format of another student's slides for a meeting with a company that was funding a research project: "The comments for improvement on the slides were to maybe change the colors of the bullets and to box the key to make it known on the graph. Knowing these things helped me in knowing what and what not to do for my presentation slides."

When Lavinia brought a copy of her research procedure and asked for help with the format, the group interpreted that request as asking how to distinguish the steps in the procedure from one another and how to arrange them in a logical flow to facilitate the audience's understanding. A question arose about the audience for the piece: was it her research advisor to whom she needed to report her procedures and commentary on the results, or was it the student researcher who would follow in the project and pick up her work after she graduates? In response to that issue, Lavinia brought two drafts representing the same material the next week. One was addressed to the research advisor; it was written in past tense, telling what she had done and giving details on the results she received. The other was written in present tense as a series of commands, telling the future researcher what steps to take and commenting about what to look for as results. Thus, Lavinia had become aware of the different readers' needs, and she understood the grammatical changes that appropriately addressed a metarhetorical audience issue.

After Lavinia's first semester in the Studio, we almost lost her. In the next semester she was still enrolled in her independent study course with her research advisor, but we discovered that she was not going to participate in RCS during what would be her final semester before graduating. She resisted the extra time RCS took, so we suggested that she should do no extra work beyond her RA's requirements and that her reflections should be written as quickly as possible. With the staff's encouragement, Lavinia did participate.

As the director of the program, with some knowledge of all the parties involved, Nancy speculated on what might have been causing Lavinia's reluctance to continue in the Studio. She wondered whether Lavinia, an African American student, had been made uncomfortable in one session during the previous semester when she brought an abstract to the group for feedback. The other students in the group included two young women, one white and one Indian, who came from professional backgrounds and good high school educations that gave them exactly the kind of experiences that would prompt an engineering research advisor to say they just "take to" research. On the day Lavinia brought her abstract, these two participants bombarded the group with their intense discussion of the reordering of Lavinia's ideas and sentences, completely taking over the session for this period. Their quick moves from one suggestion to another made it difficult for the others to follow. At that point, Nancy suggested that the group number the sentences in Lavinia's abstract and reorder them, using the numbers as tags so that all the group members could follow along.

While the two students were teaching what they had already learned, they were learners, too, in the role of passing on their experience to another student. They knew the genre of the abstract, but engagement in metadiscourse, articulating and applying the concept, made it more accessible to consciousness. By articulating their knowledge, these two students reorganized and embedded it more firmly in their own minds. In this session, the students engaged in metadiscursive discussion of the abstract before moving to the purpose and audience of this particular abstract and how that information might affect the form of the piece. One of the interesting features of the metadiscourse used by the two students as they taught Lavinia about the form of an abstract was their use of informal language, including repetitions of the term *like*, which often grates on the formal ear of an instructor. However, in a showing of a video of the event as an example of RCS in a training session for new engineering graduate student mentors, one African American graduate student pointed out that the two were using informal, everyday language to make Lavinia feel more comfortable. Here is Lavinia's reflection on that meeting:

> I received a lot of feedback on how to arrange things in my abstract, how an abstract needs to be set up, and what goes into an abstract and where it goes. Now knowing that I have to turn in an abstract that is an overview of my research

[purpose and audience] then talk about what I have done this semester with my research, I can thoroughly go through the sentences that I have already written and see what is appropriate for this situation. I think I already have everything that is needed but I do need to discuss more about what I actually did in the lab.

In the following semester, when Lavinia became the reigning experienced participant in a new small group, she remembered that session. In her later reflection, she wrote,

In last week's RCS session I contributed feedback to Anne on her task plan. In it she explained her research in how she is going to assemble and test a motor system. Her sentences were unorganized. . . .

I remember in last semester's RCS [my peers] helped [m]e organize my sentences. . . . I learned from them how to help other students organize their sentences. I put myself in the reader's shoes and tried to understand how an outside person would read Anne's task plan. After reading her task plan, I understood how others saw my paper last semester. I think after we finished rearranging Anne's task plan she could see how the structuring made a huge difference.

Near the end of her last semester in RCS, while in the throes of job-hunting, Lavinia reflected:

In my researching career, I feel that I have almost reached that mature level. I now know what is expected of a researcher and somewhat know how it needs to get done. Last semester, I did not know what my advisor really wanted me to do with the research, but now I know how he likes things done. I guess it is like getting a new professor. You have to learn their teaching styles and learn how thoroughly they want you to answer a question, especially in a class where you have to write papers.

Now I feel more comfortable talking with [my research advisor], but I am like that with any new person I meet.

I hope all of the write-ups that I am doing now will be legible for the next person that comes next year to take on my research. It really helps a lot when the person before you keep[s] good notes on what they already did so you will not repeat the same mistakes or even if you come across a problem, you can refer back to the old notes. That is why I try to record everything I do and what happened at each step so it will not be hard for the next person if they get stuck.

There are relatively few women and minority role models in engineering for those few black women, like Lavinia, who are getting engineering degrees. Social interactions in Studio spaces, which put us close enough to students for questions to arise, led to our speculation about the reasons for the difficulties they face in higher education. Even before Lavinia began participating in RCS, she had been referred to the engineering department's Professional Communications Center by one of her professors there because she was having trouble with an English course. Her difficulties were of the kind that we often encounter in English 101 students from rural South Carolina: multiple problems with grammar, spelling, and so forth, as well as "literacy" problems—a lack of familiarity with literary and academic discourse conventions. Our interaction with her led to consultation on her applications for the summer Research Experience for Undergraduates (REU) programs; we helped her understand the genre of the personal statement in order to express her research interests. She succeeded in getting an REU grant and in completing the English course. As a young black woman from a small town in South Carolina, her lack of preparation for a professional engineering career contrasts starkly with those of the young men and women who come from professional family backgrounds and who are prepared to "take to" a research career. However, Lavinia successfully sought out and used the resources provided by thirdspace programs such as the RCS and the Professional Communications Center, as well as the South Carolina Alliance for

Minority Participation (which provides professional experiences for minority students), to help her learn the communication genres required for success and to help her come to an integrated understanding of factors both internal and external to the writing tasks that she faced and will continue to face in the future.

Interpreting Assignments and Teacher's Comments

A student's first look at an instructor's assignment can be discouraging. Often writing assignments are short, terse, the teacher assuming that students have been making the same kinds of connections within a unit or project for study as the teacher, who has a more complete "text" and disciplinary, institutional, and historical understanding of the assignment. Bringing assignment instructions to the Studio for interpretation can help to lessen these distances and the sense of isolation such distances can create in student writers. Likewise, a student's first glance at the instructor's comments, which might be long and difficult to read (because the handwriting is hurried or because it is hard to tell whether the teacher is referring to content issues or relaying ideas about or choices for form, or because so many ideas are embedded in a text—kinda like this sentence with its interjection) or so short as to be cryptic—can be discouraging. Bringing a copy of the paper-with-comments to the Studio group helps students get the input of other students, as well as a group leader who is more experienced with writing, with teachers' comments, and with how to read, interpret, and respond to those comments. In essence, Studio "re-peoples" the specialized "shorthand" discourse of both assignments and comments. Thus, interpreting instructors' assignments and comments provides material for many valuable Studio sessions (as illustrated in the one-pager below). The empty mental space created—when a student can't seem to own those assignments or comments—may be filled with discussion of possible meanings, connections to previous experiences with writing (either the student writer's own or those of other group members), and potential actions to take at that particular spot in the writing process, across an entire piece of writing, or in relation to asking for further explanation from his or her instructor.

Tom Smith one-pager, November 20, 1995

In one of my sessions, one which is almost always atextual, two students in the same class came with fire in their eyes. Having just come from conferences, they were convinced that their instructor was governed by whim. I essentially let the more vocal of the two vent her frustrations. She came to Studio saying that her instructor wanted her to do a research paper in order to give the instructor advice about birth control. The student said she wanted to write about birth control, but the instructor insisted she focus on Norplant. The student seemed convinced that the instructor simply wanted to use her to get information. It seems a strange dilemma to me. In effect, it sounded like the instructor was asking specific questions about Norplant in order to create a kind of audience for the student. In effect, she was saying, "Here's what I would want to know." But the student saw herself losing authority over the project.

Studio group leaders adopt the same contextualizing approach to the work of course instructors as they do toward the work of student writers; in other words, we never allow ourselves to be drawn into debates such as "If you were grading this paper, what grade would you have given?" or sessions spent complaining about instructors. If student writing is socially constructed by complex interactions and factors, then so too is the work of composition classroom instructors, something that most of us who have served as group leaders are aware of, having been (or simultaneously occupying the position of) classroom teachers ourselves! Instructors, like students, have educational careers, disciplinary affiliations, and personality and style differences that are a part of their entire history and life. In TA training at the beginning of an academic year, one of the sessions will sometimes be a paper-grading exercise. What often emerges is the different standards that different instructors adhere to. Though the goal of such a session might be to better standardize grading approaches, no one session can fully counteract the many experiences through years of schooling that will have influenced one's grading standards. When students ask what we think about their grade or a teacher's comment, we respond in terms of the program, discipline, experience, or assignment and other relevant factors, acknowledging that there are differences in responding to and grading work (something that Studio students themselves see as they compare their returned papers, grades, and comments with other group members). Such observations open up discussion of the different fields affiliated with "English studies" from which their instructors may have come, or the generation with which an instructor identifies, or even the idea of "generations" or "paradigms" of thought within academic disciplines themselves. Students who bring limited views of academic writing (and accompanying monolithic views of good writing) typically also have little understanding of the different academic disciplines and values therein that affect writing instruction. Because they lack such information to draw on in interpreting their teacher and his or her comments about their writing, they are sometimes quick to instead attribute personal motives and attitudes to and toward their writing instructors (as we teachers sometimes do with student writers). Deconstructing monolithic views of writing is at the heart of what Studio's thirdspace teaches students and group leaders (who are often, in our programmatic experiences, also teachers).

For her 1996 ethnographic dissertation on the Writing Studio, Anita Guynn studied the role of the Writing Studio group interactions in students' revisions of their writing for English 101 courses. Guynn found that students did not so much use studio interactions to assist them in rewriting already-produced drafts for their courses; instead, they often used sessions for help in understanding the assignment or, in her terms (following Linda Flower), "task representation." Flower's research showed that "[g]iven a 'revised' task representation, students who did not normally revise extensively were able to do so" (iii). Guynn describes how she came to appreciate fully the unvoiced and assumed academic expectations of faculty, particularly in the vague instructions for assignments students receive, and the need for teachers to be critically aware of their expectations in order to make them clear to students (188). The discussion of such tacit expectations in Studio sessions can help students understand their assignments or represent their tasks to themselves more accurately; and it exemplifies the metarhetorical nature of studio work: not just to dwell metadiscursively on the surface of the text itself that students produce but to explore the shape it should take to fulfill the assignment or the genre and audience expectations brought by that teacher, and that program, in that institution. For example, Guynn's student William, who had expressed that he liked "defined" assignments (201), had trouble with the assignment to analyze a cultural artifact. His first draft of a paper about the Dallas Cowboys was essentially expressive rather than analytical, focusing on Cowboys fans. After the Studio discussion brought out specific analytical points about the cultural importance of the Cowboys, William was able to revise effectively. The revision was, in fact, a whole new paper; Guynn's analysis showed that no text from the first draft carried over into the new paper. Given a new understanding by the studio discussion of the metarhetorical expectations of the assignment to analyze a cultural artifact, he was able to produce a new, more appropriate paper (201).

This approach to deconstructing the various elements of writing assignments also dictates that just as we engage with Studio students in discussions of writing that move us into the negotiations of third-space, we also share with instructors our weekly insights into why student writers experience certain problems in their writing.

Reseeing Metadiscursive Development as Metarhetorical Awareness

In our Studio beginnings, we believed not only that the strategies discussed above would help students develop their metadiscursive abilities but that both student and staff Studio groups would then be able to theorize the cross-section of how students were comprehending and processing the metadiscourse encountered in their writing classes. But what our discussions in initial years of Studio work started (and have continued) to impress on us is not just that students lack metadiscourse but that the metadiscourse we use to talk about student writing processes and products is often too generic, that it makes for quick and easy arhetorical labeling and allows us to ignore or overlook the complexities of the different social experiences and assumptions brought by many student writers to college. In our early semesters in Studio sessions, for example, we found this to be the case with teacher comments such as the ubiquitous request for "more details" often found in the margins of student drafts and papers.

In one of our first publications about Studio research on student writing (Grego and Thompson, "Repositioning Remediation"), we reported how Studio led us to interrogate this much-used phrase in teacher commenting. We saw that it had several possible meanings, depending on the teacher, the text, and the place in the student's draft being referred to, and thus was frustrating to interpret. We recall another Studio student group from those early semesters that spent almost an entire session breaking apart a long sentence in which a student writer had tried to "add details" and, in doing so, piled up a series of clauses in one sentence. Each clause headed in a different direction. As the group members questioned the student writer about the relationships among the string of images, the student began to "unpack" her source experiences, both direct and secondhand and, therefore, how they were related to ideas that needed developing in that paper. It was as if each phrase called forth a "meeting up of histories" from her own personal and educational past. Each phrase thus had its own trajectory, and not all the phrases and trajectories were compatible or coherent with the others in that long sentence. The student writer came to see that unpacking the "histories" behind each of these phrases helped her determine what to develop in the body of her draft. She could then come back to the opening paragraph with a better sense of the overall relationships between the ideas she brought to the assignment. This same problem is discussed by another staff group leader.

Tom Smith, one-pager, November 20, 1995

I wonder sometimes about our constant harping on detail. We say, over and over, be specific, as if specificity were the paramount skill in writing. I—of course this is a typical male response to birth control!—would be bored to tears by a detailed description of Norplant. I wonder if this assertion that details are so important comes from our inability to suggest anything else (detail: semantics::grammar:syntax?)

Moreover, while most mode-teaching instructors insist upon

additions of detail in 101, they insist upon abstraction in 102 (i.e.,
don't summarize the plot). Just some thoughts.

In a recent article on the BWP at Benedict College ("Community
Archaeology"), Rhonda wrote about a Studio session spent coming
to understand how the sentence fragments that appeared only in the
opening paragraphs of a student paper were due to the student's un-
certainty about how to open an autobiographical essay: The student
had chosen to mimic the style of a voice-over narration in a movie,
and her accurate mimicry of this style included fragments. Instead of
addressing this "problem" by assigning the handbook chapter on fragments, the BWP group discussed the relationship between spoken and
written genres and conventions, as well as stylistic representations of
postmodern fragmentation versus academic culture's continued modernist preferences. These first-year students were not, of course, literary critics, but introducing the group to some of this language—and,
perhaps even more important, to some of the history and intellectual
movements with which academic culture is familiar—gave these students a different view and context within which to understand issues
of writing conventions and style.

In that same article, Rhonda reported that a BWP staff member,
Stephen Criswell, brought a student paper to our staff group and
described how he and the student group had spent a session real-
izing that the jumble of incoherent sentences on the first page was
the result of the student's earnest efforts to follow a hodgepodge of
vaguely remembered dictates from past English teachers: don't use
I, don't begin sentences with *because*, don't shift tense, use transition
words, and so forth. As the basis for the student writer's logic and reasoning came out in examination and discussion, other student group
members got their own questions answered and confusions cleared
up. And the student's paper, along with Stephen's mini narrative of
the group session at that week's staff meeting, provided BWP staff
members occasion to examine and connect their own observations
of such instances and stories of such confusions. This moment in our
interactional inquiry then fed into a short piece on such confusions

in our BWP newsletters for the first-year composition instructors. Another such instance of insight into the complexities of student writers' ideas about writing is illustrated in the complete text (below) of Rhonda's one-pager (originally cited only in part above):

Rhonda Grego, one-pager, November 6, 1998

Tuesday at my 1 P.M. BWP meeting I worked with Larry and Ryan on agreement while Kevin and David drafted papers and then with Kevin and David on brainstorming/overcoming writer's block (Kevin) and development/organization (David) while Larry and Ryan helped each other with an agreement exercise (PHEW!)—all in one short hour. After they left, I glanced at Kevin's log and read his entry:
    "I didn't learn anything today, but I got help on a paper."
I wondered (with frustration) what made Kevin perceive that learning how to use clustering to develop and organize ideas (and get past writer's block) was not learning? Was it that he saw Perry and Bryan working from the handbook and an exercise sheet on grammar—and THAT looked like "learning" because of the book and the grammar and worksheet? Is this more evidence of how so many of my students have been told for so long that they don't "know" grammar? They've been so conditioned to look outside themselves (anywhere but in their own thought processes) for what counts as "learning."
    I see this pattern in stories Emmie Davis and I have been sharing about students in our lab groups and classes who can't get the idea of "writing process." They often think that each "activity" (brainstorming, freewriting, clustering, drafting, revising, editing) is a discrete, new assignment. The result of all this disconnection (that we struggle with each day in lab groups) is that students are caught up in the surfaces and don't then have time to "go deep" into the territory where all these writing activities could interact and affect each other to improve their final written products.

Studio thirdspace allows us to see and explore the complex cultural, everyday, and popular rhetorical patterns and genres that converge and commingle in student writing, along with students' interpretations both of past teachers' advice and of their present teachers' assignments. These convergences are felt strongly by the student caught in the push-pull of the cultural, historical, disciplinary, social, and institutional forces that they represent. And as long as there are no spaces within which to stop and examine what we term the metarhetorical nature of academic writing, then every new English or composition class—no matter how well or meaningfully structured—only introduces another layer of institutionally and disciplinarily dictated directions and histories and assumptions about writing to that already compiled by each student writer throughout her or his educational history. This accumulated "meeting up" of histories, when not acknowledged by the educational system, can build frustration in student writers, so much so that even the most well-meaning and seemingly culturally sensitive labeling of a pattern of "error" in student writing can be taken negatively by the student. To that student, such labeling comes from directions unknown. Even identifying a subset of linguistic features in a student's writing as black English vernacular (BEV) patterns, which would seem to be a contextualizing act, can be taken as just another generalization, another teacherly avoidance of the complex everyday "lifeworld" that produced the writing and surrounds the student's writing development, as we saw in another significant BWP experience.

In a BWP staff meeting one week, a group leader told us about a student in one of her groups who had come to the meeting that week upset about some teacher comments on his latest paper. Since helping students work through and with teacher comments is an important activity in Studio programs, the student shared his concerns with his group. The student was in a class taught by an English department adjunct, a personable teacher who had much experience teaching English and writing classes, including some teaching in Africa. This teacher had written on the student's paper the usual editing marks and, at the end, a note that the student's writing exhibited BEV features, which could easily be worked on. The instructor invited the student to come to him for assistance, if needed. The lesser comments on content, coupled with a label that the student perceived as a "black English" seal of (societal) disapproval, made the student feel that he was being looked at narrowly as "black" by a white teacher, that his work was simply being labeled and not really read, despite the good intentions of the instructor. The student's Studio group and group leader brought their perspectives to a discussion of the instructor's possible intentions and motivations, opened up a conversation on the national-level debate over black English, including different views of those in the African American community (both national and local), and looked at what the course handbook had to say about BEV patterns.

Our ensuing staff meeting discussion focused on how the linguistic or rhetorical "accuracy" of student writing must be considered alongside the relations of power in the classroom and the "meeting up of histories" in any such interaction. The latter two issues are important in the interaction between the older white male teacher and the student because of the context of American history, the educational history of the student, and the recent social history of unfavorable attention focused on Ebonics in the popular media and even by prominent black politicians and entertainers. BWP staff meetings originated many such discussions about the ways in which the historical, social, and cultural differences between teachers or group leaders and their students affect how students perceive and what they take from the latter's statements, comments, suggestions, or teachings. The visual collage constructed by Ruby Blair, another BWP staff member and experienced teacher of first-year composition at Benedict College, illustrates just some of the student emotions, including anger, frustration, relief, confusion, defiance, and a strong personal identification with their writing, that emerge in BWP student groups as a result of these complex interactions of histories and resulting misunderstandings. (See the one-page of graphics, "The Realities of the Student Writer," in chapter 2.) Students' struggles with the histories that meet (often unseen and misunderstood by their teachers) in their writing assignments and courses can forge fierce emotions and identification with their writing.

In a 1995 *WPA* journal article on our Studio work, we hypothesized that such emotions signal submerged, complex interactions that our current vocabulary for talking about writing—our metadiscourse—frustratingly seems to ignore. Common comments, labels, terms for identifying features of writing—from genre to grammati-

cal forms—originate from Soja's secondspace world of conceptions
of writing by different disciplines (and for generations within these
disciplines) and scholarship therein, while students and their writing
are connected to even more complex worlds, including institutionalized academic culture. As compositionists we take our vocabulary
for talk about writing from fields invested in identifying the parts of
a text for the purposes of disciplinary analysis (literary criticism or
rhetoric or linguistics), but in most cases no actual analysis—at least
of student writing—will ensue. The metadiscursive commentary and
feedback that student writers receive on their work and writing come
from sources generally uninterested in the firstspace of their work,
and thus it is that student writers are cut off from themselves. They
feel the frustration of this distance, one that signals their alienation
and lack of belonging in higher education.

In *Terms of Work*, Bruce Horner recounts a similar alienation and
distancing, though on the flip side of our previous Studio examples.
Instead of working with students who are frustrated at any perceived
emptiness in the ways of talking about writing to which they've been
educated, Horner brought to his class a piece of student writing in
which he, as teacher, sensed "something happening," only to find that
the students in the class were most able to apply the ways of looking
at writing to which they'd been educated, leading them to dismiss
and ignore that "something happening." He reflects that

> as teacher I had access to other of the writer's papers and so
> could more readily see it as part of an ongoing process of "de-
> velopment." They had only the isolated, anonymous paper: It
> was only by exploring the interaction of our institutional and
> historical positionings and the different modes of the writing's
> distribution that we could do more than simply badger each
> other about whether we should condemn or praise the writer
> and the practice represented by this paper. (66)

Horner suggests that we must help students to see student writing
within its own conditions of production, and to do so we must examine the writing

> in relation to the conditions of time, the assignment, the posi-
> tioning of the student in the "intimate domestic space" of the
> course, the situation of that course and its instructor within
> the curriculum and specific institution, and the relation of
> the student's writing to available technological resources for
> the material production of the writing. (65)

In Studio student (and staff) groups, discussions will begin or
gravitate toward explicating just such contextualizing conditions and
thus can more easily maintain a focus on the classroom and nested
contexts both within and beyond as scenes for Studio students' writing. It is the "something happening" that does not always, but can
and often does, become the focus of Studio group discussions of
student writing—where that something happening may be within
the external as well as the internal pentadic scene. And an accretion
of these experiences in Studio sessions has led us to realize that it
is our and composition's essentially arhetorical treatment of student
writers and their work that needs remediation, not our student writers themselves or their work. Such Studio experiences have led us to
postmodern cultural geography for explanations of the inadequacies
we saw in the metadiscourse that we have used to talk about student
writing—for greater understanding of the distance and the disconnect
that this rhetorical inadequacy placed between ourselves and Studio
student writers.

We believe that the inadequacy of much of the metadiscourse for
talking about student writing that our discipline has co-opted from
other fields (or adopted from a literary analytical intention that is
necessarily or typically absent from composition's approach to student
writing) can be explained in part by a parallel phenomenon observed
by Soja (discussed in chapter 2) in the work of his home field of geography. On the subject of "mental maps," he wrote,

> Readers were left with the impression that the conceived space
> defined an urban reality on its own terms, the mental defined
> and indeed produced and explained the material and social
> worlds better than precise empirical descriptions. In such

illusions of transparency, as Lefebvre called them, Firstspace collapses entirely into Secondspace. The difference between them disappears. Even more significantly, also lost in the transparency of space are its fundamental historicality and sociality, any real sense of how these cognitive imageries are themselves socially produced and implicated in the relations between space, power, and knowledge. (*Thirdspace* 80)

In other words, those patterns and features of the subjects' mental maps are treated as realities separate or cut off from the larger fabric of "space, power, and knowledge."

Our Studio theorizing the cross-section showed us that our treatment of student papers—the linguistic features and rhetorical patterns we look for—may well effect a similar collapse or cutoff. Linguistic features of standard English (treated in handbook chapters on sentencing, verbs, etc.) are used to identify error and then to regard that error as sign of a lack of knowledge or ability to recognize the error. Teachers learn to ignore the fact that students do not commit the same error in every case (so that not all sentences in a draft are fragments, etc.). The potential rhetorical meaning of such features of writing as comma splices, fragments, shifts in verb tense, and problems with possessive forms in the particular moments or context in which they do occur and to which they are bound must be routinely avoided by teachers. Why? One reason is surely that interpreting grammatical "error" as a perhaps unconscious and embedded but nonetheless metarhetorical response to the convergences of relations that construct the space/place of student writing would make the job of the teacher, grader, or commenter, in the current college classroom location, unmanageable. To treat student writing with the same sophisticated attention to those convergences that we would pay to the work of a "literary" author is clearly not valued by the academy (at the levels of department or institution). Our methods of labeling the parts of different literary genres, taken from the field of literary criticism as well as from linguistics, are used as convenient formulas, but they are disconnected from the contexts out of which the writing is born. Even our use of rhetorical terms and categories, typically from classical rhetoric and particularly focusing on invention strategies, to talk about student writing is paradoxically arhetorical in that most often writing assignments pose a rhetorical setting or situation for writing outside that of the classroom or academic institution.

As Soja notes, "Lefebvre was particularly concerned with the he-gemonic power often ascribed to (and by) this idealized and elevated spatial epistemology [secondspace]. More than anything else, it made the Representations of (Second)Space what he called the dominant space, surveying and controlling both spatial practices and the lived spaces of representation" (*Thirdspace*, 80). When firstspace and sec-ondspace collapse, the "conceived" view of our daily world reigns—the "ought to be," the master narratives, and the disembodied and de-contextualized patterns ascribed to ready-made positions and plots in those narratives. In the case of composition, such conceptions are used to characterize the work of student writers in ways that allow it to be managed so that the classroom can "move on" but that may leave students frustrated, if not simply blasé, about what they can expect to obtain from the writing class in terms of "real" or "relevant" learning—or perhaps hurt by their perception of where a label is coming from.

Students see these ready-made positions and plots in instructors' reactions to their writing and in the ways we play out our class-room roles and social relations. Studio thirdspace allows these roles and relations to be articulated in an atmosphere of awareness and, therefore, negotiated by both students and, when acting as a group leader, instructors.

A Final Extended Example of a BWP Student Group

During one semester in Benedict College's BWP, Rhonda acted as leader for a group in which two of the five students were from her own freshman composition class. Her narrative report from their meeting on November 19, 1997 (with names changed) and subsequent reflections, illustrates this multilayered awareness of the meeting up of histories and renegotiation of positions and plots for writing.

Kiera read Faunta's rough draft of his exemplification paper;
Faunta needed feedback on it but did not like the idea of reading it
aloud himself. (He had missed some classes when we were working on exemplification papers/techniques. In fact, he had talked
to me after class today about English 135 being the only class
he has not dropped. He's decided to stay in school in the Spring
[19]98 semester and not let his record deal lure him away. [He is
a rap artist.] But the turmoil and indecision over this issue kept
him from fully applying himself in many classes. I assured him
that though he is behind on the third project that he has good work
otherwise and he's been making good efforts to keep up, so he will
be ok in my class.)

So Kiera read it [Faunta's draft] (we had to ask her to slow
down). In the draft, Faunta said he was trying to write about the
different ways to prepare for success and wanted to know if he
was on the "right track." The draft itself used a personification of
Success, a thinly guised story of Faunta himself and his dilemma
this semester. (During the reading of it, Lakia turned to me and
whispered loudly "Isn't that about him?")

After the reading, both Lakia and Kiera said how much they
liked his device with "success." They explained why. I said I liked
it too, that it would make a good intro for then spelling out in
more detail how success was going to "make it" and not "fail" (the
last word of the draft).

Lakia objected, saying that he [Faunta] should not change it,
that what I was saying was just like what Faunta had said happened to "success" in his paper: "Nothing was ever good enough
even though he tried hard." Basically, she objected to turning his
paper into some rigidly formulated essay, that she liked how he
"exemplified" his idea with one extended example. She had a good
point, and a really sharp one too. I heard in her voice a critique of
any suggestion that there is "one way" to do something. Being sensitive to this point, I did "say back" about her point to the group
on it [meaning that I talked through the conflict that I just narrated above with the group]. Faunta had been listening and, clearly,

thinking about it in relation to his paper. His comment was that hearing Kiera read it had let him "sit back" and hear how it communicated to others (much like he does with his rap tapes of himself). He agreed with Lakia about keeping his approach, but could see how his draft needed specifics to help a reader "see" in their mind what he was saying when he said things like, for example, "to maintain." He quickly sketched a plan for revising his draft where he'd keep his extended example of "Success," put in details about how "success" was working "to maintain" in the body, then use his current last paragraph as a conclusion.

For the rest of the lab Faunta worked on revising, I worked with Jarrod on agreement exercises/editing and Lakia and Kiera made a deal that they'd pick up and add to their own editing work before Monday's meeting if they could use the last 15 minutes to study for a big Health class exam next period.

Key to countering this collapse of first- and secondspace is to reinvest student writing with ways of discussing it that locate it as student writing, with ways of socially and disciplinarily contextualizing issues such as, in the above example, "form" in the academic essay. Embedded in Rhonda's own initial response to Faunta's essay, she later realized, were ideas put forward by her department's curriculum about teaching more "analytical" ways of developing ideas in writing (moving from more narrative to more traditionally analytical writing as English 135 progresses), as well as her institution's desire that its students do better on standardized, timed writings like those found in ETS-sponsored tests such as Praxis. "Doing better" typically refers to quickly organizing thoughts into easily recognizable essay patterns and form. The kind of shorthand that Faunta was using in the fable of "Success" might be seen as more literary than academic and, paradoxically, as weaker. Lakia's response was one that considered the integrated form and content of Faunta's essay in terms not of development but of what he was saying through the character of "Success." As Rhonda knew from the group's work together that semester, Lakia had interpreted her own history and experiences to say that teachers' comments send the message that her own writing is "never good enough." Her articulations made Rhonda see the secondspace conceptions that she was working from in her own initial responses. Lakia's comments on the position betrayed by her own comments about Faunta's draft (in her contention that Rhonda's comments only verified what Faunta had written about the struggles of "Success"), coupled with her willingness to acknowledge and share what lay behind this positioning on her part, opened up a thirdspace within which Faunta negotiated a position and an action for himself and his writing. Though such insights do not happen every day, we know from Studio experiences that many student writers—like Nancy's Carson in an example cited earlier—are sensitive to what we would term the metarhetorical relationships and positionings that underlie writing curriculum, requirements, assignments, and comments.

We may have begun our Studio program with the development of students' abilities to talk about their writing in mind, but what we found is that the implications and consequences of the outside-but-alongside positioning of Studio small groups were larger than we realized. Our initially forced spatial and institutional relocation of supplemental instruction through writing resonated with our original goals in such a way that our very understanding of student writing development itself was affected and shifted. This shift has made us wish for a similar one in the terminology available for identifying the ways that students' metarhetorical preoccupations—their best guesses and observations about and patterns for dealing with their own pentadic external-rhetorical analysis of writing assignments—influence their writing style and sentencing, organization, and development.

4 / Studio Staff and Interactional Inquiry

> Small group interaction in the lab with my colleagues during our
> Friday meeting sessions has helped me to rethink and enhance
> my abilities to teach and reach students more effectively in my
> classes. I mention our Friday reflection sessions because not
> often enough do colleagues share their experiences. Not often
> enough do we share our techniques. Not often enough do we
> share our stories without the fear of being criticized or made to
> feel inadequate. Like the students, we are the best persons to
> work together to solve the real issues that exist on our campus
> and in our classrooms.
>   —Ruby Blair, quoted in Grego, "The Bridges Writing Program"

In chapter 3 we described higher education's institutional positioning of student writers at the three institutional sites for Studio work
examined in this book. But it is not only student writers who are thus
hierarchically distanced from themselves and from understanding the
interaction of external and internal pentadic scenes within their work.
Maintaining student writers' distance from themselves and their daily
lives requires that we compositionists, too often, enact or reinforce
distances between ourselves.

Repositioning Composition Teaching and Research

The assumption of a sameness of background and even attitude toward
composition among those who teach such courses, especially at the
beginning levels of the institutional hierarchy, is largely a convenient
pretense. It is perpetuated perhaps by the fact that much published
disciplinary research on first-year composition (FYC) comes from
those working at institutions where graduate student teaching assistants (TAs) provide the teaching workforce and where composition

teachers can be relatively "homogenized" or "calibrated" by FYC writing program administrators (WPAs) charged with overseeing their training in the approaches used for FYC courses at that institutional site. We saw this attitude in operation in our work with the FYC Writing Studio at the University of South Carolina. But even here there are differences among the TAs (who have different career goals and disciplinary inclinations within English studies). It may be less the pedagogical program to which they are trained (often in their first year of graduate school) that homogenizes them than the actual physical circumstances of their teaching and classes, including the number of classes they teach and that they themselves are in graduate seminars (placing them at the upper reaches of higher education's institutional hierarchy), as well as the quality of the support and resources provided by the program and the fact that most textbooks assume a homogeneous learning environment. The influence of the material conditions at the institution commingle with the influence of one's location in higher education's institutional hierarchy, but these external pentadic influences are often ignored in favor of foregrounding the pedagogical perspective promoted by the writing program in charge.

For those graduate students who move on to positions at institutions with adequate infrastructure, where these external pentadic factors are less pressing (perhaps research institutions or those closer to that institutional class), it will be even easier for them to focus on the internal pentadic scenes of the texts studied and produced that guide their daily work. Then they can continue the patterns of privilege learned in graduate school, can discount the impact of external pentadic scenes on their own work, and perhaps become less able to understand the influence of such factors on the work of their students. They may assume (if they have to think about it at all) that the same institutional structures and mechanisms that focused their attention on disciplinary secondspace conceptions and internal pentadic life of disciplinary texts and conversations will operate in similar fashion for their current students. Engineering faculty who act as research directors for undergraduates in the Research Communications Studio in the USC College of Engineering are likely to find themselves in just such positions. Some profess a belief that a few of their undergraduate researchers just "take to" engineering better than others; the faculty may use vague language that associates such "natural" abilities with being "gifted" or having a "knack" or a "way" that echoes language we in composition have heard used about those who are better writers than others. Of course, logically we know that what we are really naming is not just what the student/writer does or does not possess but what the institutional setting has or has not made it seem important or necessary to find out.

At institutions that lack graduate research programs and TA training missions and where professionals are hired as faculty and adjuncts for teaching composition courses, keeping teachers focused on the internal pentadic elements of student writers' work is more or less difficult, depending on the infrastructure of the institution. Teachers must deal with the institutional realities of that external pentadic scene in a variety of ways. Those with a deep level of care for their students are vividly aware of the material realities that influence their ability to teach composition: realities such as large class sizes and course loads; small or ill-equipped classrooms or labs; lack of support materials such as copying facilities, paper, supplies, and handbooks, rhetorics, and readers with appropriate examples; inadequate financial resources to buy textbooks; lack of access to computers and printers; and little training in computer usage, word processing, Internet research. The list goes on. Benedict College FYC instructors certainly have felt the effects of overcrowded classes and heavy course loads: during active operation of the Bridges Writing Program (BWP) from 1997 to 2001, composition class sizes swung from thirty to more than forty-five, and teachers were regularly assigned overloads, teaching as many as five or six sections instead of the contractually designated four per semester. Though technically these instructors could have said no to these overloads, few were tenure-track, even fewer tenured, most were on yearly renewed full-time instructor contracts, and several needed extra income to supplement their salaries. Too often it is organizationally easier (or less dangerous) to find fault with what students do or do not bring in their writing than to find fault with harsh realities that the institutional setting wants us to ignore. Our profound and well-honed societal ability to ignore or sidestep issues attributable to socioeconomic class in the United States made it inevitable that we pay more disciplinary attention to developing linguistic tools for categorizing the errors in students' sentences.

Where the circumstances of teaching are poor (at least by the standards of the National Council of Teachers of English), teachers have little choice but to either supply what they are personally able to provide to make up the differences or ignore the situation and perhaps focus rigidly on the secondspace conception and the internal pentadic scenes for their students' work. The more formulaic acts of writing can result in work that at least on the surface appears the same as that at a better-off institutional site. The formulaic acts include having a certain number of sentences in each paragraph, a certain number of paragraphs in each essay, and focusing on the world of grammar and punctuation so thoroughly laid out in handbooks. Helping students in these areas allows teachers to feel that they are at least providing their students with an education similar to that at institutions of a higher class.

In each case, as we fill the space between our discipline's idea of our work and the local reality of it with ways of thinking that avoid those realities (or shoulder them as inevitable and thus inevitably sufferable burdens), we distance ourselves farther from ourselves and from each other. In fact, we may know little about who we are as (composition) teachers, English learning specialists, and Writing Center tutors and about where our ideas on writing and on student writers come from. Studio interactional inquiry helps not just student writers but also compositionists positioned as Studio student group leaders and staff researchers in these related areas:

- Studio work as group leaders has helped us to be more aware of those external pentadic factors and their influence on our work as teachers with the internal pentadic scenes of course readings and writing assignments.
- Studio staff interactional inquiry helps us to formulate our own plans and proposals for local change and helps us to see change as those actions that pry apart the collapse of first- and secondspace conceptions of our work.

- And Studio communication both with teachers and with other group leaders helps us to resist the isolation from each other encouraged by both vertical and lateral distancings of compositionists from other compositionists effected by higher education institutional structures.

Taken altogether, these outcomes of Studio interactional inquiry illustrate ways compositionists can work to make powerful institutional critique realistic and reachable on a daily basis.

The Roles of Group Leaders and Staff Members

There is in academe a kind of distancing that programs such as Bartholomae and Petrosky's seek to address. Such distancing is effected by the academic world's reliance on texts and text-based literacies to perpetuate and continue its arguments and deliberations, and even its use of text-based literacy as a colonizing metaphor, as discussed by Wysocki and Johnson-Eilola. Simply put, in the academic world, you don't have to be alive to be a part of a debate. But Bartholomae and Petrosky and others' curriculum-readings also make clear that the texts that are assumed to characterize academic culture best (because they are a part of ongoing debate on some modern topoi) are those that allow readers to focus on the realm of philosophical inquiry—a history of ideas contained by one text/argument responding to another in an ever-continuing history of debate that fills the historical scene of the internal pentadic analyses of academic and disciplinarily privileged texts in our courses. As Massey notes, "It is an old association; over and over we tame the spatial into the textual and the conceptual into representation" (*For Space* 20). Academe thus ignores the more local, or "metarhetorical," exigencies and complex sociospatial relations that construct the lives of those who engage with that text in higher education.

Being able to read, comprehend, and enter into the larger or more general academic lineage of debate is at the heart of the most seductive secondspace conceptions of academic culture and the life of the university, the siren call that lures forth most anthologies of texts considered important to defining a discipline, typically abstracting those texts (and their authors) from the firstspace of their production. Often those anthologies include excerpts of texts and thus foreshorten access to the contexts (the spatial relations) that help readers make sense of the texts themselves. They ignore the difference that contexts of production make in both the processes and products of writing. Many of the writings put before students to illustrate the nature of academic culture and debate were also rhetorically situated inside some higher education institution or system at the time of their production, but they are not typically read closely in terms of any organizational setting. Instead, that setting is usually ignored—effectively stripped away, neutralized, naturalized, neutered—to focus on the nature of the debate itself, not the context that materially enabled that debate or supported (and thereby shaped) the debaters. Indeed, it may well be this inattention to the firstspace contexts of everyday life/work that in common parlance identifies any given text as one that is valued by academe and is suitable for informing any given student's "inventing" of the university.

Approaches to help students understand a generalized view of academic culture through reading and engaging in past and present academic debates about our civic, social, or disciplinary lives abound; many rhetorics, readers, and anthologies have adopted or adapted them. Some works, like Bizzell and Herzberg's *Negotiating Difference: Cultural Case Studies for Composition*, place important texts in the context of other, less-well-known texts of their day, in the manner of new historicism. But even within a first-year college writing program that makes use of such an approach, the positioning of Studio's outside-but-alongside student groups would mean that the attitudes and assumptions that make such texts the artifacts of an academic (or disciplinary) culture would be further recontextualized by the kinds of questions and observations brought out and discussed in Studio student (and staff) sessions, including

- questions about why certain readings were chosen and observations about how they were presented and responded to in different sections of the course represented by the different students in the Studio groups;

- questions comparing that curricular program and its readings with others that the student writers had experienced in high school or with the readings and pedagogical approaches taken by other college courses Studio students are enrolled in or have taken in previous semesters (a comparison that would particularly be facilitated by beginning either in the classroom or in the Studio group with the "writing/reading history" assignment discussed in chapter 3);
- observations and recollections brought by the Studio group leader from his or her own past educational experiences, both as student and as teacher, pertaining to
  - different reasons for how and why such readings and writing assignments are chosen and articulated,
  - how such assignments are connected
    - to that institution's or writing program's educational curriculum, both in the present and historically,
    - to the structure of "learning" in higher education institutions more generally (perhaps relating something about the history or intent of general-education movements or about the liberal arts tradition at that college),
    - to larger societal assumptions about what it means to be educated, in terms of what one reads and writes in college (versus what one reads on his or her own),
    - to issues that are of particular, defining interest to those in a particular discipline, or
    - to the group leader's own responses to similar assignments or readings when he or she was a student, perhaps at different points in his or her educational career or at another institutional site.

Here the importance of the Studio group leader position is apparent. The facilitative and perspective-sharing role of that group leader is key to putting a current and local flesh-and-bone body (with all its attendant confusions, insecurities, and contradictions) on the work required of student writers, as well as depicting that body as one that walks and breathes and eats in that particular institution's campus-and-buildings environment. It is not that classroom teachers do not broach these kinds of issues in their classes; but one of the major purposes of Studio group leaders is to pull such questions out as context for each student's specific writing development and to address the metarhetorical connections that a classroom teacher may have little time to acknowledge, much less address. As a classroom teacher I may teach the same topic, content, and assignment two, three, four, or more times in any given week, but repeating my own thoughts and words is different from hearing the sense that students are making of their classroom encounters.

Stephen Criswell, one-pager, September 24, 1999

. . . . I noticed a common problem this week among my group members' essays. Many of their drafts, both rough and polished, lacked focus. While this is a common problem among first-year college writers, after talking with my group members, I think we English instructors are partly to blame. Too often we make assignments like "write a narrative" or "compose a draft of a comparison-contrast paper" but we forget to (or just don't) say why or for whom. So the students tell a story, or they tell how something is similar to and different from something else, but they don't know why they are doing it—and it shows. They ramble; their papers lack coherence or focus; and it is because they really don't know where they are going. They often don't have a clear idea why they are writing what they are writing. And all too often, if pressed, I can't tell them; I'm not sure why they are writing what they are writing. I keep coming back to this realization that your freshman year of college is about the only time in your adult life that you write this kind of audience-less, even purpose-less, prose. . . . But I myself am guilty of this. I have told my students, "Just tell me a story," and then penalized them for not having a thesis. I guess one could argue that much of what students write in freshman com-

> position has a purpose similar to calisthenics. They are practice
> pieces for real-world writing. But scrimmage games don't count.

In his dissertation, *The Writing Studio: A Qualitative Study Contextu-alized within the Freshman Composition Program at the University of South Carolina*, Michael Barnes, who served as a Studio group leader from 1996 to 1998, as acting director in 1997, and as associate director in 1998, analyzes the different roles Studio staff take in leading their sessions. After a careful ethnographic analysis of a Studio session in comparison with class presentation, Barnes presents a set of categories, or domains, describing the multiple roles a Studio staff leader can take on in the thirdspace of Studio: The Conductor maintains productive group dynamics; the Contextualizer brings in relevant student (and teacher) academic and experiential background to make the connection between everyday life, the academic environment, and student writing within; the Negotiator redefines student and "teacher" roles as they play out in Studio groups while also acknowledging and dealing with student resistance; the Supporter generally validates student positions without necessarily confirming them and admits affective elements into the learning environment; and the Translator helps students understand the "language," terminology, and teacher talk of the academy while also identifying insights about everyday life as relevant to academic work (178–92). In the Research Communications Studio (RCS) project, graduate student Lori Donath identifies another role of the staff leader in her dissertation study: that of "elicitation of critique." In her analysis of a videotaped RCS session led by Nancy, Donath found that 50 percent of Nancy's contributions to the sessions were eliciting comments from the participants (Donath, Spray, Thompson, Alford, Craig, and Matthews).

Heightened awareness of these factors and their influences on student writers' work brings a commensurate awareness of their influence on us as classroom teachers, lab specialists or tutors, and Studio group leaders. Helping students become good group members helps us be more sensitive to the differences among us and the reasons for those differences in terms of both professional and life experiences. Of course, Studio staff dynamics will differ according to variations in institutional class discussed earlier in this chapter, but this heightened awareness of the multiplicity of spaces brought by each of us to interactional inquiry enriches how we see each other and what we do—and enables us to work together for needed local change rather than against each other.

The BWP at Benedict College provides a good example of the importance of this aspect of Studio interactional inquiry. In the years immediately prior to BWP, the college had sustained a new president and several new administrators, particularly deans. There had been turmoil at the end of the previous president's regime, and faculty were factionalized and suspicious of the motives of newcomers. Administrators brought in by a new president at a small, open-admissions, private, and tuition-driven HBCU could easily be expected to "clean house" of long-time faculty. Within the English, Foreign Languages, and (then) Media Arts Department, there were a few tenured faculty close to retirement, another group of long-time instructors, and an English learning specialist who had been hired to staff the newly centralized BCCARES (Benedict College Center for Academic Reinforcement, Enhancement, and Support) academic services area in the 1980s when the previously classroom-tied writing, reading, and speech labs were abandoned. Top-down program and curriculum changes abounded. In particular, the new president enacted a pilot program in which students who would otherwise have been enrolled in remedial writing and reading classes were instead mainstreamed into a regular FYC course with an attendant lab section run by the English learning specialist. When the results seemed to be that these students performed as well in their FYC course as did other "regular" students, a second English learning specialists was hired with the idea that the program would be expanded and all remedial writing courses would be abandoned. A similar plan was followed for remedial math courses.

The desire to mainstream these remedial students in this case was driven, at least in part, by the issue of tuition. Students required to spend a first semester or year in remedial math and English courses would have fewer federal dollars with which to complete regular program-required courses for their bachelor's degrees at the college. At that point, Rhonda was hired by the college as a visiting associate professor, and when her new dean heard about her involvement with the FYC Writing Studio at the University of South Carolina, he encouraged her to write a proposal for a grant from FIPSE (Fund for the Improvement for Postsecondary Education). The resulting money was combined with funding from the American Council of Learned Societies to provide a computer-lab, administrative assistance, a copier, supplies, and, most important, release time for faculty to work as BWP staff and group leaders.

Rhonda insisted that English faculty and learning specialists be involved in planning for the grant proposal and in adapting Studio approaches to the institutional site. To these ends she called open meetings to discuss drafts, conferred individually with faculty and administrators, engaged advanced-level English majors in researching the history of the English curriculum (specifically composition courses and labs) at Benedict College, and, in order to address the concerns of faculty who were more familiar with large lab sections and the use of skill-and-drill workbooks, helped facilitate an initial year of BWP in which half of student participants were put into large lab sections and used a basic skills workbook and the other half were placed into more Studio-styled small groups. Rhonda herself worked as a group leader as well as program administrator, but she made clear her view of the supportive and facilitative role of an administrator by providing whatever services and documents were needed by BWP faculty and group leaders, not in the sense of currying favor and building a power base to advance along with newly hired administrators. Nancy served as grant consultant to provide ongoing formative assessment. Her local reputation as a caring and dedicated teacher also sent a strong message about the intent of the program to involve "ground-level" teachers in decision making. All weekly report forms, the student BWP contract, midterm, and final report forms, as well as departmental newsletter and summer writing-across-the-curriculum workshops (with Marie Wilson Nelson as workshop leader) were planned and executed by Rhonda, Nancy, and Cheryl Jackson (administrative specialist) under the direction and with the input and guidance of English faculty and administrators, BWP group leaders, and English learning specialists.

Even so, it took some time before suspicions and factions began to ease and BWP group leaders began to trust and respect each other's very different professional backgrounds. Among those teachers and learning specialists who served as BWP group leaders were an ABD (all but dissertation) scholar in English who was a playwright on the side, a master's graduate who had retired from teaching eighth-grade grammar and had graduated from Benedict College in the 1940s, a Benedict College alumnus from the 1980s who had a master's degree in teaching, a recent alumnus of Voorhees College (another South Carolina HBCU) with a master's in English, a local creative writer with a master's degree in fine arts and teaching certification, a recent graduate of Benedict College with a B.A. in English, a Ph.D. scholar in folklore studies, a Ph.D. scholar in linguistics, and Rhonda, with a Ph.D. in composition and rhetoric.

As mentioned in chapter 3, when the president took decision-making power away from the faculty and mandated that labs replace remedial courses, some faculty developed suspicions about activities "over there" in the now separate BCCARES English lab area. Nevertheless, after the first year of operation, English faculty felt comfortable enough with the Studio small groups to move the next year's BWP operation to an all-small-group format without an accompanying workbook. Concerned faculty could see that grammar concerns were not being abandoned but that attention to more rhetorical issues of audience and purpose and evaluation of research sources, as well as issues associated with writing process (invention, development, organization, etc.) arising from the use of a reader as well as a handbook in the course, were helpful to their students' writing development. Still, among the most traditional, "old school" faculty there were concerns that making room for rhetorical and writing process issues meant that "reality" issues (the need to produce what Geneva Smitherman terms "Standard Written English" and even older school concerns, for example, that students be able to write in legible, straight lines on blank paper as they once had to do on job applications) would be left behind. These concerns arose particularly from those faculty who themselves had lived through a time in Columbia when any little problem could be pointed to as evidence that an African American young man or woman was not "good enough" for a job. Students who were not drilled hard enough on the basics might fall prey to what older faculty referred to as "the Black Trap."

The distances between faculty and learning specialists who served as BWP group leaders, that is, our different experiences with the politics of language use, were bridged over the years by the weeks and days of our service together in BWP student and staff interactional inquiry groups. But the differences were still there, and misunderstandings erupted even in our last year of full BWP operation. Below Rhonda describes one such controversy.

> *Rhonda Grego, one-pager, October 1, 1999*
>
> *After reading Mrs. Taylor's one-pager from our BWP meeting on Friday, September 24, 1999, concerns were raised by our group. Mrs. Taylor was upset. She related that she had returned student papers and that one student had brought her paper to her BWP group meeting and returned to Mrs. Taylor with disagreement from the lab group leader about the grade received on the paper. Mrs. Taylor's one-pager stated: "I do not want my English 135 students to be victims of the Black Trap. If you, BWP Group Leaders, don't agree with the grade I put on students' papers, please tell me. Don't write on the student's paper that this should have been an A." Mrs. Taylor said that she did not have the student's paper itself; she suspected that the handwriting on the students' paper was that of Ms. Colgate [a BWP group leader and one of the two English learning specialists], who was not present at the staff meeting.*
>
> *On Tuesday, September 28, I asked Ms. Colgate about Mrs. Taylor's report. Since seeing Mrs. Taylor's one-pager on Monday, Ms. Colgate had gone through her files to determine which student's work was at the center of this controversy. The only paper she found in her files that seemed like it might be that described was the attached work (and lab log). She noted that this was the only case that seemed close to what Mrs. Taylor described. (She could not recall at any time writing "should have been an A" on a student's paper in lab.)*

See the paper entitled "My Remarkable Grandmother," attached. The student had brought the paper to lab, asking "why did I get a C?" Ms. Colgate looked at the paragraph with the student group, telling her the things that are jotted in the margin at the top left of the page: "too general," "need more specifics," "describe, make the reader taste, smell, hear, see, feel." When the student was still wondering why she got a "C," Ms. Colgate replied (and wrote) that the student should ask Mrs. Taylor "What is her criteria for a C—why not a B or an A?" Ms. Colgate's intent was not to question Mrs. Taylor's grade but to suggest to the student the kind of questions she might ask her teacher so that the student could gain better understanding of her grade from the teacher's perspective.

Clearly Ms. Colgate was not saying that the paper should have received an A," since she had also written notes on serious deficiencies in the paragraph prior to the question at the bottom of the page. Our discussion of these interactions at that week's BWP staff meeting reminded us all that even with all that we had learned about each other as teachers and as BWP group leaders, our basic assumptions and differences could still leave us feeling vulnerable. It was a sign of the years we had spent in inquiry meetings with each other that we could discuss the motivations of both: Mrs. Taylor, the retired eighth-grade teacher and Benedict alumna, speaking and teaching from her concerns about the continued racism faced by Benedict students, and Anne Colgate, the creative writer originally from New York, working to empower her BWP students to seek answers, to ask the "why" questions that she herself was so good at asking, as she too worked to equip students with the approaches she believed they needed to make it in the world. And we reiterated a valuable lesson learned over and over in BWP Studio meetings: always look beyond the surface of the story, at what Massey terms the "multiplicity of spaces" that construct our work.

The Products of Interactional Inquiry: Local Change

We have two contrasting but overlapping images in mind to depict the contrast that between higher-ed's secondspace conception of itself and the Studio's interactional inquiry. The first image represents the traditional higher education scale to which we have been referring: that of a ladder (with rungs to be climbed to get to the top, with the emotions and relations that assist the individual in that climb clearly absented from the picture) with perhaps (whimsically speaking) a gold bell to be rung only once the climber gets to the top. But the image that interactional inquiry superimposes on that ladder is something more like a spiraling helix swinging widely around the ladder, embracing all those sociospatial relations that surround our movements and work at different points in our higher education institutions, all those matrices of experience and position and differing points of view that are there every time we enter another classroom, office, or space. The spirals become wider as they circle toward the top, with the accretion of sociospatial relations being carried upward as layers of context, for knowledge production becomes more and more complex as institutional systems of academic culture work to organize the efforts of people across both time and space. In this spiraling image there is no bell to be rung at the top, as if to announce the claiming of a prize, or that another academic angel has earned his or her wings. Instead, there are connections (or opportunities to make connections), both up and down, between the successive levels of the spirals, connections representing Massey's definition of place as that held within the "specificity of the mix of links and interconnections to 'the beyond'" (*Space* 5).

In Studio student and staff groups, we seek to be more aware of the ways in which writing assignments, comments, terminologies, assessments, and so forth are constructed from a complex intersection of personal and professional backgrounds, disciplinary rationales, institutional experiences, and higher education processes; to be more aware of the ways in which our work with student writers is just one stage on which the history and politics of our larger society (including continuing inequities), as well as intellectual movements and disciplinary trends, are being played out. Studio seeks to bring to bear a sense of place that is, as Massey says, "extra-verted" to our work with both student and staff group inquiry, to open up a thirdspace where the voices of those intersections at the lower levels of the academic hierarchy can be heard, where connections can be explored. To give full context to Massey's definition of place:

> [T]he particularity of any place is . . . constructed not by placing boundaries around it and defining its identity through counter-position to the other which lies beyond, but precisely (in part) through the specificity of the mix of links and interconnections to that "beyond." Places viewed this way are open and porous. (*Space* 5)

Interactional inquiry provides the organizational scaffold for staff group operation, staff thirdspaces depending, as with student groups, on the mix of faculty and staff in any given semester, as well as on the surrounding institutional environment. Staff meetings keep us in touch with issues of conducting groups, while also bringing to the table issues related to student participants, making us all more reflective about the patterns and interactions that we are a part of in the student group meetings where we act as leaders. But Studio staff interactional inquiry also alerts us to our connections with the larger institutional setting, including the ways in which institutional systems (including administrative layers) structure student and teacher behaviors, and not always for the better. There were several times over the years of BWP staff meetings, for example, when we would "turn off the tape recorder" so that everyone felt more comfortable talking about recent administrative decisions and policies—typically made with little faculty input—that we felt impacted negatively on students. Decisions about increasing class sizes, not hiring enough faculty to teach courses so that overloads were assigned, the lack of staffing needed in other labs, and concerns about our students' increasing levels of debt were issues we discussed but could do little about except make sure that students in our small groups were informed about their own rights, that we helped students know whom to ask questions of, that we were proactive in communicating to faculty, via our biweekly newsletter, our own ideas formed in our biweekly staff meetings about "best practices" in working with student writers, and that we modeled what we agreed on in our own teaching and in our committee-chosen course texts and revisions of our common course outlines.

In other words, the "products" of Writing Studio interactional inquiry will not always or predictably be the normal results of typically located research, though such products as graduate student dissertation work and our occasional articles and conference presentations have resulted from Studio programs with which we've worked. But the primary goals of Writing Studio interactional inquiry are not interpretive or critical—they are not scholarly in the sense recognized by that traditional higher education institutional hierarchy. Echoing Dobrin and Weisser's discussion of what differentiates ecocomposition from ecocriticism, we might say that Studio and interactional inquiry are not interpretive models so much as productive ones. Interactional inquiry, in particular, is an action: helping student writers and teachers with their work, not to "gain knowledge" but to provide settings in which the knowledges of participants can operate through their interactions, to provide settings in which the effects of institutionalized expectations and assumptions can be seen as such.

Useful here is a distinction made by Michel Foucault and Gilles Deleuze about relations between theory and practice and a postmodern view of the role of the intellectual in society. In a conversation published under the title "Intellectuals and Power," they discuss how in modern times "practice" was the application of "theory," useful for extending theory and at times becoming the basis for creation of new theories. (This would be the view from the more traditional higher-ed hierarchy that we began with in chapter 1.) But in postmodern times, as Deleuze explains, the relationship between theory and practice is less delineated and less hierarchical:

> [F]rom the moment a theory moves into its proper domain, it begins to encounter obstacles, walls, and blockages which require its relay by another type of discourse (it is through this other discourse that it eventually passes to a different domain). Practice is a set of relays from one theoretical point to another, and theory is a relay from one practice to another. No theory can develop without eventually encountering a wall,

and practice is necessary for piercing that wall. (Foucault, "Intellectuals and Power" 206)

This has been the rhythm that we have found over time in Studio staff interactional inquiry groups in particular: the professionals in these staff groups bring both theoretical and practical awarenesses that help us "relay" from one point to another as our group works to "theorize the cross-section" of weekly interactions and to figure out how to proceed from there.

Deleuze points to Foucault's analysis of asylums and confinement in nineteenth-century capitalist society and his accompanying work to organize a group to "create conditions that permit the prisoners themselves to speak" (Foucault, "Intellectuals and Power" 206). He asserts, "This was not an application; nor was it a project for initiating reforms or enquiry in the traditional sense. The emphasis was altogether different: a system of relays within a larger sphere, within a multiplicity of parts that are both theoretical and practical" (206). We see Writing Studio program organization operating along with spatial theory and interactional inquiry as just such a system. The purpose of this "system of relays" in the case of Studio is to penetrate the "wall" thrown up by our institutionally normalized inattention to the effects of composition's institutional locations and situations. Foucault writes that since the events of May 1968 in France, he sees how

the intellectual discovered that the masses no longer need him to gain knowledge: they *know* perfectly well, without illusion; they know far better than he and they are certainly capable of expressing themselves. But there exists a system of power which blocks, prohibits, and invalidates this discourse and this knowledge, a power not only found in the manifest authority of censorship, but one that profoundly and subtly penetrates an entire societal network. Intellectuals are themselves agents of this system of power—the idea of their responsibility for "consciousness" and discourse forms part of the system. The intellectual's role is no longer to place himself "somewhat ahead and to the side" in order to express the stifled truth

of the collectivity; rather, it is to struggle against the forms
of power that transform him into its object and instrument
in the sphere of "knowledge," "truth," "consciousness," and
"discourse." (207–8; emphasis in the original)

Another product, then, of Studio work would be to use the group
intelligence found within student and staff groups to help composition
in its similar struggle against those forms of institutional power that
transform compositionists into just another disciplinary object and
instrument of that power. Foucault notes,

This is a struggle against power, a struggle aimed at reveal-
ing and undermining power where it is most invisible and
insidious. It is not to "awaken consciousness" that we struggle
(the masses have been aware for some time that consciousness is a form of knowledge; and consciousness as the basis
of subjectivity is a prerogative of the bourgeoisie), but to sap
power, to take power; it is an activity conducted alongside
those who struggle for power, and not their illumination
from a safe distance. A "theory" is the regional system of this
struggle. (208)

The products of such struggle will be thus necessarily different for
different "regional systems" or, in our case, for different manifestations of Studio's use of interactional inquiry at different institutional
sites. At the original FYC Writing Studio at the University of South
Carolina, the graduate student TAs who were Studio group leaders
were themselves a part of the institutional hierarchy that privileges
research at its upper reaches; so we drew heavily on the language of
research and that mission as the lingua franca of that site. At Benedict College, however, research activities were to some suspect either
because they made subjects of those who have historical reasons to
suspect "outside" experts or simply because research was just less
familiar, since research activities were the province of faculty who
had the luxury of more time because they taught smaller upper-level
courses and typically not those teaching at beginning levels. In our

work with BWP staff groups, we became sensitive to this difference and adopted the language of "conversations" suggested by the group to talk about interactional inquiry. In RCS, the culture of discourse about education in engineering dictated that Nancy and Libby adapt to the use of cognitive science terminology and frames for research to talk about the features of interactional inquiry for that audience. The documents that the various Writing Studio programs produce have also certainly reflected differences in position within higher-ed's institutional hierarchy, as well as the local institutional manifestations of power within which we were working and the means through which we could find to work "outside but alongside" the systems in place.

The interpretation of experience within interactional inquiry happens collaboratively, as group participants (whether students or staff) engage in regular sessions in which they share, largely through talk and stories, their experiences, letting the life of their weekly everyday work gather force by finding similarities and common ground through a cross-sectional analysis. But because our approach thus privileges talk over writing, it has been difficult to use these documents to unearth examples with which to illustrate (much less provide evidence in any traditional sense) of the results or effects that we claim for Studio interactional inquiry. Like much actual writing that references local systems or situations, and where the people who experience what is being written about are present and reachable for further dialogue, explanation, and clarification, Studio dialogue sheets and one-pagers often reference specific stories in general terms, without the particular details that bring scenarios "alive" in ways that narratives must do for readers who were not "there." What interactional inquiry is intended to do (and what we believe it does) is build experiences with and validate knowledges about writing, experiences and knowledges that, as Foucault and Deleuze might say, struggle with the institution's desire to turn our students and ourselves into its objects and instruments of power, struggle with too easy acceptance of generalized assumptions and languages for identifying student writing, for identifying the motivations behind our work with student writers.

Our interactional inquiry activities have certainly been undertaken "alongside those who struggle for power"—those who are ourselves and our students. And we have certainly "sapped power," because we have used interactional inquiry as the means to take a good measure of professional control over situations at all three institutional sites, not always (or even usually) in ways pleasing to administrators. In USC's FYC Writing Studio, our close proximity to the designated places/ spaces for disciplinary knowledge making meant that the language of assessment and research was even more present and available. Part of sapping power at that site was to co-opt this language for our own ends. We were conscious of doing so from the start, in our first proposal to the department for the original Studio and then in our first-year report on its operation, in which we focused on both recent trends in higher education assessment and qualitative research in composition, as well as the department's mission to train its graduate student teachers. And, as the original Studio progressed through its years of staff interactional inquiry, the graduate TAs who formed each year's Studio staff began to consistently focus on some concern that is persistent and complex enough to keep considering it week after week, from the multiple perspectives brought through different student and staff participants and forged within the crucible of weekly everyday experiences with students in Studio sessions. One such focus was the topic of "engage-ment." In 1999, this concept was identified by a staff group as an important topic: What constitutes engagement in the small group? How can you tell if a student is engaged? If the student says nothing in response to another student's paper but follows the conversation, is the student engaged? How do you rate behavior that is distracting to other group members? How could we structure our group work to get a high level of engagement from each student? What, exactly, is the effect of a high level of engagement on a student's work?

The next year, the new staff group, which consisted of some former members as well as new members (an important situation for bringing in new ideas to staff groups), took up the problem of engage-ment again. Throughout the first part of the semester, intense weekly discussions revolved around how to define engagement and identify it in ways that could be measured with a Likert scale. Finally, after several drafts, an acceptable scale was created by the staff, and each staff member then was able to numerically rate each student each week on a four-point Likert scale of (4) high, (3) medium, (2) low, or (1) no engagement. In general, an engaged student is one who is "involved in a session, who makes frequent revision suggestions to others and acknowledges the suggestions of his or her peers" (Thompson and Sutton). A "3" on engagement characterizes the student's suggestions as generally high in quality, including formal, stylistic, grammatical, meta-awareness, or content suggestions, and indicates that the student is considered by the group leader to be an important member of the group ("Student Engagement in Studio Group Meetings"). The final averages of the weekly ratings for each student indicated that a higher engagement score correlated with successful participation in Studio and a higher English 101 grade. Of those students who demonstrated engagement by attending Studio seven or more times during the semester (a number that itself resulted from intense discussion by the staff) and who received a high engagement score (defined as 2.5 or higher on the 4-point scale), 80 percent received a B or better in English 101, with almost half receiving A's. By contrast, low engagement scores generally correlated with low English 101 grades.

In this example, the interactional inquiry group was its own agent in creating and owning a research study to help us both understand and illustrate results of the small group student work. It was also an activity that taught the staff much about research, as Terry Carter's comments illustrate.

Terry Carter, one-pager, December 6, 2000

Well, I have to admit that I was a bit skeptical about the possibilities of interactional inquiry, but I have now come to respect its possibilities. I remember when the idea about the rating scale for engagement first began and how we spent at least three meeting[s] discussing how we would and would not be able to measure engagement—I felt like we were not going to reach an agreement because of the varying ideas about what constituted student engagement. Now what really stood out in my mind was that what we were doing was actually the initial steps to conducting research. I am not sure why I always think of research as something other than what we do in composition environments like this; I think

> *that I naturally think of research in term[s] of science, and if I do*
> *not see visible measuring tools, then research does not naturally*
> *surface as a descriptor of [what] we do in composition studies.*

On several levels, the engagement study was an interactional inquiry that grew organically out of the work of the Writing Studio staff and thus had meaning and staying power for the staff groups.

In other words, Studio interactional inquiry opens up the third-space that lies between the collapse of firstspace perceptions and secondspace conceptions, in part by "listening" to persistent local problems that, by their persistence, seem to be "telling us" something, either about ourselves or about student writing, or about both. In finding practical solutions or approaches to these concerns, issues, and problems, we provide our own infrastructures for making more visible and accessible those "links and connections" that traditional institutional hierarchy and attendant mechanisms of distancing would tend to ignore or make difficult to see. Those actions and interactions that our specific institutional geographies at our specific sites make "difficult" but that make sense to those who work together daily within a site reveal not only the hegemonic nature and operation of those institutional hierarchies but also the "fissures" through which institutional critique and change can be constructed.

This idea operated very simply in another problem the Writing Studio staff group tackled: the need for students to bring multiple copies of their papers so all group participants could see the writing, not just hear it read aloud. Studio "publishing" of student writers' drafts and texts each week is an important part of opening up the positional silences that surround work at the "lower" levels of academic culture. But it was always difficult to get students to bring copies; even one copy is hard to get from them, and asking them to bring several copies is even more complicated because of the time and expense involved. Though we had access to a photocopy machine at the other end of the hallway in the Writing Center, it took precious minutes of the hourlong meeting to gather the papers, run down the hall, make the copies, and sort them for the participants. Even a copy machine in our own environment would take time. Thus, staff members discussed and researched possibilities for providing a visual component for the writing that students bring. Finally we settled on a computer with a monitor large enough for all group members to see, which could connect with any student's e-mail or with any Internet information. With the computer and an Elmo projector attached, students could access their writing, and any paper (i.e., hard-copy draft with teacher comments) could be projected through the monitor with the Elmo. This technology gave our group access to pieces of writing for on-the-spot discussions. The technology and the successful in-house grant proposal the staff wrote to fund it were important elements of the Studio experience, and we often shared ideas in staff meetings about how we used the technology in our groups. Students liked it too, in the same way that it is fun for them to "surf the net" and see or hear the voices of others on a variety of topics. The large-screen computer gave the groups the best of both worlds: looking at student texts in a visual medium much like that facilitated by discussion boards and digital drop boxes in online courses but still being face-to-face, with the resulting ease of opening up questions that stray afield of the "text" itself and getting into matters of "task representation" and other subjective factors that are also an important part of revision and writing development.

These examples illustrate how the interactional inquiry of staff meetings is the group space in which we dwell in the program—creating and recreating the program from week to week and from year to year. As the program continues—but staff members change—from year to year, Soja's concept of "social formation and reformation" is enacted. Each year, the work of the interactional inquiry staff is formed and reformed, depending on the attitudes, interests, and abilities of the different staff members. As some staff members stay on from one year to another, continuity and memory of issues from the previous staff make their way into a new staff and a new group applies its intellect to a continuing issue. One of the most experienced Writing Studio group leaders, Mark Sutton, produced the following eloquent reflection at the end of three years of working as a group leader and student administrator:

Mark Sutton, Final one-pager, December 4, 2001

Studio has helped me see how tremendously complicated and varied teaching and academia can be. Studio's position in third space allows us to see how many different teachers approach the same subject. Some of their ideas I want to emulate; others bother me. In order to help these teachers' students, the Studio has to learn to adapt to all these styles, and there are so many.

While the Studio is generally comfortable accepting this complexity, we don't want to leave it unchanged. Studio tends to be activist; we want to make First-Year English and the University better for students. Making changes without force, however, can be hard. We have to plan our ideas very carefully. Studio has shown me how those solutions are not as easy to reach as we may hope. They contain drawbacks, consequences, and other problems that we must consider. Interactional inquiry requires us to accept all points of view, to honor the complexity of the academic world. Nancy once described it as "the extended time of a semester that gives us the opportunity to think about the good places and the rough spots in our program; the extended time to bring them up, leave them a while, come back to them after we've lived a little more, had a few more experiences, and bring them up again with a new perspective to a group of other people whose perspectives have also changed." This means we work slowly but deliberately.

For example, the Engagement Scale was developed over two intense (and stimulating) hour and a half meetings. The staff that year wanted as accurate a scale as possible, and the time was, in my opinion, worth it.

Of course, the scale isn't perfect, as L. pointed out at orientation. This brings up another lesson Studio has taught me: teaching undergoes constant revision. Everything about it changes as life moves on. We've talked about revising the diagnostic, just like the previous staffs. We've talked about other changes as well; now, the next staff will pick up some of them, building on them while developing their own. This constant state of change makes Studio very hard to define. It tends to be both the past and the future, things that have been done, things that need to be done, and things that should be done. Throughout, our work is dominated by one central question: "How can we help our students?"

Both these examples of Studio staff interactional inquiry—around issues of engagement (not just superficial "access") and facilitating communication about student texts to show that they are as important as those found in our rhetorics and readers (or those studied and argued over by literary critics and academics across disciplines)—illustrate the ways in which Studio interactional inquiry pushes us to support everyday communication across and within group boundaries, laterally as well as vertically within our institutional hierarchy of higher education, and how Studio is pushed from within to find ways to make the voices and experiences of those in these positions heard within everyday academic culture.

Of course, as the previous accounts and our own collaborative history make clear, Studio interactional inquiry also results in the more traditional kinds of publications valued by higher education's institutionalization of academic culture: conference papers, dissertations, book chapters, journal articles, and this book—all arising from collections of or reflections on our everyday work in Studio sessions. In all these ways, Studio programs with which we've worked have tried to bring "Other" positions and voices from the lower reaches of life on higher ed's institutional scale into the upper reaches of knowledge construction and publication in academe. The writing and communicating process draws us into reflection on our work and the productive activity of articulating insights—though for ourselves and our students, first and foremost.

In the case of RCS, working with staff that includes both comprhet and linguistics graduate students, as well as graduate students and faculty in engineering, is a way to continue learning how to teach writing and communications in disciplines across the university. Doing Studio or teaching communications within a discipline different from our own provides the opportunity to dwell there long enough to learn its culture, to engage in what former RCS codirector Libby Alford calls "research by walking around." Running into instructors on a daily basis in the halls provides a personal connection with others and a venue for getting and giving relevant information, as Libby discovered when, as a composition-rhetoric faculty member, she began to dwell in the University of South Carolina's College of Engineering and Information Technology. By dwelling in another discipline, without being a "natural" part of that discipline, we can better see the demands made of student writers, and Studio sessions organize a space/place in which we can work closely with those writers to open up and negotiate those demands: introductions in writing and speaking that tie research into the general societal and technological value of a project, the format of the scientific method, the pared-down logical style of the language used to communicate, the infusion of visuals and graphics into the writing, the different types of genres students must write—and the accompanying differences in the social relations of that discipline.

In the accompanying differences in social relations within a discipline is where we find the first hint of those external pentadic scenes that swirl around the textual concerns that are more internal to the engineering disciplines: At this more advanced level in the institutional hierarchy, the genres of communication are more obviously and more closely linked to disciplinary research and knowledge-making activities; that proximity is testified to by general engineering faculty's ideas that the students who have reached this level are ready to perform as proficient communicators, as if having reached this level carries an automatic or natural readiness to speak and write like an engineer. But of course not all are, and no one who appears ready is naturally so, though the assumption of a thus naturalized being can easily make those without such an apparent naturalness feel as if they do not belong. On one level, RCS helps those who feel like outsiders because they do not have cultural backgrounds that match those of the traditional white, male engineer. Yet on another level, all RCS students need help articulating the larger contexts in which the research they are participating in matters to the discipline, and this larger historical context is not always made apparent to undergraduate researcher assistants. There is no official course mechanism to do so: the historical context for a research study would necessarily involve references to the context of work at that particular institutional site and the circumstances surrounding the advancement of a particular kind of research at that institution. Since there is no course for undergraduates to provide that kind of context, they are left to discover it largely on their own, even though such knowledge is vital to the documents that they are required to provide as part of their research experience.

RCS interactional inquiry for staff groups thus brings out knowledges that are assumed at higher levels in the institutional hierarchy but that in fact have not been taught and perhaps might never be, formally, because the curriculum at those advanced undergraduate levels is focused on the internal pentadic scene of disciplinary knowledges. At these levels, knowledge of pentadic scene of both the internal and external varieties is largely assumed, and this is where RCS and interactional inquiry can help both advanced undergraduate students who need these knowledges to communicate well at these advanced levels and the graduate students and faculty who either possess in practice but cannot articulate these knowledges or who are using these articulations as the basis for their research into the rhetoric and linguistics of a discipline different from their own.

Composition and rhetoric graduate students and faculty in the engineering RCS have learned the lay of this land—a land that includes its own silences and thirdspace fissures specific to its position in the academic scale. In engineering fields, silences surround social relations that construct the practices of everyday place/space. These silences can create less familiar/friendly working environments for women students and staff, because their social ways of being (and thus their social construction of space/place) can seem excluded from those work environments, thereby seeming to exclude them as well. It is clear that the positional silences about social relations at lower levels of the higher-ed institutional hierarchy, plus traditional associations of certain fields in the sciences with higher levels of objective research (particularly authority carried by those in the hard sciences), are those typically associated with gender or class differences. Silences about issues of gender difference, or seeing these issues of gender style differences as necessary, "must be so" differences, mean that there is room also in upper-level undergraduate learning environments for the thirdspace functions of Studio, where up-close examination of everyday practices, combined with the advocacy role of the group leader and Studio staff, can create openings for articulating the social relations that are being silenced by lack of institutional attention to and awareness of those traditional silences.

Resisting Institutional Distancings

Higher education's institutional organization dictates that knowledge-making activities at the top of the scale are those that should most heavily influence and inform the content of texts and courses at lower levels in the scale. Such publications and accompanying influence on educational programs and curricula are typically the products of graduate-degree-granting institutions where faculty members are specifically given lighter teaching loads to facilitate such work—in what we would see as a kind of backdoor acknowledgment of how consuming involvement in the everyday sociospatial relations of learning/teaching can be, and how distracting for researchers. Such publications typically work hard to convince readers of the universal nature of the knowledges presented; it is rare for academic researchers to acknowledge the rhetorical influence or impact of the space/place that informs their work, since all graduate students are typically taught to assume that where they as researchers are located is immaterial to the results, as long as the research methods are sound. Indeed, for research methods to be "sound," they must control for the potential biases of the researcher.

The problem is that higher education institutions do not see themselves as a space/place of bias; they do not see themselves in terms of a "scale" of positions or in terms of Massey's accompanying socio-spatial relations. This is a key part of higher education's secondspace conception of itself. The social relations and affective dimensions of research at these upper levels or at the particular higher education institution (if acknowledged at all) are articulated, codified, and contained within debates over the hows and whys of research methodologies that typically become the subject of articles/publications separate from the publication of the research results themselves. Even in such discussions, however, the influence that the home higher education institution has on the research is rarely mentioned. Thus the resulting publication of research often does not reflect openly on the full complexity of the sociospatial relations at that researcher's position in the higher-ed scale. Unless the writer/researcher is working from one of the Other areas in higher education, traditional silences and hierarchies of influence are maintained.

Yet all kinds of work/writing—that of the "world of work," of academic experts, and of student writers—are organizationally contextualized. What differs are the organizational contexts we choose to attend to and those we choose to ignore: compositionists attend to the organizational contexts for writing in the world of work and in the fields of technical and business writing, looking at different kinds of organizational settings and environments and the effects of these differences on the conventions of writing—and vice versa. But we have generally chosen to ignore (at least in our curricula) the different kinds of higher education organizations themselves as similarly particularized organizational contexts for writing. This ignorance—really more the kind of politeness typical of situations in which we find ourselves confronting but not wanting to openly acknowledge differences in socioeconomic class and means—is crucial to maintaining secondspace conceptions of the universal nature of ideas/arguments and communication in academe, but it has kept our understanding of student writing and writing program structure stagnant.

One of the benefits of Studio work is that the outside-but-alongside positioning brings awareness of these influences and affects. It has made us look carefully at why higher education institutions enjoy different relationships with generalized, secondspace conceptions of academe (such as Bartholomae's "inventing the university") and with each other. What will differ from institution to institution is distance between those who teach writing and the sanctioned "knowledge-making" positions in the higher-ed scale. Herein we find the root of differences in Studio programs from one institution to the next. The social relations at each institutional site are also different because of different institutional prior history and the place occupied by different institutions on higher education's "scale" of being, a scale that distances faculty (and thereby, writing curriculum, student populations, staff, etc.) who are from those different institutions. And, because many of those who "speak" most in our discipline's national, professional spaces are from four-year state-affiliated, selective admissions or research institutions, faculty at smaller, more teaching-oriented colleges or open-admissions schools can find themselves struggling to overcome the distance between themselves (with their firstspace experiences) and the predominant views, pedagogies, and approaches in their discipline. The farther away the faculty and institution are from the upper end of the scale/hierarchy of knowledge making in any discipline, the more generic the curriculum and view of writing handed down from loftier spaces/places may become—not because of any lack of faculty expertise but because the curriculum forged at the upper end of a scale will be ill-equipped to deal with firstspace life at other places on the hierarchical scale.

Looking at student writing from an external pentadic or metarhetorical standpoint means not just explicating the stretched-out social relations that are a part of academe's text-based culture and that surround texts therein but also communicating about this academic cultural mode of interaction to students who are themselves several more degrees removed from the world and culture that support those relations. The greater the distance between knowledge-making positions in the higher education hierarchy and those faculty who teach writing at any given institution, the bigger the teaching load and the less able those faculty, loaded with more courses and more students in those classes, are to carry out the kind of metarhetorical examination that could open up and explicate the everyday social relations that construct such knowledges and texts. Faculty at these Other institutions are thus often forced to be more reliant on a generic curriculum, the most arhetorical manifestation of which is treatment of handbooks as texts instead of reference tools. Different relations with and distances from privileged positions in higher ed's scale make for different mechanisms of silence and require different approaches to opening up those silences.

Thus, in each Studio program manifestation, time/place/staff configurations are shaped by the institutional spaces in which the program lives, with a common element of an attitude of interactional inquiry taken by each staff group. In the USC Writing Studio, staff members were graduate TAs in literature, linguistics, or composition and rhetoric who applied to participate in the program. Instead of teaching one course, these graduate students chose the Studio staff group assignment of conducting five one-hour groups each week along with staff meetings and communications with instructors regarding their Studio students. A program that brings together graduate TAs from different English areas immerses them in interactional inquiry, which can help to overcome the distances between those from different backgrounds and in a departmental environment of professors jockeying for graduate students' time, energies, and loyalties. In the BWP at Benedict College, staff members were regular faculty who taught the introductory English 135 and 137 courses, along with two learning specialists who staffed the writing center; faculty were given release time to participate as facilitators of groups, financed by a FIPSE grant (which also paid Nancy as an assessment consultant). In the Opportunity Scholars Studio at USC, Director Ruth Strickland kept a staff of experienced Opportunity Scholars Program (OSP) students as tutors, and these peer tutors (often two per group) staffed the studio groups. In RCS, an NSF grant paid for composition and rhetoric and linguistics graduate students, engineering graduate student mentors, and communications faculty to staff the program.

These different staff group scenarios illustrate how the institutional space in which the program arises shapes its own Studio. In each of these cases, Studio takes advantage of the "distributed cognition" (Winsor; Salomon) of the different staff members available in the particular environment in the same way that distributed cognition operates among students with different areas of expertise or different social backgrounds and interrelations in student groups. Taking advantage of these different knowledges and experiences is an especially important part of the way that Studio acknowledges the sociospatial multiplicities that construct each site: In the RCS, graduate student staff members from engineering were included to provide near-peer technical help to undergraduate students. In BWP, it was important to value the knowledge of African American instructors who have extensive experience in teaching minority students at an HBCU. In OSP, the distributed cognition includes the experienced peer tutors who have themselves been through the program and thus often can understand first-year students' needs better than experienced instructors. In the original USC FYC Writing Studio program, experienced graduate TAs brought their different backgrounds in literature, composition and rhetoric, and linguistics to the table as we discussed our student and program issues each week in staff meetings.

Studio's bottom-up communication pathway, operating from within the academic scale-of-being itself, thus contrasts with the top-down communication pathway that typically structures and influences work within higher-ed institutions. Studio looks for ways to help unheard voices speak into the silences more immediately and directly located within their own institutional spaces/places. The challenge here is great, because it is not just a matter of asking or prodding people to speak or to voice their experiences within the sociospatial relations that construct everyday work/life. It is a matter of working with students and staff as they unlearn silences and ways of avoiding saying anything except what they believe is expected, and as they deal with the fact that the institutional system that governs their daily lives has determinedly (though in ways that can differ) ignored their Other experiences. As an extended example of a Studio encounter with academe's institutional narcissism, we offer the following examination of our experiences with the BWP at Benedict College.

An Extended Example: Benedict College's BWP

Though group leaders in Benedict College's BWP acted in capacities similar to those in USC's Writing Studio and RCS, their experience base and institutional setting were very different from those of the graduate TAs at USC and the staff of the RCS. BWP's group leaders included faculty who taught the freshman composition courses and learning specialists who staffed the English lab in the BCCARES student services area where the Bridges program held both its weekly student meetings and its bimonthly staff meetings. At Benedict, those who worked as group leaders or BWP staff were also classroom teachers, receiving a one-course release time from their typical four- (sometimes five-) course teaching load per semester in exchange for serving as a Bridges group leader for five groups per week, plus attending staff meetings and keeping track of required program record-keeping and paperwork duties.

The USC first-year composition program, like most programs at four-year graduate-degree-granting institutions, depended on a guiding philosophy/pedagogical approach that its teachers were in the process of learning while enacting to give its program overall coherence. But writing programs at colleges like Benedict, where faculty already have degrees and often considerable experience, may have a very general guiding philosophy/pedagogy (often identified by our field as "current-traditional") that relies heavily on the experience of the faculty in working with the social/cultural factors (and socio-spatial relations) that influence students' learning and retention in college. However, their experiential and cultural knowledges were not captured by either the generic curriculum or texts that were in evidence when Rhonda first came to Benedict College in fall 1996. As a university-trained compositionist-rhetorician who had previously worked/taught in a four-year state-supported research institution with graduate programs, Rhonda saw the common outlines guiding the two first-year composition courses as woefully inadequate, consisting of a single course text—a handbook—and a course outline that featured week-by-week assignments in different chapters in the handbook. The handbook was—or appeared to be—the curriculum. Undoubtedly in some instances, this was the complete curriculum, particularly in the case of faculty who were less than dedicated to the educational mission of this open admissions HBCU. But it was definitely *not* the complete curriculum for those faculty who came to work in the BWP as Studio group leaders.

When Rhonda first introduced the idea of a Studio small-group "outside-but-alongside" structure to deal with the problems created by the large lab sections with which President Swinton had replaced previous basic writing courses, the idea was met with antagonism from some faculty who were suspicious of outsiders and of pedagogical approaches that they saw as coming from institutional settings that

had little experience (or interest) in working with the student population found at Benedict College. Other faculty, however, including
those who were Benedict alumni and who had worked in writing and
reading labs that, in the 1980s, had been physically connected to the
classrooms where composition courses were taught, saw the Studio
proposal as a return to a more closely connected and linked relationship between the classroom and the "lab" that had been successful
in the freshman composition program's past. Rhonda worked with
these faculty to put together a Studio proposal—the Bridges Writing
Program—that could function within the structure and history of
Benedict College as an institutional site. With the FIPSE funding,
BWP began operation in fall 1997.

At first, faculty at Benedict, like those we have encountered in
the audiences of conference presentations about Studio over the years,
wanted to keep some of the trappings of a traditional classroom approach, including a workbook with "fill in the blank" exercises that
had been used in previous large labs and as a resource by some teachers (for what old-schoolers call "seat work"). The fear was—and still
can be—that there wouldn't be "enough" to do in Studio-type sessions,
that students wouldn't have work to bring, that students needed to be
kept busy, and so on. But what Rhonda—and Nancy, in her capacity
as outside assessment consultant—saw, as Studio interactional inquiry
progressed over the three years of the grant-funding, is that faculty,
particularly those who volunteered to work as BWP staff student group
leaders, possessed rich knowledges about Benedict's African American
student population, about their lives and the social/familial/personal
conflicts that affected their development and their work as writers in
the first-year composition courses and as students in courses across
the curriculum as well. And we saw how the standard, generic, current-traditional curriculum that had been in place when Rhonda
came to the college was less a reflection of the actual content of those
teachers' courses than it was a reflection of the extent to which those
discipline-sanctioned vehicles for the teaching of writing simply did
not touch/address the complex firstspace of these students' everyday
lives, of these students' writing development, and of these teachers'

cultural and pedagogical experience working with Benedict College's almost 100 percent African American student population.

Buried in the big metal cabinets that made the English lab room look more like a warehouse than a place of current vitality, Rhonda found further historical artifacts of past curriculum and testing, and tapes for teaching the "parts" and "rhetorics" of correct academic discourse, including SAT and CAT (California Achievement Tests) materials and a forgotten book on testing. As she enacted a therapeutic clean sweep of these cabinets and their dusty contents to make room for BWP student meeting reports, student group files, copies of student writing shared with weekly groups, staff meeting one-pagers, and program supplies, she had a palpable sense of how these faculty and Others like them had, for so long, been wading through the strong currents of another culture, through curriculum and materials and texts designed for those for whom the sociospatial relations of academic culture so nearly matched that of their own everyday lives that it was invisible, as unseen and light as the air they breathed. But for Benedict faculty and their Other students, that air was strangling. She contrasted this image with BWP staff meetings where they all had the time and energy to really talk and examine together specific student writing behaviors and attitudes, and ways of working holistically with student writing development at Benedict College.

While USC's Writing Studio used the Studio dialogue sheets and placement activities to help TAs learn about teaching, the Bridges program used program activities to help experienced but busy and overloaded faculty have the time to reflect, communicate, and share ideas with each other. Whereas USC's Writing Studio made use of dialogue sheets from Studio staff to course instructors, the BWP required students to write a reflection at the end of each weekly student session, asked staff to file a weekly meeting report with attendance data needed for the program as well as a brief narrative of each session, and then asked students and their group leaders to jointly prepare a midterm and final report that was sent to each student's classroom course instructor. These midterm and final reports included the staff/group leader's verification of the attendance and participation points earned by the student, as well as a paragraph, constructed and written by the student, reflecting on his or her BWP experiences thus far. In addition, as program director, Rhonda culled examples, ideas, and suggestions from weekly meeting reports and staff meetings—as well as attendance data and qualitative data about writing concerns/issues in the groups and in staff meetings—for a bimonthly BWP newsletter sent just to first-year writing instructors and other faculty in the Department of English, Foreign Languages, and Mass Communication.

Benedict faculty and learning specialists possessed a wealth of untapped knowledges about the everyday, sociospatial relations and issues surrounding student writing development, and how to work within these relations at what one of the more outspoken faculty members termed the "reality level." And, in addition to personal experience as students from a culture, class, or race not well reflected in the upper echelons of academic culture, these faculty also brought professional expertise in a variety of English areas. In the case of the BWP, it was clear that the job of administration would be to provide scaffolding for voicing and sharing those knowledges, as well as a thirdspace in which our multiplicity of sociospatial relations to societal, institutional, and academic "norms" could find voice. The richness of our BWP interactional inquiry and the administrative procedures for inclusion that were at the heart of our work in the program were evident in improved retention of BWP students in the English 135 and 137 first-year composition course sequence (compared with non-lab-placed students; see Grego, "Community Archaeology"). The richness of these interactions was also maintained through several faculty initiatives that have since resulted from the mutual respect for both articulated and unarticulated knowledges brought to the table in BWP, including choosing a rhetoric/reader and eventually putting together our own custom reader for the two courses, a reader that reflects the knowledges and mutual respect for the knowledges of Benedict faculty about what works and how to negotiate a hybridity between academe's text-based culture and our African American students' everyday encounters with life at Benedict College.

Nancy's final assessment overview—a key document in the final BWP FIPSE report prepared for the U.S. Department of Education in

2000—gives an excellent overview of the different work accomplished by BWP as a Studio program that operated from the basis of awareness of, rather than ignoring, institutional/organizational differences that influence student writing development and that should influence writing program development and design. Over the three years of the FIPSE funding, Nancy attended weekly and then bimonthly staff meetings, tape-recording the meetings (with the approval of the group), taking notes, and bringing her own one-pager to the table, reflecting on what she was seeing as an "outside-insider," participating in the interactional inquiry of the group from yet another perspective. The opening paragraphs from her report (below; qtd. in Grego, "Bridges") address the ways that a Studio program facilitates the negotiation of a first and secondspace conception of higher education that plays out differently at an institutional site that is academically, disciplinarily, and socially distanced or "Othered."

Good Conversations, the Basis of Inquiry

A staff member of the Bridges Writing Program characterizes BWP staff meetings as "good conversations." In that program, good conversations, rather than the earlier language of "theorizing the cross-section," were the form of interactional inquiry there.

Our good conversations did not occur in a haphazard environment. They arose out of the weekly scheduled staff meetings that were a crucial component of the program. Meeting at noon, sitting around the table with our shared potluck lunches, we gathered each week to bring our observations and concerns to the table. Those, also, didn't occur in a haphazard fashion, but arose in the one-page informal piece of writing that we each bring (with copies for everyone) as our anticipation of, preparation for, and initial contribution to the meeting. Thus, everyone's voice is represented as the meeting begins. From there, we discuss the most pressing concerns brought to the table, making the effort to respond to each person's one-pager, but also leaving openings for the related concerns and ideas and creative thinking that emerge from this organic beginning. These staff meetings open the space for our conversations, through which we conduct our action research project that continues each week to build and refine the program. In HBCU environments like Benedict, as in other educational environments as well, we must move along with the times, making changes to fit the context in which we find ourselves at the moment. The old scripts are insufficient, even counterproductive, for educating a new generation of young people. . . .

We came to call our action research "interactional inquiry" because it depends on the interactions of all the members to make the program run productively. Decisions about topics that come "to the table" are based on the different points of view that staff members bring and on "theorizing the cross-section" to construct best practices from collective wisdom. The result of action research is the refinement of the program through rounds and rounds of considering directions to take. Since this is a research environment and faculty are encouraged and expected to build their research knowledge, we work to gradually extend the research program through adding layers of writing to the discussion. Following a pattern similar to the small groups set up to help students in their inquiry-writing processes, the research that begins in the informal one-pagers and the conversations staff members bring to the table then moves to drafting more formal papers presented at conferences and finally to article- and book-length research publications.

The weekly meetings bring out what staff members know, which of their teaching approaches work best, and what they understand about students and colleagues across the institution. The meetings provide a forum for staff members to offer suggestions for additions or changes to the program. They are a place to talk about the positive things as well as the frustrations of working in the institution. These meetings never could have succeeded without the staff members' willingness to hash things out, to question, to consider multiple perspectives, to share knowledge and observations.

In this outside-but-alongside thirdspace place, we step just far enough outside the traditional institutional structures to gain perspective on our student groups and our administrative structure. We create an open and safe place for ourselves to bring to the table creative ideas, programmatic concerns, and institutional struggles. With the help of all staff members, we alternate solving logistical problems of the program with thinking creatively and philosophically about program directions. In the same way that the students in their small groups engage in intellectual discussions about writing, the staff, too, engage in intellectual discussions about teaching, research, and program administration. This is the stuff of our "good conversations."

The program director provides a strong but nondirective style of leadership that allows the action to flow from the environment and the people in it. The director provides scaffolding and structure for the program but at each step lays ideas out on the table so that staff members can see the possibilities and add insights from their knowledge of this institution. The approach is to bring out in the open the history and attitudes of the institution that must be considered in running the program and, perhaps more important, to identify and articulate the considerable strengths of the faculty and writing specialists who serve as staff for the BWP. The strengths of these faculty become a major component of the collective wisdom that coalesces to run the program. By opening the program administration to the group, the director is able to combine her own strengths with those of others in the program. This combination forms a powerful coalition of faculty intelligence. (Thompson qtd. in Grego, "Bridges")

Among the topics of conversation around which Nancy organized this section of her report were program logistics, attitude about "research," interpretation of courses and assignments, pushing inside students' experience to open out details, and social ecologies of learning. Within the section on attitude about "research," the way that interactional inquiry worked to assure faculty that this program was here to recognize their metarhetorical knowledges is clear, just as in the section on pushing inside students' experience we can hear how Studio worked to break new ground in developing all of our metarhetorical awareness of student work:

Attitude about "Research"

The staff were slow to take to the idea of research because they saw "research" in the traditional sense of the outside researcher who does not respect the knowledge of those who are being "researched," or of "research" as ideas from outside that are unrelated to the HBCU context. Through many conversations the concept of research began to change, as we worked to reflect back to staff members their interests that could be possible research topics. We recognized during the second year that interesting stories about work in small groups with students were emerging from the group. It is from these multiple stories that we were able, then, to gather a large body of information from our "good conversations" with which we could then "theorize the cross-section."

As we continued focusing on action inquiry, staff members began to engage in the inquiry. Early in the project staff members were reluctant to write one-pagers for meetings, but in the second and third years much more enthusiasm and self-confidence were evident in the one-pagers representing their "local knowledge" that contributed to programmatic decision making. Another thing that has helped give form to the research component of the program is that the hours of BWP staff meetings could be reported as part of the in-house faculty development component in Benedict's evaluation system.

The knowledge we generated and the group processes we learned through our "good conversations" were disseminated to other Benedict faculty in summer workshops on writing across the curriculum, in reporting at conferences, and in working on pieces of writing for a book on the project. Staff took on an attitude of research; systematic record keeping contributed a sense of palpability and a database for further research. . . .

Pushing Inside Student Experiences to Open Out the Details

One of the most productive ongoing conversations involved stories of students' work in small groups or classes, opening out details of their lives to see into the reasons for the difficulties they have getting to class or producing their work. Often specific students' stories became the focus of good conversations. We came to understand better how the everyday events in students' lives affect their performance, such as the family problems that take attention away from the college studies, which sometimes pale in importance compared with family crises. One staff member [Ruby Blair] composed a page of expressive computer-generated "stick-figures" to illustrate an array of students' affective states. This attuned all of us to the factors that distract students from their work and to the need to help them handle life situations better. This staff member's visual representation of local knowledge gathered over a long teaching career at Benedict gives that knowledge shape and makes it available as a part of the collective knowledge of the group. We came to understand how necessary it is to acknowledge students' feelings and problems and to talk through them in order to get beyond what's blocking creative processes, but that there also has to be a limit so students realize they must move beyond their difficulties to accomplish academic work. (Thompson qtd. in Grego, "Bridges")

As these sections from Nancy's report show, over many staff meetings—"good conversations" rather than "theorizing the cross-section" was our language here—we came to see that the distances that separated us were often due to mythologized terminologies, or ways of talking about/identifying features of student writing that were so distanced from the firstspace realms of our everyday work with students in BWP sessions (and other Studio sessions), that they felt much less meaningful than our shared stories about those everyday experiences in our everyday spaces on campus. And while there were/ are still differences between us (not only in demographics but in matters of pedagogy as well), we came to forge common bonds through a common vocabulary of caring for our students and the dilemmas that they faced, as well as the dilemmas that we faced together.

As we got to know each other and to articulate and open out more of the complexities of our everyday work with student writers, we laughed together about how references to "they" and to "taboo" ("turn off the tape recorder!") topics arose more and more in our staff meetings as we came to see the institution's role in constructing and maintaining distance between students and writing/learning. We saw how administrators paralleled the top-down cultural geography of academic knowledge making with their own top-down policies. Administrators' general lack of communication with teachers and the false assumptions about students/writing upon which they founded institutional policies and positions became dominant topics of our staff meeting discussions. The group talked often about the need for better lines of communication with administration, and as BWP project and grant director, Rhonda occupied a position in which she worked to open these lines of communication through reports, presentations, conferences, summer workshops with faculty across the curriculum, and even communication with FIPSE about problems in program and grant administration specific to small, open-admissions colleges like Benedict. The summer workshops effectively engaged faculty across the curriculum in interactional inquiry into their own writing and into how their course curricula and disciplinary programs of study as manifested at Benedict College affected the development of student writing.

Each new academic year at this small, enrollment-driven college brought administrative or administrator changes that impinged upon the operations of the program. Many conversations in the staff meetings concerned struggles to take in stride the edicts of new administrators, each of whom brought an agenda from the outside to enact and an assumption of the "sameness" of some areas of work in higher-ed

institutions that seemed to prevent them from seeking input about
the programs already operating at our particular site. These changes
brought endless frustration and made clear how much more beneficial
it would be if administrators tried to identify and understand what
is already in place and support that which is successful. New admin-
istrations could more productively encourage articulation of what is
going on and bring to the activities already in place a new coherence,
building from the bottom up rather than importing new programs
from the top down. Bringing our frustrations to the table, venting,
and pushing inside what seemed like unreasonable administrative
changes and expectations allowed the staff to develop and share, as
Massey would say, an "extra-verted" sense of place, a sense of the way
in which larger ends and flows of power were at work in our everyday
lives. Even this gave us greater understanding of how our student
writers—who are also caught in the ebb and flow of tides beyond
their immediate control back in their composition classrooms—feel
as they struggle with their assignments.

We did what we could, working to solve everyday problems of
student/teacher participation and attendance by forging reporting/re-
flecting/communication mechanisms. During discussions of how to
set up our forms, newsletters, and reports, we began to come together
over the realities of our students' work, their misunderstandings in
the classroom, and the classroom's misunderstandings of them. Tell-
ingly, we talked much about student emotions and attitudes, and in
the process of discussing/probing what lay behind them, we came
together even more, leaving behind some of the distances created by
"error" vocabulary alone between ourselves and student writing. We
emerged with better appreciation and respect for the lifeworlds behind
our professional differences than our comp/rhet/literature/linguistics
disciplines had given us to work from. Understanding of distances
lessens them. And even though remnants of the BWP small group
program struggled once grant funding ended, what has lasted are the
bonds of understanding among the faculty that resulted not only in
coming together over choices of readers and readings (hand-selecting
individual pieces for our own Mercury Reader anthology) but also
in advocating with upper administration for smaller class sizes and

additional pay for increased classroom hours of teaching, as well as lobbying for our own writing program assessment design.

Conclusion

Studio articulation of thirdspace is built on communications. At the beginning those communications are characterized by the intimacy of personal exchange, often in close proximity, that is, sitting beside one another or across the table from one another, particularly when the two of us, taking over an unused room that eventually became the Studio space, began collaborating daily in our work to create the Writing Studio at USC.

According to James Moffett's communication theory, the difficulty of discoursing is based on abstraction in the form of variation of distance in time and space between the speaker, the listener, and the subject. He relates the degree of particularity or generality to communications between persons: from the particularity of face-to-face, or I-thou, communications to the generality or abstraction that occurs as the communication expands out in space and time to become more impersonalized, the I-it relationship (Moffett 11). In the Studio, the most personal and concrete is the discussion that occurs between and among the people sitting at the table where there is immediate feedback, verbal and visual. As communications spiral out, the difficulty becomes making effective connections that will feed back into the program. Since a thirdspace program depends on its effective ongoing communications (rather than an official designated space in the academy), the efforts and energies put into communication are vital for the program's existence. The spiraling out and feeding back are the essence of the interactional inquiry that produces change to keep the program lively in the dynamic ecologies of differing institutional environments. Through the interactional inquiry, or action research, the communication circles back into the conceptual and practical improvements we made in Studio processes from week to week and year to year.

One of the questions directed to us from the beginning was how to use the Studio model in a program run with faculty rather than graduate TAs. Our experiences at Benedict, above, provide one answer. As we consult with faculty in more traditional institutions and departments, we see that the positional silences of higher education manifest themselves in different ways. And as Studio has moved into other disciplines, we've seen how the cultures and languages of different disciplines clash. Words carry different meanings, different connotations, different baggage from one discipline or institutional site to another. Ways of approaching one another differ. By going outside to other campuses, we obtain more views of the program and its various changes as it grows in other institutional environments. Interaction with Cindy Lewiecki-Wilson and John Tassoni at Miami–Middletown, for example, has made us look at the social construction of critical pedagogy—in terms of programs rather than individuals or individual classrooms. Our articles on the program in *WPA* and *CCC* and our conference presentations have also brought feedback from compositionists at many other institutions. Their questions feed back into our program, helping us think through our program's implications, just as the inclusion of new staff members each year is a benefit. The presence of a new person, a new voice, a new element in the evolving sociospatial relations that is the focus of Studio disrupts what we might come to see as status quo by presenting the need to explain and therefore revisit issues that we might have considered closed. A new person asks questions and brings new perspectives to what we thought we already knew. In our explanations and answers to questions, we build further and farther on what we already know, as we have done here and as we hope to continue doing as our Studio experiences continue to grow.

Epilogue: Eulogy and Prolegomenon

[Thirdspace] does not derive simply from an additive combination of its binary antecedents but rather from a disordering,
deconstruction, and tentative reconstitution of their presumed
totalization producing an open alternative that is both similar
and strikingly different

> —Edward Soja, *Thirdspace: Journeys to*
> *Los Angeles and Other Real-and-Imagined Places*

This is space as the sphere of a dynamic simultaneity, constantly
disconnected by new arrivals, constantly waiting to be determined (and therefore always undermined) by the construction of
new relations. It is always being made and always therefore, in a
sense, unfinished (except that "finishing" is not on the agenda).
. . . The "always" is rather that there are always connections yet
to be made, juxtapositions yet to flower into interaction, or not,
potential links which may never be established. Loose ends and
ongoing stories. "Space," then, can never be that completed simultaneity in which all interconnections have been established,
in which everywhere is already (and at that moment unchang-
ingly) linked to everywhere else.

> —Doreen Massey, *For Space*

A system takes a lot of trouble. A system must be devised and
implemented. To be sure, much of its design is tacit, its imple-
mentation an extension of usual modes of comfortable life. That
is why most people who are uncomfortable in a system experience frustration. That is also why uncomfortable people can
often change a system. They can see it.

> —J. Elspeth Stuckey, *The Violence of Literacy*

Academe, institutions, and disciplines—though relationships within each of these systems overlap, each names a scene that has been and is being rhetorically constructed through an ever-changing set of relationships, for an ever-changing set of exigencies, past and present and future. Academe names a long-standing set of (generally liberal) ideas about the advancement of knowledge for the sake of understanding our world and improving our lives as a human community. Composition's own liberal activism on issues of, for example, greater access to higher education for nontraditional student populations is rhetorically supported by these ideals of academic culture and research—despite the social pressures that have worked specifically against actual access at different times and places in our nation's history.

Institutions such as colleges and universities in higher education are the actual physical spaces/places where disciplinary and academic work is embodied on a daily basis, constructed by intersections between academe and disciplinary discourses (shaped by current assumptions about "should be"), along with the specific relationships between faculty, staff, students, and administrators in classrooms, labs, offices, dorms, and so on. As such, institutions may tend toward conservatism; their purview involves issues of budget and buildings, territories, and the management of the people and material conditions needed to operationalize and implement academic culture and disciplinarity. Institutions thus speak of "assessment" of programs and courses, leaving "research" to designate activities within disciplines that advance those knowledges regarded as independent of specific institutional sites and thus valued by academe and disciplinary culture at what Porter and colleagues term the "macro-level" (622).

Indeed, it is through the macro-level discourses of "academe" and "disciplinarity" that we academics escape our institutionally bound spaces, our institutional bodies—encompassing our very local situations and interrelations and all the attendant new arrivals, disconnections, loose ends, and ongoing stories of which Doreen Massey writes. Of course, composition's disciplinary subject (the teaching of writing) seems to determinedly focus our gaze on just those institutional interrelations and bodies, but even we have found ways to escape dealing with the complexity that the differences in our various institutional spaces/places entail. In some ways, the very activism of our discipline is a part of that escape: in focusing on the plight of nontraditional students or of those adjunct faculty and compositionists who are academe's "women in the basement" (Crowley), we have allowed that which is defined as "traditional" and "mainstream" (Burke's "parlor room" in the front of the house) to avoid (or avert) our critical rhetorical gaze. We are, after all, well-mannered radicals.

But as Studio work got us moving across and behind the typical administrative roles in higher education that composition has come to know and be comfortable with—structures such as first-year composition (FYC), writing across the curriculum, writing in the disciplines, or Writing Centers—we saw how crossing composition's administrative roles with institutional and disciplinary ideals of research apparently meant we'd forgotten our place. In our original Studio, in the University of South Carolina's FYC program (and English Department), for example, "disciplinarity" contributed both more and less to the survival of Studio space: With a Ph.D. program in composition and rhetoric in the same department, the original Studio was supported initially because of our collaborative directorship and efforts, from 1992 to 2000, to frame the disorder and deconstruction created by Studio as a research program, as a space/place for disciplinary theorizing-based-on-research beneficial to graduate students and programs. Three graduate students (two in composition and rhetoric and one in linguistics) completed doctoral dissertation projects from within this original Studio. The initial Studio program produced conference presentations, and both faculty and staff (graduate student researchers) produced publications through which we hoped to construct the legitimacy of our work within the comp-rhet program. We thus drew on the value that our institution, as an environment for academe, claimed to have for research.

But disciplinarity for composition can be a two-edged sword, one not meant to be pulled from its foundational stone. Studio positioning at USC conflicted with institutional hierarchy and history (as discussed in chapter 3) and with composition's departmental administrative positioning. Though many FYC programs in large state universities with comp-rhet graduate programs, such as the University of South Carolina, are theory-driven, that relationship is typically one in which theoretical approaches (often those favored by or palatable to the other English disciplines represented in such departments) "trickle down" to shape the choice of assignments and textbooks/readers in FYC courses. These theory-driven pedagogies are often used as the basis for training graduate student teaching assistants (often literature/linguistics TAs outnumbering those in composition/rhetoric), and serve in part to legitimize their teaching as a component of their graduate education.

Studio, however, operates/d on a different model, one in which we at least in part reject the "presumed totalization" (Soja, *Thirdspace* 61) and accompanying comfort and legitimization offered by such discourse-theory-driven shaping of course content/curriculum. We worked to "trickle up" and, thus apparently defying the gravity of our positioning, "rudely" sought out research methodology and theory outside that of the liaisons typically respected by or represented in English departments (see chapter 1). We moved toward approaches and theories that help get at "meta" views that made sense of the specific location and interrelationships in which we found ourselves (interactional inquiry), that recollect the embodied insights ignored by institutionalized disciplines (memory work). In other words, Studio represented our taking ourselves playfully-seriously as composition-ists, as "thirders" within the university and our department, and looking for research approaches and models that would help us do just that. By not allowing us to escape composition's embodiment within higher education's institutional life, Studio positioned us to see that though we may not avoid institutional complicity, composition does enact a "thirding" that we can be attentive to if we focus more determinedly on not only differences in institutional environment but also the nexus of relationships that rhetorically construct the space/place within which teachers and students reside in any given institutional environment. Though located in an institutionally mandated FYC program driven by disciplinarily approved theory, Studio staffing and staff meetings were framed by interactional inquiry and memory-work approaches that were informed by methodologically focused theory and, most important, that sought those "tentative reconstitutions" (Soja, *Thirdspace* 61) that can be achieved by organizing participants (students and staff) as they come together to engage in activities and theorize the cross-section of their experiences to form provisional bases for further actions and work.

And though at first some compositionists may have regarded our work as a kind of traitor to struggles in other states to keep a place for basic writing programs, courses, and students in certain state institutions, others became interested in aspects of our work that resonated with their own. John Paul Tassoni and Cynthia Lewiecki-Wilson at Miami University–Middletown were asking "How [can] we change the entrenched practices of the teaching of basic writing at our university?" (69) before they heard one of our earlier CCCC presentations and went home to begin their own version of Studio. Our dialogue with these two dedicated professionals over the years has certainly enriched our own understanding of both Studio and composition's space/place within different institutional structures and histories. (See Tassoni and Lewiecki-Wilson's excellent analysis and account of their Studio experiences.)

Others who became interested in and cited Studio work—Peter Elbow and Ira Shor—are typically thought to represent very different, even opposite, ideologies of composition's work. Though at first we felt that the interest of both meant that we had not well articulated the difference of our Studio work, we came to realize that both their approaches also tap into this "thirding" that is the essence of composition, that both have advocated writing program administration based also on methodologically focused theory or approaches and that it was their recognition of this kinship, of this similar-yet-different quality, that sparked their interest in Studio work. From Elbow's perspective, Studio groups provide a supportive space for student writers facing the kinds of frustrations that he has spoken so many times about facing on his own in graduate school and which led him to his workshop (versus a more "content" or linguistically oriented) approach for all writers, as well as FYC curricula. From Shor's perspective, Studio provides an alternative to basic writing and "the testing regimes that drive BW [basic writing] enrollments" that he believes "should be abolished by mainstreaming basic writers into untracked comp classes expanded with extra hours and tutorial services to meet all students' needs, based in the themes and idioms they bring to class" (104). Shor's approach, like Elbow's, grew from frustrations with the institutionalized systems that surrounded composition and FYC; both these responses to Studio (and similar programs) are born out of a similar disciplinary boundary-crossing into institutional territory—and an accompanying heightened awareness and critique of institutional spaces/places for "learning" writing.

Thus, as we went into the mid- to late 1990s with the Studio program at the University of South Carolina, there were visible (and fairly traditional) signs of our success in programmatically operating Studio's hybrid/thirdspace—a success charged by our use of disciplinary and academic research to frame a space typically defined by institutional structurings as "mere service" or, at most, teaching located at the lowest level of higher education's institutionalized spatial scale. But, however much composition's disciplinarity thus meant to the initial success of our Studio program work, in the long run framing Studio work as a research program tested the limits of the respect that higher education institutions can have for the discipline of composition—or the limits of disciplinarity in accepting composition's heightened attention to the space/place of institutional scene. Seen from the thirdspace perspective of Studio work, composition is positioned to facilitate an external pentadic analysis of institutionalized life, while strict disciplinarity would prefer internal pentadic analyses of the discourse through which we construct our various subjects.

The conservatism of USC's English Department in the 1990s, along with the conservatism innate to that large state university as an institution, both finally worked against sustaining Studio space, as well as a career within the English Department. In May 1995 Rhonda was denied tenure, and though any such instance certainly represents a "meeting up" of many histories and reasons, her case was fraught with signs of the university's ambivalence toward an assistant professor's career in which the usual boundaries of disciplinary and institutional work were blurred. On the basis of her Studio work and then recent publications out of that work, the department majority voted in her favor, but influential literature faculty with traditional ideas of disciplinary contributions in the fields of literature and bibliography conjoined with the doubts of one of her own outside reviewers (who asked, "Why is she going outside of the field of basic writing for theoretical grounding?"). Though in the numerical minority, disapproval from without and within prevailed outside and above the departmental level, solidified no doubt by the conservatism inherent in the institution if not also in academic culture itself. Our use of the Writing Program Administrators statement on how to value the administrative work of a compositionist did not help Rhonda's case. Even calling Studio work "administrative" put it in binary opposition to "disciplinary research" and worked against all the arguments we had framed for the hybridity of this thirdspace venture as disciplinary research: in higher education, administrators assess, disciplinary scholars research.

Nonetheless, the FYC Studio persisted, with Nancy and an advanced graduate student in composition and rhetoric serving as directors, until the final blow to our original Studio program came in 2001. As Nancy was preparing to retire from the English Department (while also working on a National Science Foundation [NSF] grant proposal to create another version of Studio in the College of Engineering and Information Technology), a decision was made to fold the Writing Studio into the Writing Center. For a transitional year, experienced graduate student Mark Sutton, who had previously been assistant director of the Writing Studio, became an assistant director for the Writing Center and was given the task of shepherding the Studio into the Writing Center, with Nancy's help. The newly appointed Writing Center director was expected to develop the Writing Center as a program to demonstrate to university administration the English Department's commitment to service—not as a research arm of the composition and rhetoric program. With the Studio's new locus of control in the Writing Center director, the energy and commitment to interactional inquiry required to keep Studio as an open alternative that is similar but different from the Writing Center were effectively, institutionally dissipated. As Nancy and Mark Sutton explained in a memo to the department chair on October 22, 2001,

Despite everyone's best intentions, the present arrangement of merging the Studio with the Writing Center has not worked well. The change was hurriedly made in the face of possible budget cuts last spring and without discussion that could have avoided the clash of the Writing Center's more hierarchical style with the Studio's collective administration practice. The model of the Center has forced Center staff members, who were not informed in advance, to teach Studio groups whether they chose to or not. In contrast, participatory inquiry programs like the Studio cannot function by force. The model calls for a small, dedicated staff (of 3–4 members) who are committed to working out the day-to-day procedures and willing to engage with and find solutions to administrative and educational issues that arise. In this way, the Studio is an action research project that gives graduate students administrative experience in designing and redesigning the program. This feature, along with experience in small-group teaching, provides our graduate students a unique and valuable expertise that enhances their applications for academic positions. (Thompson and Sutton, October 22, 2001)

Especially destructive was the requirement that all Writing Center consultants also participate as Studio leaders whether they chose to or not, justified as a way to equalize graduate student positions and therefore make program administration more efficient. Rather than three to five dedicated staff members, the Studio now had a dozen Writing Center staff members, some of whom were resistant to conducting small groups and who were definitely distanced from attitudes of inquiry or research. Without dedicated staff meetings and leadership in supporting and modeling continuous interactional inquiry, there was no way to keep Studio's research focus intact. Writing Center/Studio staff meetings that included all tutors (those working with individuals as well as small groups) brought out the negative attitudes of those who were assigned to small groups but who had no interest in working in or understanding this hybrid space. And with a Writing Center director who was not trained in composition and who was directed by the department chair to focus on efficiency and numbers, there was little support for theorizing the cross-section when problems or frustrations arose, to arrive at those tentative reconstitutions that allow those of us who occupy thirdspaces to live within a state of "constantly waiting to be determined (and therefore always undermined) by the construction of new relations."

The chair who had hired this Writing Center director was responsible for moving the department in directions that would help the university toward its stated goal of Research 1 status and AAU (Association of American Universities) institutional recognition. At that time, there was no patience for hearing how the commitment (at whatever level) required to keep Studio space open could be a benefit, despite Nancy and Mark's attempts (illustrated at the end of the memo passage quoted above) to remind the department of the way in which Studio work realized the research mission of the disciplines, the department, and the institution. Despite the shift away from old-school New Criticism and bibliography work and toward postmodern critical, feminist, and rhetorical theory in new departmental faculty hires through the end of the 1990s and into the new millennium, the conservatism of the institution—at least with respect to composition—overrode this repositioning of the department's disciplinary profiles. After one semester of that transitional year, Mark and Nancy preemptively removed their support for trying to make Studio "work" in the Writing Center, because they saw that the program had become too compromised in that environment.

In the meantime, Nancy and Libby Alford (a former graduate student who had earned her comp-rhet doctoral degree through the department) had applied for an NSF grant to use Studio approaches to help undergraduate engineering students communicate their research and learn about the discourse of professionals in engineering fields. This grant came through, and thus the Studio sent a runner underground to sprout up at the Research Communications Studio (RCS) in the College of Engineering and Information Technology, where it operated through its four years of funding.

At Benedict College, a very different institution, composition's claims to disciplinarity meant little from the start: for the time that the Studio-modeled Bridges Writing Program existed in full operation (from 1997 to 2001), it was in large part the faculty and staff's re-memorying of their previous work in similar lab hybrid thirdspaces at the institution that professionally fueled the success of the program. At Benedict College, "disciplinarity" was at first one of many obstacles that the teaching faculty and English lab staff who were to work with the supplemental Studio-based program (funded by FIPSE [Fund for the Improvement of Postsecondary Education]) had to face. Each faculty member had different areas of English studies, teaching, or even educational administration that constituted the "disciplinary" affiliation of their graduate degree programs. For some, middle or high school teaching was a more recent affiliation for their work as composition instructors. Several faculty were initially suspicious of Rhonda, an outsider with an unusual degree (in composition and rhetoric), from whom they expected a program based on foreign content or assumptions about student writing that did not mesh with their experience with student writers at, as one faculty member adamantly and repeatedly put it, "the reality level."

Issues of race were coded everywhere, including the juxtaposition set up between what works "out there" at the large, predominantly white state university a mile down the road (to which, after forced desegregation in the 1960s, Benedict College lost academically gifted African American students—the "cream of the crop," as one alumnus said). This racialized institutional history was materially manifested in the race and institutional positioning of those departmental faculty and staff involved in the initial planning for the program: white faculty included Rhonda and two male faculty, with the highest levels of graduate education—and tenure—and one of the two English lab learning specialists (herself a writer), while the majority of the faculty were black, including at that time four women and one man who were long-time instructors in Benedict's FYC courses—none with tenure. These racial histories conjoined with the racialized histories of the city and of the continued inequities in the state's educational system in such a way that composition's liberal attitudes toward issues such as grammar and usage were seen as equivalent to the white privilege long enjoyed by the university (USC) that housed the state's doctoral

degree in comp-rhet. Discipline and institution were regarded as one
and the same, both coded "white," neither one regarded as capable
of understanding the needs of "our students" at Benedict College "at
the reality level."

In this small, liberal arts, open-admissions, historically black
college, many faculty felt they were already in a kind of thirdspace:
at an institution dedicated to educating students whom our public
school systems had neglected and most other colleges would not accept. Initial work within the Studio-style Bridges Writing Program
(BWP) there included acknowledging the history and ancestry of
past programs at the college that were home to similar outside-but-
alongside work. We presented the results of these explorations at the
South Carolina Writing Center Association Conference sessions in
1997, 1998, and 1999 (Blair, Colgate, Criswell, Greene, Grego, and
Thompson), where faculty discussed the previous kinds of writing lab
and lab-classroom partnerships undertaken at the college, including
those during the 1970s and 1980s, when there were reading, writing,
and speech lab rooms connected directly to the classrooms in which
these courses were taught, there was a fluid flow between activities
in the classroom and the lab, and there was instantaneous collaboration, or a "dynamic simultaneity," between the classroom teacher, the
student, and lab staff.

As Benedict College faculty shared the insights that they had
gained from this and other previous hybrid space work with student
writers, Studio interactional inquiry in our weekly staff meetings was
able to make use of these insights, as they were adapted to the new
(and rapidly changing) institutional environments created as part
of the college's efforts to increase student enrollment and retention.
As Benedict College moved from a student population of about one
thousand to just over two thousand during BWP's FIPSE funding from
1997 to 2000 and then departmental funding from 2000 to fall 2001,
the BWP became a place in which that re-memoried institutional past,
along with the experience of some of the Benedict College faculty with
composition process pedagogy in the 1970s (as part of the grant that
began USC's original Writing Center), were combined with the interactional inquiry of our experiences in student and staff small groups

to create a program that engaged both student writers and faculty and staff in the pursuit of deeper understandings of student writing development and histories thereof. As discussed before, particularly in chapter 4, we developed our program through interactional inquiry and were able to gather assessment results showing that the BWP increased student retention in FYC courses (Grego, "Community Archaeology"). These results allayed some (but certainly not all) of the negative educational effects of rising numbers of students assigned to composition course sections and classrooms (from the high twenties and low thirties per classroom to the midforties and more between 1997 and 2001). As we theorized the cross-section of our everyday work with student writers, we began to forge insights into the complex dynamics of student writers' struggles, insights that took us beyond polarized and polarizing process versus product or linguistic/literary versus rhetorical analyses—and beyond the racialized binaries that always oversimplify and can easily block communication.

For one year and a half after FIPSE funding ended, BWP faculty, group leaders, and learning specialists struggled to continue the program with dwindling institutional support. But starting in spring 2002, the college's failure to provide the infrastructure (though modest) required to run the program, plus the overloading of FYC courses in both numbers of students per section and the number of courses taught by each faculty instructor, as well as the loss of one of two English learning specialists, overwhelmed our ability to keep the BWP fully operational. Spring 2002 also brought controversial policies, instituted by upper administration to retain students, an important goal for institutions whose budgets are tuition-driven. Considerable national attention was paid to the conflict over one of these policies. Originally termed SEE, for "Success Equals Effort," the policy required that "effort" activities account for 60 percent of the grade in freshman courses and 50 percent in sophomore courses, in addition to the more traditional knowledge indicators typically used to award the majority of a student's course grade. Though Benedict College administrators argue that this is an innovative educational policy that seeks to teach "disadvantaged" students how to put forward the effort necessary for success, this policy has raised concerns about academic freedom of college teachers to determine the basis for course grades. During this same time, the English lab was moved more firmly under the umbrella of an Academic Support Services unit that included counseling and testing, and lab specialists' time was routinely taken away from English instruction and applied to more general institutional matters such as calling students about class attendance.

Nonetheless, until the end of fall 2005, when she took a job elsewhere, the remaining English learning specialist, Anne Colgate, worked valiantly to keep BWP-like small groups going, though faculty had less and less time to support her efforts. And from 2002 to 2005, those of us in English who had worked as BWP group leaders retained our sense of solidarity gained through shared experiences and insights. We used what we had learned together to compile our own reader for FYC courses, to work together on writing assessment in the program in ways that resisted upper-level administrators' attempts to determine procedures, and to conduct research and produce reports on institutional problems such as faculty and lab staff attrition and burgeoning class sizes. Our BWP experiences gave us a grounding that comes with a long-range understanding of ourselves within our disciplinary and institutional scenes, and thus a stronger basis for continued professional collaboration than we would otherwise have had.

And, as at USC, the concepts of Studio programs—particularly other ways to use "outside-but-alongside" approaches to support student achievement and staff development—migrated into other areas at the College. For instance, the Student Leadership Development unit runs one-hour seminar courses, required of Benedict students every semester during their four-year matriculation, through which students earn the majority of their 120 hours of required service learning before graduation. Service-learning projects, not just at off-campus sites but within the institution itself, open up spaces within which students, teachers, and staff realize the complexity of their interrelationships and the ways writing practice and pedagogy are shaped within the specific institutional spaces/places constructed by those relationships. A further FIPSE-funded project, titled "Composing Academic Identities: Writing and Serving-to-Learn across the Curriculum at Benedict

College" (Greene and Grego), extended original BWP interactional inquiry and the outside-but-alongside educational model to faculty working with service-learning projects in disciplinary-specific courses that involve student research. This work has also extended into explorations of on-campus service-learning projects. For example, a technical writing class takes on a project of researching, designing, writing, and conducting user tests of a brochure outlining classroom etiquette that could be provided to new first-year students in a campus orientation session. In researching such guidelines on other campuses, interviewing and surveying faculty and students on our own campus, and working with orientation staff, these students encounter the complexity of actual institutional spaces/places such as their own campus. They have to wrestle with the real-world difficulty of forming a text from within both internal and external pentadic analyses of higher education's institutionalized scene. They must examine the complexity of the campus as an organizational and material setting and their education as an embodied set of experiences. And, perhaps as important, we academics who work with students on such projects have to see our work as embodied, in terms of the specific institutional complexities of space/place and interrelationships therein.

In addition to institutional change from within, Rhonda also worked outside the department (as an officer in Benedict College's chapter of the AAUP [American Association of University Professors]) to argue for the importance of sincere and significant faculty input in matters of policy that affect educational courses and programs. In June 2005 the AAUP–Benedict College chapter was awarded the AAUP Beatrice Konheim Award for exemplary efforts to promote academic freedom, and Benedict College now has the rare distinction of being "double-censured" by the AAUP. Unfortunately, the combination of all these efforts made life at Benedict College increasingly uncomfortable. Understanding just how much our work with student writers is influenced by institutional geographies of composition and unable to face such a counterproductive teaching environment for yet another year, Rhonda left the college in July 2006 and is currently teaching at nearby Midlands Technical College.

An Open Future: The Dynamism of Real Life

What we intend the previous stories to illustrate is the push-pull of beginnings and endings that is attendant on life in academically institutionalized thirdspace. "This is a space of loose ends and missing links. For the future to be open, space must be open too" (Massey, *For Space* 12). What it means for a space to be open is that the connections that sustain it may be cut off, at least in material ways, so that they cease to grow or so that the relationships thus forged may change as other connections are made, as we have experienced in our work with Studio programs. Despite the coming and going of the various Studios with which we've worked, we appreciate the alternative spatial imagining of higher education and writing instruction therein that this work has brought us to. It is this spatial imagining that we believe can lead to composition's own "[re]inventing" of the university as a space/place that is not constructed solely by attention to the internal pentadic analyses and production of texts.

Locating ourselves in our particular spaces via Studio sessions with students and staff over the years in different institutional sites, we have developed a cumulative sense of what we might term, à la Patricia Mann and Porter et al., the "microrhetorics" of our daily works and lives, accompanied by a sense that the spatial dynamics of these microrhetorics are not always as compatible with the temporal, idealized master narratives, with those disciplinarily preferred or institutionally simplified "macrorhetorics," as we are asked to pretend when we attend conferences, read our journals, or implement writing programs and assessments thereof. Massey's arguments about the relationship between space and "representation" open up a provocative metarhetorical awareness of composition's space/place in academe and higher education—and point the way to the kinds of "thirding" and institutional critique embedded in composition's own being that we have experienced in Studio interactional inquiry within student and staff groups.

In tracing the long history of our preference for historicism and temporally focused master narratives, Massey notes, "It is an old association; over and over we tame the spatial into the textual and the conceptual; into representation" (*For Space* 20). She argues that our modernist privileging of time (as a rich concept) and our reduction of space to a mere surface, to a territory without its own histories and trajectories, ready to be conquered and colonized, can be connected to the valorizing of science and scientific research—and the role played by writing in constructing the relationships central to modern academic culture. For a spatial explication of connections between science and writing, Massey turns to the work of Michel de Certeau in *The Practice of Everyday Life*:

> For de Certeau, the emergence of writing (as distinct from orality) and of modern scientific method involved precisely the obliteration of temporal dynamic, the creation of a blank space (*un espace propre*) both of the object of knowledge and as a place for inscription, and the act of writing (on that space). These three processes are intimately associated. Narrative, stories, trajectories are all suppressed in the emergence of science as the writing of the world. And that process of writing, more generally of making a mark upon the blank space of a page, is what removes the dynamism of "real life." (*For Space* 25)

In response to this suppression of "narratives, stories, and trajectories," Massey believes, time was valorized:

> Maybe the misreading of space, its relegation to the outer darkness of fixity and closure, came about in part because of social scientists' and philosophers' reactions to natural science's intransigence on the matter of time. It was as a result of science's intransigence [holding that time was reversible, that scientific experiments and events could replicate/repeat themselves, and that thus the world was a closed system] that some philosophers sought a way around its propositions. If time was to be asserted as open and creative, then that business that science got up to, pinning things down (writing them down), and taking the life out of them, must be its opposite—which they called "space." (*For Space* 32)

Thus the sense of "writing" with which composition has grown up in higher education is that associated with the despatialization of our academic worlds: a despatializing effected by the privileging of time and narrative (narrative being the world of the humanities), on the one hand, but, on the other, by a concomitant institutionalization of the sciences through the ways in which ideas of "objectivity," "empirical method," and "progress" dominated the structure, reorganization, and growth of early-twentieth-century higher education institutions and preferred definitions of "discipline" therein. In a fascinating way, composition is a discipline that has always existed within both these worlds: work in science and technical writing has been around in higher education about as long as has composition (see Grego "Science"). This both/and existence uniquely positioned composition to embrace the work of Thomas Kuhn—even applying the language of "paradigm shift" liberally in naming our own disciplinary developments.

But in doing so we reveal that we are still a part of a larger modernist academic narrative that sees "science as the writing of the world"—and that we too have been shaped by academe's construction (or conceptual obliteration) of its space through the values and perspectives of scientific method, by science's use of writing (or "pinning things down") and the ways that its distancing hierarchy works to "remove the dynamism of 'real life'" (Massey, *For Space* 25). Despite our postmodern critical reverence for narrative and stories, we remain mired in science's preferred timelessness of space and a view of life (of our students and their writing) that is limited by the extent to which our academic institutions continue to be structured (through their daily material practices and territories) by a powerful reverence for objective scientific method, and by an accompanying disregard for the "dynamism of 'real life'" that thirdspaces like Studio persistently and urgently bring to our awareness.

Our both/and lives as compositionists help explain how our reliance on the institutional valorizing of disciplinary research (described in the USC and Benedict stories with which we began this chapter) both did and did not "work" to keep our original Studio spaces alive and well. To the extent that disciplines within higher education institutions have come to value narratives, stories, and trajectories, Studio can be valued as an extension of that work, as a resurrecting of academe's "space" through the "meeting up of histories" therein. To the extent that higher education institutions themselves are still conservatively structured around science's "writing of the world" and are not equipped to deal with the details, multiplicities, and heterogeneities that constitute the "dynamism of 'real life,'" Studio may not be tolerated too long in any particular institutional space/place because it transgresses into those details, into the "loose ends and missing links" (Massey, *For Space* 11–12) that do not make for neat assessments or happy-ending stories of student (or program or faculty) successes, that do not fit into the expectations, tolerances, or timeframes that the academy or a particularly institutional site may have for either research or program administration. The kinds of connections that Studio interactional inquiry asks us to examine between institutional mechanisms, policies, and structures, on the one hand, and the daily work of student writers and teachers, on the other, may not be welcome. Institutional critique advanced by connecting relationships between external and internal pentadic scenes, as our experiences show, will by definition be vulnerable to those higher education politics that encourage individuals in positions of power to act on behalf of institutional preservation and then makes these actions more palatable by encouraging them to place responsibility on institutional systems and by rewarding intellectual escape into internal pentadic scenes.

Our Compositional Situation

We end by urging greater attention to what we term our "compositional situation." An admittedly awkward play on "rhetorical situation"—a foundational phrase for our discipline—"compositional situation" seems nonetheless the clearest way to name the external pentadic counterpoint to the internal pentadic analyses of that discourse through which our institutional lives are constructed. Internal pentadic analyses of student writing assignments were, of course, promoted by college composition's "rhetorical revival" in the middle of the twentieth century. Lloyd Bitzer's 1968 explication of the concept of "rhetorical situation" in the pages of *Philosophy and Rhetoric* was followed by important rhetorical reexaminations of the concept of "audience" by compositionists such as Douglas Park, Andrea Lunsford and Lisa Ede, Peter Elbow, and others. A now-foundational interest in the tenets of classical rhetoric and the ensuing history of Western rhetoric, including the "New Rhetorics" and those theorists such as Burke (along with Ong and Booth) who bridged the rhetoric/literature gap gave intellectual grounding to numerous Ph.D. programs in composition and rhetoric that were forged in the 1970s and 1980s—and to the still burgeoning subfield of technical writing and communication, or professional writing. In other words, composition as a discipline has gained considerable support by enacting an internal analysis of writing assignments, programs, and disciplinary writing that is in keeping with its Rhetorical heritage. (Here we use *Rhetorical* with a capital *R* to designate its discipline-defining status.)

Still today, numerous references to "the rhetorical situation" and the anthologizing of debates about the concept of "audience" in resource books for writing teachers indicate the extent to which we rely on an assumed understanding of exactly what is being referenced by "rhetorical situation" and "audience" in the discussion and assignment of writing in college classrooms. Most discussions seem to refer to influences internal to the reading/writing assigned, ignoring the numerous layers of complexity that such assignments first present to our students (and instructors) who live primarily and first within the unresolved and ever-shifting scene of the institutional setting and accompanying relationships, a scene external to (or at least several layers distanced from) the work internal to the texts of any given assignment. For students whose home cultures and backgrounds are not part of academe's mainstream culture, the journey that they must make through several external scenes to those internal to the texts that they are to read and produce is one much different from (and "longer" than) that assumed by an academic culture that privileges ignoring its own everyday embodiments. These students are enmeshed in a complex "compositional situation," needing to understand the whys and whats of an assignment, of the class, the teacher, and their own responses (learned and reinforced) to these more immediate features of composition's space/place.

Porter and colleagues are, for understandable reasons, frustrated with the extent to which our "field's identity is so immersed in first-year composition" (615). They argue, "For one thing, such critique usually focuses on a limited set of organization spaces: the composition classroom, the first-year composition curriculum, the English department," and desire to "look at institutional writing spaces outside the university" (625). But we end with a different position. The application of our Studio experiences and alternative research methods to students (and faculty) working "outside but alongside" composition classes (or upper-level undergraduate research writing experiences) provided the openings and orientations from which the richness of our "compositional situation" becomes more visible and more integral to our work with writing. Thus, we argue that more concerted attention be paid to the different compositional situations in which both teachers and students find themselves, to the great variety of factors that influence the very different shapes and relationships within writing programs across institutions both in the United States and abroad, and to the ways in which these complex factors might bring us to a rhetoric of student writing that is respectful of those exigencies. If we learn to better understand our own interrelations with our institutional spaces/places, we will become more relevant to needed work not only in college composition but in K–12 on this same issue—and we will be more effective champions of social justice within our own home institutions, as well as in the larger world of higher education and beyond.

Studio experiences reinforce the need to regard our work within first-year composition (and writing across the curriculum, writing in the disciplines, and writing centers) with the same rhetorical acumen—and a renewed attention to space/place—that we apply to writing in other organizational settings outside those immediate to our own discipline. Composition is, to return to where we began, itself a space/place that can generate institutional critique. Facing that challenge must mean that we extend greater metarhetorical awareness not only to the work of student writers but also to our own work to "[re]invent" the university and our particular institutional sites. In her conclusion to *The Violence of Literacy*, J. Elspeth Stuckey simply urges that "those to whom we must listen must ultimately become ourselves. In this way, the change that many of us want may become the change that all of us require" (127). But what she asks—that we become "those to whom we must listen"—is not made simple by higher education's institutional structures and their self-preserving distancings. How are we to accomplish this? What can we do? Stuckey says, "It may be that the most likely way change will ever happen is incremental, local, one person at a time" (126), and we have certainly seen the truth of this statement as we have applied our individual/collaborative energies to various difficult situations over the years. But are there no undisciplined disciplinary ways to move? Attending more systematically and systemically to the different ways that higher education's institutional spaces/places are peopled, and honing a finer-tuned respect for and understanding of the "meeting up of histories" that construct composition's daily work and that influence both the teaching and production of writing: we believe that such moves can open up space and the possibilities of our future.

Bibliography

Index

Bibliography

Aristotle. *Aristotle on Memory.* Trans. Richard Sorabji. Providence: Brown UP, 1972.

———. *Aristotle on Rhetoric.* Trans. George A. Kennedy. New York: Oxford UP, 1991.

Barnes, Michael. "The Writing Studio: A Qualitative Study Contextualized within the Freshman Composition Program at the University of South Carolina." Diss. U of South Carolina, 2000.

Bartholomae, David. "Inventing the University." *Perspectives on Literacy.* Ed. Eugene R. Kintgen, Barry M. Kroll, and Mike Rose. Carbondale: Southern Illinois UP, 1988. 273–85.

———. "The Tidy House: Basic Writing in the American Curriculum." *Journal of Basic Writing* 12.1 (1993): 4–21.

Bartholomae, David, and Anthony Petrosky. *Facts, Artifacts, and Counterfacts: Theory and Method for a Reading and Writing Course.* Portsmouth, NH: Boynton, 1986.

Bazerman, Charles. *Shaping Written Knowledge: The Genre and Activity of the Experimental Article in Science.* Madison: U of Wisconsin P, 1988.

Belenky, Mary Field, Blythe McVicker Clinchy, Nancy Rule Goldberger, and Jill Mattuck Tarule. *Women's Ways of Knowing.* New York: Basic, 1986.

Bhabha, Homi K. *The Location of Culture.* London: Routledge, 1994.

Bitzer, Lloyd. "The Rhetorical Situation." *Philosophy and Rhetoric* 1 (1968): 1–15.

Bizzell, Patricia. "The Intellectual Work of 'Mixed' Forms of Academic Discourses." *ALT DIS: Alternative Discourses and the Academy.* Ed. Christopher Schroeder, Helen Fox, Patricia Bizzell. Portsmouth, NH: Boynton, 2002. 1–10.

———. "What Is a Discourse Community?" *Academic Discourse and Critical Consciousness.* Pittsburgh: U of Pittsburgh P, 1992. 222–37.

Bizzell, Patricia, and Bruce Herzberg. *Negotiating Difference: Cultural Case Studies for Composition.* New York: Bedford, 1995.

Blair, Ruby. "The Realities of the Student Writer." Southeast Regional Writing Center Association Conference. Charleston, SC. 4 Feb. 1999.

Blair, Ruby, Anne Colgate, Stephen Criswell, Doris Greene, Rhonda Grego, and Nancy Thompson. "Outside-Alongside-Inside: A Third Space." Southeast Regional Writing Center Association Conference. Charleston, SC. 4 Feb. 1999.

Booth, Wayne. *The Rhetoric of Fiction.* Chicago: U of Chicago P, 1961.

Bourdieu, Pierre, Jean-Claude Passeron, and Monique de Saint Martin. *Academic Discourse: Linguistic Misunderstanding and Professorial Power.* Trans. Richard Teese. Stanford, CA: Stanford UP, 1994.

Brandt, Deborah. *Literacy as Involvement: The Acts of Writers, Readers, and Texts.* Carbondale: Southern Illinois UP, 1990.

Brooke, Robert. "Underlife and Writing Instruction." *College Composition and Communication* 38 (1987): 141–52.

———. *Writing and Sense of Self: Identity Negotiation in Writing Workshops.* Urbana, IL: NCTE, 1991.

Brooke, Robert, Ruth Mirtz, and Rich Evans. *Small Groups in Writing Workshops.* Urbana, IL: NCTE, 1994.

Burke, Kenneth. *A Grammar of Motives.* New York: Prentice Hall, 1945.

———. *The Philosophy of Literary Forms: Studies in Symbolic Action.* 2nd ed. Baton Rouge: Louisiana State UP, 1967.

Butler, Paul. "Composition as Countermonument: Toward a New Space in Writing Classrooms and Curricula." *WPA* 29.3 (2006): 11–25.

Caputo, John, and Mark Yount. "Introduction." *Foucault and the Critique of Institutions.* Ed. John Caputo and Mark Yount. University Park: Pennsylvania State UP, 1993. 3–23.

Certeau, Michael de. *The Practice of Everyday Life.* Trans. Steven Rendall. Berkeley: U of California P, 1984.

Chiseri-Strater, Elizabeth. *Academic Literacies: The Public and Private Discourse of University Students.* Portsmouth, NH: Heinemann, 1991.

Cleary, Linda Miller. *From the Other Side of the Desk: Students Speak Out about Writing.* Portsmouth, NH: Heinemann, 1991.

Crawford, June, Susan Kippax, Jenny Onyx, Una Gault, and Pam Benton. *Emotion and Gender, Constructing Meaning from Memory.* London: Sage, 1992.

Daly, Mary. *Outercourse.* San Francisco: Harper, 1992.

DiMedio, Gregory Lawrence. "Aligning Perception with Purpose: The Development of Two Writing Centers." Thesis. U of South Carolina, 1994.

Dobrin, Sidney I., and Christian R. Weisser. *Natural Discourse: Toward Ecocomposition.* Albany: SUNY P, 2002.

Donath, Lori, Roxanne Spray, Nancy Thompson, Elisabeth Alford, Nadia Craig, Michael Matthews. "Characterizing Discourse among Undergraduate Researchers in an Inquiry-Based Community of Practice." *Journal of Engineering Education,* 94.4 (2005): 403–17.

Ede, Lisa, and Andrea Lunsford. "Audience Addressed/Audience Invoked: The Role of Audience in Composition Theory and Pedagogy." *College Composition and Communication* 35 (1984): 155–71.

Elbow, Peter. "Basic Utopia." Conference on Redefining Basic Skills: Transforming New Approaches into Pedagogy. Adelphi University, Garden City, NY. 6 Nov. 1993.

———. "Closing My Eyes as I Speak: An Argument for Ignoring Audience." *College English* 49 (1987): 50–69.

———. *Writing without Teachers*. New York: Oxford UP, 1973.

———. *Writing with Power*. New York: Oxford UP, 1981.

Elbow, Peter, and Pat Belanoff. *A Community of Writers*. New York: McGraw-Hill, 1989.

Emig, Janet. *The Composing Processes of Twelfth Graders*. NCTE Research Report no. 13. Urbana, IL: NCTE, 1971.

Flower, Linda. "TR06. The Role of Task Representation in Reading-to-Write." National Center for the Study of Writing and Literacy, Technical Report, June 1984, 35 pp. 9 Mar. 2005 <http://www.writing project.org/cs/nwpp/print/nwpr/592>.

Flynn, Elizabeth A. "Composing as a Woman." *College Composition and Communication* 39 (1988): 423–35.

Foss, Sonja K., Karen A. Foss, and Robert Trapp. *Contemporary Perspectives on Rhetoric*. Prospect Heights, IL: Waveland, 1985.

Foucault, Michel. "Intellectuals and Power: A Conversation between Michel Foucault and Gilles Deleuze." *Language, Counter-Memory, Practice: Selected Essays and Interviews*. Ed. Donald F. Bouchard. Ithaca, NY: Cornell UP, 1977. 205–17.

———. "Of Other Spaces." *Diacritics* 16 (1986): 22–27.

Fox, Tom. "Basic Writing as Cultural Conflict." *Journal of Education* 172.1 (1990): 65–83.

Freebody, P., A. Luke, and P. Gilbert. "Reading Positions and Practices in the Classroom." *Curriculum Inquiry* 21 (1991): 435–57.

Gee, James. *Social Linguistics and Literacies: Ideology in Discourses*. 2nd ed. London: Taylor, 1996.

Gere, Anne Ruggles. "Talking in Writing Groups." *Perspectives on Talk and Learning*. Ed. Susan Hynds and Donald L. Rubin. Urbana, IL: NCTE, 1990. 115–28.

———. *Writing Groups: History, Theory, and Implications*. Carbondale: Southern Illinois UP, 1987.

Giddens, Anthony. *The Consequences of Modernity*. Cambridge: Polity, 1990.

Gleason, Barbara. "Evaluating Writing Programs in Real Time: The Politics of Remediation." *College Composition and Communication* 51 (2000): 560–88.

Goffman, E. *Asylums: Essays on the Social Situation of Mental Patients and Other Inmates*. New York: Anchor, 1961.

Gray-Rosendale, Laura. *Rethinking Basic Writing: Exploring Identity, Politics, and Community in Interaction*. Mahwah, NJ: Erlbaum, 2000.

Greene, Gwenda, and Rhonda Grego. "Composing Academic Identities: Writing and Serving-to-Learn across the Curriculum at Benedict College." FIPSE grant. Oct. 2000–Aug. 2001. #P116B000571.

Grego, Rhonda. "Benedict College Writing Program/English Lab History." South Carolina Writing Center Association Meeting. 6 Feb. 1998. Charleston, SC.

——. "The Bridges Writing Program (BWP) at Benedict College: Participatory Inquiry for Student-, Faculty-, and Program-Development." Fund for Improvement of Postsecondary Education. U.S. Department of Education Grant #P116B971289. Final Report. Washington, D.C. June 2000. (Unpublished report available from FIPSE.)

——. "Community Archaeology: An Historically Black College Deconstructs Basic Writing." *Included in English Studies: Learning Climates That Cultivate Racial and Ethnic Diversity.* Ed. Shelli B. Fowler and Victor Vitanza. Washington, DC: AAHE/NCTE, 2002.

——. "Recollecting Student Ethos: Rhetorical Education from a Third Space Perspective." Rhetorical Education in America Conference. Pennsylvania State University, University Park, PA. 7 July 1999.

——. *Recollection and Its Return.* Unpublished manuscript, 1992.

——. "Rhetorics of Tradition and the Rhetorical Tradition in the Radical University, 1873–1877." Conf. on Coll. Composition and Communication Convention. Chicago. 4 Apr. 1998.

——. "Science, Late Nineteenth-Century Rhetoric, and the Beginnings of Technical Writing Instruction in America." *Journal of Technical Writing and Communication* 1.1 (1987): 63–78.

——. "The Textual Nature of Memory and Particular Texts: Rediscovering a Lost Canon of Rhetoric." Diss. Pennsylvania State U, 1989.

Grego, Rhonda, and Nancy Thompson. "Forging New Academic Identities in a Third Space." Conf. of South Africa Association for Research and Development in Higher Education. Penninsula Technikon, Cape Town. 1 July 1999.

——. "Locating Qualitative Research across the Global Community." *English International* 4.1 (June 1996): 5–10.

——. "Repositioning Remediation: Renegotiating Composition's Work in the Academy." *College Composition and Communication* 47 (Feb. 1996): 62–84.

——. "The Writing Studio Project at the University of South Carolina." National Conference on Redefining Basic Skills. Adelphi University, Garden City, NY. Nov. 1993.

——. "The Writing Studio Program: Reconfiguring Basic Writing/Freshman Composition." *Writing Program Administration* 19.1 (1995): 66–79.

Gresham, Morgan, and Kathleen Blake Yancey. "New Studio Composition: New Sites for Writing, New Forms of Composition, New Cultures of Learning." *WPA* 28.1–2 (2004): 9–28.

Gutierrez, Kris, Betsy Rymes, and Joanne Larson. "Script, Counterscript, and Underlife in the Classroom: James Brown versus *Brown v. Board of Education.*" *Harvard Educational Review* 65 (1995): 452–53.

Guynn, Anita. *Student Revisions in Complex Contexts: The Role of Writing Studio.* Diss. U of South Carolina, 1996.

Haug, Frigga, et al. *Female Sexualisation: A Collective Work of Memory.* Trans. Erica Carter. London: Verso, 1987.

Heidegger, Martin. "Building Dwelling Thinking." *Poetry, Language, Thought.* Trans. Albert Hofstadter. New York: Harper, 1971.

Hollis, Daniel Walker. *University of South Carolina.* Columbia: U of South Carolina P, 1956.

hooks, bell. *Talking Back: Thinking Feminist, Thinking Black.* Boston: South End, 1989.

———. *Yearning: Race, Gender, and Cultural Politics.* Boston: South End, 1990.

Horner, Bruce. *Terms of Work for Composition: A Materialist Critique.* Albany: SUNY P, 2000.

Horner, Bruce, and Min-Zhan Lu. *Representing the "Other": Basic Writers and the Teaching of Basic Writing.* Urbana, IL: NCTE, 1999.

Hynds, Susan, and Donald L. Rubin, eds. *Perspectives on Talk and Learning.* Urbana, IL: NCTE, 1990.

Hull, Glynda, and Mike Rose. "Rethinking Remediation: Towards a Social-Cognitive Understanding of Problematic Reading and Writing." *Written Communication* 6.2 (1989): 139–54.

Iotova, Albena. RCS Web page. 5 Sept. 2006 <http://www.che.sc.edu/centers/RCS/iotova3/SolarCells page.html>.

Kirsch, Gesa E., ed. *Women Writing the Academy: Audience, Authority, and Transformation.* Carbondale: Southern Illinois UP, 1993.

Kutz, Eleanor. *Exploring Literacy: A Guide to Reading, Writing, and Research.* New York: Longman, 2003.

Kutz, Eleanor, and Hephzibah Roskelly. *An Unquiet Pedagogy: Transforming Practice in the English Classroom.* Portsmouth, NH: Heinemann, 1991.

Kutz, Eleanor, Suzy W. Groden, and Vivian Zamel. *The Discovery of Competence: Teaching and Learning with Diverse Student Writers.* Portsmouth, NH: Heinemann, 1993.

Lalicker, William B. "A Basic Introduction to Basic Writing Program Structures: A Baseline and Five Alternatives." *Basic Writing e-Journal* 1.2 (1999). <http://www.asu.edu/clas/english/composition/cbs/bwe_fall_1999.html>.

Launspach, Sonja. *Interactional Strategies and the Role of Questions in the Acquisition of Academic Discourse.* Diss. U of South Carolina, 1998.

Lave, Jean. "Situating Learning in Communities of Practice." *Perspectives on Socially Shared Cognition.* Ed. L. Resnick, J. Levine, and S. Teasley. Washington, DC: American Psychological Association, 1991. 63–82.

Lefebvre, Henri. *The Production of Space.* Cambridge, MA: Blackwell, 1991.

Light, Richard J. *The Harvard Assessment Seminars, Second Report.* Cambridge: Harvard U Graduate School of Education and Kennedy School of Government, 1992.

Macauley, William John, Jr. *Studio Pedagogy and First-Year Composition: A Qualitative Study of Studio-Based Learning, Student Empowerment, and the Application of Studio Pedagogies to College-Level Composition*. Diss. Indiana U of Pennsylvania, May 1999.

Mahala, Daniel, and Jody Swilky. "Constructing Disciplinary Space: The Borders, Boundaries, and Zones of English." *JAC* 23.4 (2003): 765–97.

Mann, Patricia. *Micro-Politics: Agency in a Postfeminist Era*. Minneapolis: U of Minnesota P, 1994.

Massey, Doreen. *For Space*. London: Sage, 2005.

———. "Power Geometry and a Progressive Sense of Place." *Mapping the Futures: Local Cultures, Global Change*. Ed. Jon Bird, Barry Curtis, Tim Putnam, George Robertson, and Lisa Tickner. New York: Routledge, 1992. 59–69.

———. *Space, Place, and Gender*. Minneapolis: U of Minnesota P, 1994.

Matthews, Luke. RCS Web page. 5 Sept. 2006. <http://www.che.sc.edu/centers/RCS/matthews2/research%20background.htm>.

Mauk, Johnathon. "Location, Location, Location: The 'Real' (E)states of Being, Writing, and Thinking in Composition." *College English* 65.4 (2003): 368–88.

McNenny, Gerri, ed. *Mainstreaming Basic Writers: Politics and Pedagogies of Access*. Mahwah, NJ: Erlbaum, 2001.

Miller, D. W. "The New Urban Studies." *Chronicle of Higher Education* 46.50 (2000): A15–A16.

Miller, Susan. *Textual Carnivals: The Politics of Composition*. Carbondale: Southern Illinois UP, 1993.

Moffett, James. *Teaching the Universe of Discourse*. Boston: Houghton, 1968.

Morrison, Toni. *Beloved*. New York: Penguin, 1987.

Mountford, Roxanne. *The Gendered Pulpit: Preaching in American Protestant Spaces*. Carbondale: Southern Illinois UP, 2003.

Mutnick, Deborah. *Writing in an Alien World*. Portsmouth, NH: Heinemann, 1996.

Nelson, Marie Wilson. *At the Point of Need: Teaching Basic and ESL Writers*. Portsmouth, NH: Heinemann, 1991.

Ong, Walter J. "From Mimesis to Irony: The Distancing of Voice." *The Horizon of Literature*. Ed. Paul Hernadi. Lincoln: U of Nebraska P, 1982.

Park, Douglas B. "The Meanings of 'Audience.'" *College English* 44 (March 1982): 247–57.

Plato. *Phaedrus*. Trans. W. C. Helmbold and W. G. Rabinowitz. Indianapolis: Bobbs-Merrill, 1956.

Porter, James E., Patricia Sullivan, Stuart Blythe, Jeffrey T. Grabill, and Libby Miles. "Institutional Critique: A Rhetorical Methodology for Change." *College Composition and Communication* 51 (2000): 610–42.

Ray, Ruth. *The Practice of Theory: Teacher Research in Composition*. Urbana, IL: NCTE, 1993.

Reason, Peter, ed. *Human Inquiry in Action, Developments in New Paradigm Research.* London: Sage, 1988.

Reason, Peter, and John Rowan, eds. *Human Inquiry, a Sourcebook of New Paradigm Research.* Chichester, Eng.: Wiley, 1981.

Research Communications Studio Web site <www.che.sc.edu/centers/RCS/rcsmain.htm>.

Reynolds, Nedra. "Composition's Imagined Geographies: The Politics of Space in the Frontier, City, and Cyberspace." *CCC* 50 (1998): 12–35.

———. *Geographies of Writing: Inhabiting Places and Encountering Difference.* Carbondale: Southern Illinois UP, 2004.

Ritchie, Joy. "Confronting the 'Essential' Problem: Reconnecting Feminist Theory and Pedagogy." *Journal of Advanced Composition* 10 (1990): 249–73.

Robinson, Marilynne. *Housekeeping.* New York: Bantam, 1982.

Rodby, Judith, and Tom Fox. "Basic Work and Material Acts: The Ironies, Discrepancies, and Disjunctures of Basic Writing and Mainstreaming." *Journal of Basic Writing* 19.1 (2000): 84–99.

Rose, Mike. "The Language of Exclusion: Writing Instruction at the University." *College English* 47.4 (1985): 341–59.

Rose, Shirley K., and Irwin Weiser. *The Writing Program Administrator as Researcher: Inquiry in Action and Reflection.* Portsmouth, NH: Heinemann, 1999.

Rouse, Joseph. "Foucault and the Natural Sciences." *Foucault and the Critique of Institutions.* Ed. John Caputo and Mark Yount. University Park: Pennsylvania State UP, 1993. 137–62.

Rubin, Donald, and William M. Dodd. *Talking into Writing: Exercises for Basic Writers.* Urbana, IL: NCTE and ERIC, 1987.

Salomon, Gavriel. "No Distribution with Individuals' Cognition: A Dynamic Interactional View." *Distributed Cognitions: Psychological and Educational Considerations.* Ed. G. Salomon. Cambridge: Cambridge UP, 1993. 111–38.

Schmelzer, Mary. "Panopticism and Postmodern Pedagogy." *Foucault and the Critique of Institutions.* Ed. John Caputo and Mark Yount. University Park: Pennsylvania State UP, 1993. 127–36.

Schroeder, Christopher, Helen Fox, and Patricia Bizzell. *ALT DIS: Alternative Discourses and the Academy.* Portsmouth, NH: Boynton, 2002.

Shaughnessy, Mina. *Errors and Expectations.* New York: Oxford UP, 1977.

Shor, Ira, ed. *Freire for the Classroom: A Sourcebook for Liberatory Teaching.* Portsmouth, NH: Heinemann, 1987.

———. "Illegal Literacy." *Journal of Basic Writing* 19.1 (2000): 100–12.

Sledd, James. "Return to Service." *Composition Studies* 28.2 (Fall 2000): 11–32.

Smith, Dorothy. *The Everyday World as Problematic: A Feminist Sociology.* Boston: Northeastern UP, 1987.

Snider, Renate M., Teresa Trupiano Barry, and Sharon K. Thomas. "Using the Peer Response Model for Graduate Student Writing Groups in the Sciences." *Michigan Academician* 31 (1999): 359–69.

Soja, Edward W. "Planning in/for Postmodernity." *Space and Social Theory*. Ed. Georges Benko and Ulf Strohmayer. Malden, MA: Blackwell, 1997. 236–49.

———. *Postmodern Geographies: The Reassertion of Space in Critical Social Theory*. New York: Verso, 1989.

———. *Thirdspace: Journeys to Los Angeles and Other Real-and-Imagined Places*. Cambridge, MA: Blackwell, 1996.

Soja, Edward, and Barbara Hooper. "The Spaces that Difference Makes, Some Notes on the Geographical Margins of the New Cultural Politics." *Place and the Politics of Identity*. London: Routledge, 1993.

Soliday, Mary. "Class Dismissed." *College English* 61 (July 1999): 731–51.

———. "From the Margins to the Mainstream: Reconceiving Remediation." *College Composition and Communication* 47 (Feb. 1996): 85–100.

Stevens, Scott. "Nowhere to Go: Basic Writing and the Scapegoating of Civic Failure." *Journal of Basic Writing* 19.1 (2000): 3–15.

Street, Brian. "What's 'New' in New Literacy Studies? Critical Approaches to Literacy in Theory and Practice." Vandenberg, Hum, and Clary-Lemon 50–71.

Stuckey, J. Elspeth. *The Violence of Literacy*. Portsmouth, NH: Boynton, 1991.

"Student Engagement in Studio Group Meetings." Final Engagement Study Rubric. Fall 2000 (unpublished report).

Sunstein, Bonnie Stone, and Elizabeth Chiseri-Strater. *FieldWorking: Reading and Writing Research*. Boston: Bedford, 2002.

Tassoni, John Paul, and Cynthia Lewiecki-Wilson. "Not Just Anywhere, Anywhen: Mapping Change through Studio Work." *Journal of Basic Writing* 24.1 (2005): 68–92.

Thompson, Nancy S. "Effects of Verbal Ability, Audio-Pictorial Stimuli, and Print-Verbal Stimuli on the Reading and Writing Abilities of Early Adolescent Students." ERIC Document ED289162, 1988 (Abstract).

———. "Imaging, Literacy, and Sylvia Ashton-Warner." *Images in Language, Media, and Mind*. Ed. Roy F. Fox. Urbana, IL: NCTE, 1994. 29–41.

Thompson, Nancy, and Rhonda Grego. "Forging New Academic Identities in a Third Space." Conf. of South Africa Association for Research and Development in Higher Education. Penninsula Technikon. Cape Town. 1 July 1999.

———. "Locating Qualitative Research across the Global Community." *English International* 4.1 (1996): 5–10.

———. "Repositioning Remediation: Renegotiating Composition's Work in the Academy." *College Composition and Communication* 47 (Feb. 1996): 62–84.

———. "The Writing Studio Program: Reconfiguring Basic Writing/Freshman Composition." *Writing Program Administration* 19.1 (1995): 66–79.

————. "The Writing Studio Project at the University of South Carolina." National Conference on Redefining Basic Skills. Adelphi University, Garden City, NY. Nov. 1993.

Thompson, Nancy, and Mark Sutton. "Planning for the Future of the Writing Studio." Memo to Steven Lynn, English Department chair, U of South Carolina. 22 Oct. 2001.

————. "Report of Writing Studio Operations." Final report submitted to Steven Lynn, English Department chair, U of South Carolina. Fall 2000–Spring 2001.

Thompson, Nancy, Elisabeth Alford, Changyong Liao, Robert Johnson, and Michael Matthews. "Integrating Undergraduate Research into Engineering: A Communications Approach to Holistic Education." *Journal of Engineering Education* 94.3 (July 2005): 297–307.

Tobin, Lad. *Writing Relationships: What Really Happens in the Composition Class.* Portsmouth, NH: Boynton, 1993.

USC Writing Studio Web site. NSF EEC 0212244. 4 May 2005 <http://www.cas. sc.edu/engl/studio>.

Vandenberg, Peter, Sue Hum, and Jennifer Clary-Lemon, eds. *Relations, Locations, Positions: Composition Theory for Writing Teachers.* Urbana, IL: NCTE, 2006.

Vygotsky, L. S. *Thought and Language.* Cambridge, MA: MIT P, 1962.

Weese, Katherine L, Stephen L. Fox, and Stuart Green, eds. *Teaching Academic Literacy: The Uses of Teacher-Research in Developing a Writing Program.* Mahwah, NJ: Erlbaum, 1999.

Wilson, Anita. "There Is No Escape from Third-space Theory: Borderland Discourse and the 'In-Between' Literacies of Prisons." *Situated Literacies: Reading and Writing in Context.* Ed. David Barton, Mary Hamilton, and Roz Ivanic. London: Routledge, 2000. 54–69.

Winsor, Dorothy. "Learning to Do Knowledge Work in Systems of Distributed Cognition." *Journal of Business and Technical Communication* 15.1 (2001): 5–28.

Wysocki, Anne, and Johndan Johnson-Eilola. "Blinded by the Letter: Why Are We Using Literacy as a Metaphor for Everything Else?" In *Passions, Pedagogies and 21st Century Technologies.* Ed. Gail E. Hawisher and Cynthia L. Selfe. Salt Lake City: Utah State UP and NCTE, 1999.

Young, James. *The Texture of Memory.* New Haven: Yale UP, 1993.

Index

academe: distancing in, 47–48, 74, 98–99, 160, 198; hierarchies within, 38–40; institutionalization of, 35–36; top-down policies of, 198
academic culture, 160–62
academic discourse, 40–41, 60–62, 72, 150, 160–61
action research, 194, 196
administration, 39, 171–72, 204–5
African American students, 101, 110, 211. *See also* Bridges Writing Program (BWP)
African American studies, 102
Alford, Libby, 21, 85, 98, 113, 181–82, 210
Allen University, 108
American Association of University Professors (AAUP), 215
American Council of Learned Societies, 166
analysis: pentadic, external vs. internal, 63–66, 70–71, 219; of print advertisements, 128–29; rhetorical, 62; as scene, 62–63, 84
anthologies, 160–61
Ariail, Jennie, 113
artifacts, use of, 116, 126–34
Ashton-Warner, Sylvia, 53
At the Point of Need (Nelson), 48–49
"at the point of need" assistance, 105–6
audience, concept of, 220

Barnes, Michael, 98, 164
Bartholomae, David, 5, 160
basic writing courses: alternatives to, 206–7; approaches to, 3–6; construct of, 76; defining dilemma of, 14–15; GI Bill and, 101; learning environments for, 31; mainstreaming debate over, 16;

movement away from, 2–3, 91, 102; research on, 30, 156–57; and unwelcome student groups, 101–2
BCCARES (Benedict College Center for Academic Reinforcement, Enhancement, and Support), 110–11, 166
Belanoff, Pat, 51
Beloved (Morrison), 46, 56
Benedict College: AAUP double censure of, 215; disciplinarity at, 210–11; educational opportunities at, 108–9; faculty of, 190, 192; FYC at, 108–11; initial response to Studio at, 189–90; and interactional inquiry, 174–75; open admissions recruitment at, 117; racial and racialized histories at, 211–12. *See also* Bridges Writing Program (BWP)
Benton, Pam, 54
BEV (black English vernacular) patterns, 147–48
Bhabha, Homi, 23, 75–77
Bitzer, Lloyd, 219–20
Bizzell, Patricia, 40–41
Black Trap, 168–69
Blair, Ruby, 67–68, 109, 148, 156
Blythe, Stuart, 26
boundary crossing, 207–8
Bourdieu, Pierre, 103–4
Bridges Writing Program (BWP): African American instructors in, 187–88; assessment of, 192–93, 213; design of, 6, 166; faculty of, 167–68, 212; group leaders of, 167; interactional inquiry in, 165–69, 212–13; midterm and final reports for, 191–92; staff members in, 188–200; starvation of, 21, 214; student group in, 152–55; summer workshops at, 198; writing-history assignment in, 117–18

235

Rhonda C. Grego is a full-time instructor at Midlands Technical College in Columbia, South Carolina, where she teaches first-year composition courses and serves as English Department liaison for writing support services. Previously she held positions as assistant professor of English at the University of South Carolina and as tenured associate professor of English at Benedict College, both in Columbia. Her conference presentations, journal and book articles, and grant work have explored the effect of organizational history and geography on the shape of writing instruction and attendant programs in higher education institutions, as well as the ways that rhetorical and feminist theories of memory and alternative research methodologies help articulate the influence of place and space on writing and composition's work with college student writers. Ongoing research interests are in composition and higher education history in South Carolina and the slave narratives, folklore, and fiction of the historically black communities in and around Congaree National Park near Columbia. Special honors include the AAUP Konheim Award, Benedict College Outstanding Faculty Member of the Year, 2001–2002, and the TWIN Leadership Award, YWCA, spring 2001.

Nancy S. Thompson is a professor emerita in the English Department at the University of South Carolina. Through several years of her career in English at USC, she was in charge of the course on the teaching of writing required of secondary-teachers-in-training. Another scholarly project that occupied her for several years was recuperation of the fictional and pedagogical writings of the prominent New Zealand educator Sylvia Ashton-Warner, research that has also resulted in several publications. After retiring from the USC English Department, Thompson worked with another colleague to write a National Science Foundation proposal that resulted in funding for the Research Communications Studio in Engineering. Each of these projects has resulted in publications, conference and workshop presentations, and consultations with other universities. Most notable professional achievements include her roles as media editor for *English Journal,* 1975–80, and as chair of the NCTE International Assembly in 1987, 1988, and 1994. At her retirement, the USC Composition/Rhetoric Association established the Nancy Thompson Achievement Award for Enduring Enthusiasm and Service to the Field. She is currently continuing her career as an educator in the Peace Corps.

Other Books in the Studies in Writing & Rhetoric Series

*African American Literacies Unleashed: Vernacular English
and the Composition Classroom*
Arnetha F. Ball and Ted Lardner

Rhetoric and Reality: Writing Instruction in American Colleges, 1900–1985
James A. Berlin

Writing Instruction in Nineteenth-Century American Colleges
James A. Berlin

Something Old, Something New: College Writing Teachers and Classroom Change
Wendy Bishop

The Variables of Composition: Process and Product in a Business Setting
Glenn J. Broadhead and Richard C. Freed

Audience Expectations and Teacher Demands
Robert Brooke and John Hendricks

*Archives of Instruction: Nineteenth-Century Rhetorics, Readers,
and Composition Books in the Unites States*
Jean Ferguson Carr, Stephen L. Carr, and Lucille M. Schultz

Rehearsing New Roles: How College Students Develop as Writers
Lee Ann Carroll

*Dialogue, Dialectic, and Conversation: A Social Perspective
on the Function of Writing*
Gregory Clark

Toward a Grammar of Passages
Richard M. Coe

A Communion of Friendship: Literacy, Spiritual Practice, and Women in Recovery
Beth Daniell

Rural Literacies
Kim Donehower, Charlotte Hogg, and Eileen E. Schell

Embodied Literacies: Imageword and a Poetics of Teaching
Kristie S. Fleckenstein

Writing with Authority: Students' Roles as Writers in Cross-National Perspective
David Foster

Writing Groups: History, Theory, and Implications
Anne Ruggles Gere

Sexuality and the Politics of Ethos in the Writing Classroom
Zan Meyer Gonçalves